MW00827740

Redefining Latin American Historical Fiction

Redefining Latin American Historical Fiction

The Impact of Feminism and Postcolonialism

Edited by Helene Carol Weldt-Basson

First published in 2013 by
PALGRAVE MACMILLAN®
in the United States—a division of St. Martin's Press LLC,
175 Fifth Avenue, New York, NY 10010.

Where this book is distributed in the UK, Europe and the rest of the World,
this is by Palgrave Macmillan, a division of Macmillan Publishers Limited,
registered in England, company number 785998, of Houndmills,
Basingstoke, Hampshire RG21 6XS.

Palgrave Macmillan is the global academic imprint of the above
companies and has companies and representatives throughout the world.

Palgrave® and Macmillan® are registered trademarks in the United
States, the United Kingdom, Europe and other countries.

ISBN: 978–1–137–27756–5

Library of Congress Cataloging-in-Publication Data

Redefining Latin American historical fiction : the impact of feminism and
    postcolonialism / edited by Helene Carol Weldt-Basson.
      pages   cm
    ISBN 978–1–137–27756–5 (alk. paper)
    1. Historical fiction, Latin American—History and criticism.
    2. Feminism and literature—Latin America.   3. Postmodernism
    (Literature)—Latin America.   I. Weldt-Basson, Helene Carol, 1958–
    PQ7082.H57R43 2013
    863'.0810998—dc23   2012048701

A catalogue record of the book is available from the British Library.

Design by Integra Software Services

First edition: June 2013

10 9 8 7 6 5 4 3 2 1

Transferred to Digital Printing in 2013

For Marc, with love on our twentieth anniversary

Contents

List of Tables

Acknowledgments

Many thanks go to the numerous people who contributed to the publication of this book. First, I would like to thank Michigan State University, whose award of a Humanities and Arts Research Program (HARP) grant enabled the timely completion of this manuscript. Second, I would like to acknowledge the hard work of the volume's contributors, without whom this book would not have been possible. Finally, I would like to acknowledge the journal *Acta Literaria* for giving me permission to print a translation of the article written by Marcelo Coddou, "Santa Evita, historia, mito, ficción: una narrativa a partir del Otro Lado," *Acta Literaria* 35 (2007): 59–75.

I

Introduction: Feminism and Postcolonialism—New Directions in Latin American Historical Fiction

Helene Carol Weldt-Basson

Theoretical Overview of the Historical Novel

The evolution of historical fiction throughout the twentieth century has been the topic of numerous studies. The principal tendency of contemporary scholarship on the topic is to trace the impact of postmodernism on recent manifestations of the genre. For those unfamiliar with the term *postmodernism*, it refers to both a period (the era following modernism) and a philosophy. According to Linda Hutcheon and Jean-François Lyotard (Lyotard, 34), the following characteristics can generally be attributed to postmodern fiction or art:

(1) postmodernism rejects elitism, political conservatism, and the autonomy of art associated with its predecessor, modernism, in favor of cultural democratization and a generally contestatory stance;

(2) postmodernism views all knowledge as subjective, a human construct, thus questioning the transparent relationship between history and reality;

(3) postmodernism is centered on the concept of difference, recognizing distinctions of class, race, gender, sexual orientation, and

deconstructing binary oppositions that schematize human nature (Hutcheon, 3–53);

(4) postmodernism opposes all master or metanarratives with their pretension to absolute truth (Lyotard, 34).

This postmodern stance, which has dominated (albeit overlapping with modernism) the literary scene since the 1980s, explains to a large degree many of the changes wrought on historical fiction, both inside and outside Latin America. As we will see in the following pages, most of the current studies on Latin American historical fiction focus precisely on changes evidenced in the Latin American New Novel to the traditional model of the historical novel as defined by the Marxist critic Georg Lukács in the 1930s, in his landmark book *The Historical Novel*. Lukács largely defines the classical form of the genre on the basis of the nineteenth-century works of Sir Walter Scott. The essential characteristics of the genre include representation of a distant past, historical figures as minor rather than major characters, the hero as an average man who represents social trends and historical forces (the "world-historical individual" in Hegel's words), past historical events as a prehistory of the present, and adherence to historical facts (Lukács, 21–61).

Although most studies begin their discussions with Lukács's work, the Italian writer Alessandro Manzoni was an important precursor to Lukács's study. Manzoni was both a writer of historical fiction and a theorist who contemplated the contradictions inherent in historical fiction in his nineteenth-century book *On the Historical Novel*. According to the critic Sandra Bermann, Manzoni built his work on a scrupulous adherence to history (Bermann, 21). For Manzoni, the only real difference between historical fiction and history proper was that the former had the poetic license to fill in the "interstices of history" (Bermann, 23), the gaps in words, thoughts, and feelings of historical subjects that do not appear in the historical record. Nonetheless, Manzoni was torn between the exigencies of remaining true to historical fact and those of writing a piece of fiction. This essential contradiction between the didactic value of the historical novel and the reality that historical fiction "lies" through invention led Manzoni to predict the eventual decline of the historical novel (Manzoni, 126). Paradoxically, to some degree, we can think of Manzoni's ideas on historical fiction as a very early anticipation of the postmodernist notion of post-history: there can be no complete adherence to historical fact because "facts" are subjective, based on individual perceptions and interpretations, and thus the concept of history is negated. I will return to this idea later on in my discussion of the effects of postmodernism on the Latin American historical novel.

After Lukács's study, there was a large temporal gap in important theoretical studies on the historical novel until Joseph Turner's article "The Kinds of Historical Fiction: An Essay in Definition and Methodology" appeared in 1979. By that time, many years had passed since the publication of Lukács's book, leading Turner to take a totally different theoretical approach to the historical novel, largely focusing on the different ways in which invention is employed in historical fiction. Turner defines three types of historical novels (Turner, 337–345):

(1) the disguised historical novel, which includes no actual historical characters or events, but creates parallels between its characters and historical figures;

(2) the invented historical novel, which refers back to a distant past (the world before the author was born). Since the characters and events are removed from the author's experience, even though they are invented, they acquire a historical nature; and

(3) the documented historical novel, in which real historical figures appear, and in which the novelist is in a position similar to that of the historian, but may fill in the gaps in recorded history with invented details.

Turner ultimately makes an interesting observation regarding the different purposes of historical novelists. He suggests that they may write in the "original mode," in which their aim is to create a compelling vision of the past; or they may write in the "reflective mode," in which the gap between past and present is recognized and bridged; or they may write in the "philosophical mode," in which their concern is if or how history itself is possible (an anticipation of Hayden White's concept of metahistory).[1] Turner's study is of value because it defines a new set of aims for historical fiction that go beyond Lukács's embodiment of social trends and forces to reflect upon the concept of history itself.

Another gap followed Turner's article, and no major new reflection on the concept of the historical novel appeared until 1986, when the noted Latin Americanist Daniel Balderston published *The Historical Novel in Latin America: A Symposium*.[2] This book compiles a number of interesting studies on the historical novel, featuring a theoretical study of the genre by the noted scholar Noé Jitrik. Jitrik proposes a broad definition of the historical novel that includes works that focus on local customs, social psychology, and sociopolitical issues. According to Jitrik,

La novela histórica se propone representar conflictos sociales... pero también... podrían entrar manifestaciones costumbristas, de crítica social o política y aun de psicología social...en tal abanico, una constante insoslayable sería la referencia a hechos históricos...En suma...lo que peculiarzaría la noción de novela histórica es la referencia a un momento considerado como histórico y...cierto apoyo documental realizado por quien se propone tal representación.

(Jitrik, 20–21)

[The historical novel proposes the representation of social conflicts...but also...manifestations of *costumbrismo,* social or political criticism or even social psychology could enter into this category....In this spectrum an inescapable constant would be the reference to historical events....In sum...what would be peculiar to the notion of historical novel is the reference to a moment that is considered historical...and...certain documentary support achieved by the one who proposes such a representation.]

(my translation)

The common denominator shared by all these different varieties of historical novel (political, sociological, psychological, and *costumbrista*) is their reliance on a historical referent and historical documentation.

In the early 1990s, at least three major studies of the historical novel were published: Naomi Jacobs's *The Character of Truth: Historical Figures in Contemporary Fiction* (1990), Roberto González-Echeverría's *Myth and Archive: A Theory of Latin American Narrative* (1990), and Seymour Menton's *Latin America's New Historical Novel* (1993). All three are extremely important, because for the first time, these works took into account the significant changes that had begun to occur in the content and style of historical fiction as a result of formal innovation and experimentation in the novel, especially in Latin America, beginning in the 1940s and 1950s.

Although Jacobs does not speak specifically about the Latin American historical novel, the categories she defines are important for its analysis. Jacobs defines three types of contemporary historical fiction (Jacobs, xx):

(1) *Fiction biographies:* fictional works that treat a time period in the life of a single historical figure. These works employ both modernist and postmodernist techniques and do not subscribe to the objectivity of historical biography although they may include historical facts;

(2) *Fiction histories:* fictional works in which historical figures are representative of "unchanging patterns of human behavior" and thus reduced to simplified types. Real characters are present to aid the writer's satirical cultural analysis, and not to bring history to life;

(3) *Recombinant fiction:* fictional works that mix historical and mythical figures to destroy all boundaries between fiction and history.

What is of particular interest in Jacobs's study is that she is one of the first critics to include works that mix history with myth or fantastic elements within the category of historical fiction. In Latin America, such novels are generally considered "magical realist" works, and, as we shall see, they have been specifically excluded from the historical novel genre by such critics as María Cristina Pons in her book *Memorias del olvido: la novela histórica de fines del siglo XX* (1996) (Pons, 101).

Although González-Echeverría does not focus on contemporary Latin American fiction in *Myth and Archive* (with the exception of Gabriel García Márquez's *Cien años soledad* [*One Hundred Years of Solitude*]), he defines several of the major characteristics that will come to be associated with the postmodern historical novel. González-Echeverría asserts that "the new narrative unwinds the history told in the old chronicles by showing that history was made up of a series of conventional topics whose coherence and authority depend on the codified beliefs of a period whose ideological structure is no longer current" (15). In other words, González-Echeverría points to the deconstruction of history, and the exposure of its ideological subjectivity, and is thus among the first to suggest the postmodern view of history that permeates the contemporary Latin American historical novel. González-Ecehverría also pioneers the discussion of the historical novel's use of documents, both legal and scientific, which he refers to in his study as the "archive."

Seymour Menton's *Latin America's New Historical Novel* (1993) is the first book that actually attempts to identify the moments of evolution or change in the Latin American historical novel and define the characteristics of what he terms the "New Historical Novel." Menton identifies the birth of the new historical novel with the works of the Cuban writer Alejo Carpentier, specifically in 1949, the year of publication of *El reino de este mundo* [*The Kingdom of This World*] (Menton, 22). Subsequent critics, such as María Cristina Pons, disagree with Menton's chronology, citing Carpentier as more of an aberration than as the initiator of a new trend (Pons, 105). According to Menton, this new novel is characterized by six important traits:

(1) The subordination of the mimetic recreation of history to the illustration of three philosophical ideas: the impossibility of ascertaining the truth value of history, history's cyclical nature, and the unpredictability of history;

(2) The conscious distortion of history through omissions, exaggerations, and anachronisms;

(3) Famous historical figures as protagonists instead of minor characters;

(4) Metafiction (reference to the writer's own creative process);

(5) Intertextuality with other texts and historical documents; and

(6) Dialogism, parody, the carnivalesque, and heteroglossia as defined by Mikhail Bakhtin.[3]

Menton's study, like González-Echeverría's, is among the first to chronicle the shift in Latin American historical fiction toward postmodernism.

The ideas of these critics are later echoed by a number of other scholars, such as Peter Elmore, who in *La fábrica de la memoria: la crisis de la representación en la novela histórica latinoamericana* (1997) focuses on how historical fiction uses past historical moments, such as the Conquest and Independence, to reflect on contemporary historical events and crises, emphasizing the contestatory dimension of such historical fiction. Several years later, Mark Hernández made similar observations in his study titled *Figural Conquistadors* (2006), which focuses on the re-reading of the chronicles by post-boom writers in order to articulate a counterdiscourse to official history on the conquest.

I have already cited the important work of María Cristina Pons, *Memorias del olvido: la novela historica de fines del siglo XX* (1996), for her dissention with other critics on the historical novel. Although Pons notes the important effect of postmodernism on the Latin American historical novel, she does not focus on this aspect of contemporary historical fiction as do most of other critics, and instead, turns her attention to delimiting the concept of historical fiction. Pons asserts that the presence of history is not a determining factor of the historical novel, but rather what is significant is the purpose of employing history in the novel. If history serves a merely decorative purpose, then a novel should not be considered historical. History must have a structural role in the novel for it to be viewed as truly historical. According to Pons, historical novels are inevitably political, and no distinction should be made between historical, political, and testimonial novels.[4] Pons disagrees with Lukács that the historical novel must refer to a distant past, but emphasizes that it must adhere to a linear time, to Bakhtin's time–space chronotope, and thus cannot present a mythical or cyclical time. In this way, Pons excludes magical realist novels from her definition of historical fiction, dissenting with González-Echeverría's, Menton's, and Jacobs's definitions of the genre and excluding all the "Boom" novels (with the exception of Carpentier's) from the category of historical novel. Pons also cites the use of historical documents or textualized history in the contemporary Latin American historical novel. Finally, she defines several important differences in the evolution of the Latin American historical novel vis-á-vis that of Europe. In contrast to Scott's nostalgia for the past and essential conservatism, the Latin American historical novel has been characterized by both the search for identity during the chaos of the post-independence era and an essentially liberal ideology (Pons, 27–101).

Most of the other critics who wrote about historical fiction since 1998 have emphasized the role of postmodernism in the historical novel. Both Celia Fernández Prieto in *Historia y novela: poética de la novela histórica* (1998) and Magdalena Perkowska in *Historias híbridas: la nueva novela histórica latinoamericana* (1985–2000, [2008]) focus purely on the postmodern character of the most recent Latin American historical fiction. Prieto defines two basic kinds of historical fiction: novels that follow the traditional model (Scott's) and those that are postmodern. The postmodern novel distorts historical material and proposes

> historias alternativas, apócrifas o contradictorias sobre sucesos o personajes de gran relevancia histórica: De hecho estas novelas presentan los hechos desde la perspectiva de los perdedores, de las minorías marginadas o excluídas de la Historia, mostrando así que privilegiar una tradición textual implica aceptar una específica versión de la realidad histórica a expensas de otras versiones diferentes. (150)

> [alternate, false or contradictory histories about events or characters of great historical relevance. In fact these novels present events from the perspective of the losers, the marginalized minorities or those excluded from history, showing that privileging a textual tradition implies accepting a specific version of historical reality at the cost of other different versions.]
>
> (my translation)

Prieto emphasizes an important dimension of postmodern historical fiction: the fact that postmodern historical novels give voice to the historical other, to marginalized beings such as the colonial subject and women. Thus, Prieto indirectly suggests the important direction of the contemporary historical fiction that will be developed in this book.

Similarly, although Perkowska's *Historias híbridas* (2008) acknowledges the importance of postcolonialism in the contemporary historical novel, she states "opto por privelgiar un enfoque posmoderno" [I opt for privileging a postmodern focus], which she uses to specifically attempt to answer two questions within her study: "¿Es posible hablar de la muerte o disolución de la historicidad y de la historia en y desde América Latina? ¿Qué visión de la historia transmite la novela histórica en las postrimerías del siglo XX?" (Perkowska, 20) [Is it possible to speak of the death or dissolution of historicity and of history in and from Latin America? What vision of history does the historical novel at the end of the twentieth century transmit?]. Through the analyses conducted in her book, Perkowska refutes Jameson's idea that postmodernism signals the end of history, showing that the Latin American postmodern historical novel proposes a provisional rather than an absolute truth, situated "en la confrontación con otras verdades" (73) [situated within the confrontation with other truths]. With regard to her second question, Perkowska proposes that the historical novel written after re-democratization in Latin America is the construction of "hybrid histories," which, according to Canclini, combine both elements of postindustrial society with those of pre-modern oral culture (Perkowska, 100). According to Perkowska, while the novel of the 1960s–1980s is subversive in nature, the novel of post-democratization attempts to conserve the "utopic spirit" (Perkowska, 104). Perkowska, like Prieto, acknowledges the significance of postcolonialism but does not choose to pursue its importance in her study. She states:

> La idea de "una lectura diferenciada" o la re-significación desde un lugar geocultural periférico señala la presencia del enfoque poscolonial, subrayada adicionalmente por el uso de términos o conceptos centrales en las teorías poscoloniales (la hibridez, el subalterno, el locus diferencial de enunciación, la mirada doble, el entre-lugar, el discurso intermedio)... Esto se debe en parte al hecho de que las teorías posmodernas y poscoloniales comparten muchas características y algunas agendas. (28–29)

> [The idea of "a differentiated reading" or the re-signification from a peripheral geocultural place signals the presence of a postcolonial focus, additionally underlined by the use of terms and concepts central to postcolonial theories (hybridity, the subaltern, the differential locus of enunciation, the double look, the inter-place, the intermediate discourse)... This is due in part to the fact that postcolonial and postmodern theories share many of the same characteristics and agendas.]

(my translation)

Perkowska limits herself to underscoring the similarities between postmodernism and postcolonialism without delving into the specificity or impact of postcolonial theory. Moreover, the subversive nature of feminism and postcolonialism appear to contradict her notion of the "utopic spirit" of the literature produced in the 1990s.

Michael Rössner's article "De la utopía histórica a la historia utópica: reflexiones sobre la nueva novela histórica como re-escritura de textos históricos" (1999) also defines the "Latin American new historical novel" on the basis of its postmodern character. Rössner states that this new novel is a "reanimation" of history through a "re-escritura, el repensamiento de la Historia . . . fracturada en una imagen polifacética de voces y contravoces" (Rössner, 76–77) [the rewriting, the rethinking of History . . . fractured into a multifaceted image of voices and countervoices]. Rössner concurs with the idea that Latin American historical fiction represents a search for identity, but its encounter with history is both ludic and demystifying (73). However, Rössner, like Pons, feels that in the magical realist fiction of the boom, "no había lugar para la historia" (69) [there was no room for history].

One of the most recent books on historical fiction, Jerome de Groot's *The Historical Novel: The New Critical Idiom* (2010), gives an exhaustive overview of the development of the historical novel. De Groot emphasizes the subversive potential of the historical novel and also focuses on the postmodern nature of the contemporary historical genre. According to de Groot (citing Linda Hutcheon), historical fiction is the clearest artistic expression of postmodernism (de Groot, 120), and there has been a shift toward intertextuality, contradiction, self-reflexivity, and narrative problems in historical fiction since the 1960s (de Groot, 119). De Groot, like Perkowska, dissents with Jameson's notion that postmodernism is devoid of political influence and leads to a total dissolution of history (139). Like Pons, he cites the importance of the question of national identity in historical fiction. De Groot's study is one of the few that mentions women's writing with regard to the historical novel; he cites Evelyn Waugh's comment about the commonalities between postmodernism and feminism, because both "disrupt traditional boundaries particularly between the dominant and marginal culture" (de Groot, 133). He also discusses some works by women writers as precursors to Scott. Another book that specifically dedicates itself to the question of the relationship between historical fiction and women writers is Diana Wallace's *The Woman's Historical Novel (British Women Writers, 1900–2000)* published in 2005. Although Wallace studies only British fiction by women writers, many of her observations are applicable to Latin America as well. Wallace argues that "the historical novel has been *par excellence* the form which has enabled women to write about men and the male world of politics and warfare" (22). It is curious that there have been no similar studies made to date on historical fiction by Latin American women writers.[5]

Feminism and Postcolonialism

As this chapter overview illustrates, current scholarship on the Latin American historical fiction genre has failed to adequately take into account the impact of two major contemporary discourses: feminism and postcolonialism. These two movements have significantly influenced the development of the contemporary Latin American historical novel over the past 50 years, but have largely been subsumed under the general rubric of postmodernism. While, as various critics have pointed out, feminism and postcolonialism share certain techniques and agendas with postmodernism, they are not synonymous with postmodernism and merit their own consideration with regard to the development of the most recent historical novel in Latin America.

Before delving into my own theory and definition of the historical novel and the impact that feminism and postcolonialism have had on the genre, it is necessary to briefly define these two terms, which like postmodernism, mean different things to different critics. Jane Freedman has defined feminism as concerning itself "with women's inferior position in society and with discrimination encountered by women because of their sex. Furthermore, one could argue that feminists call for changes in the social, economic, political or cultural order, to reduce and eventually overcome the discrimination against women" (Freedman, 212). Freedman is careful when she refers to feminisms in the plural, in order to emphasize the variety of feminist philosophies and approaches that abound. Historically, three waves of feminism have been defined. First-wave feminism refers to the suffrage movement of the 1920s in the United States (later in Latin America, where women's right to vote was obtained during the period 1949–1960); second-wave feminism refers to the women's liberation movement of the 1960s and 1970s, when women fought for equality; and third-wave feminism, beginning in the 1980s and 1990s, refers to the movement that combats essentialist ideas about women and emphasizes female diversity through race, class, age, and the like. Feminism becomes postmodern and performative in nature in its most recent phase. Elaine Showalter, in her landmark article "Feminist Criticism in the Wilderness" (1985), discusses the two types of feminist literary criticism that emerge from first- and second-wave feminism: woman as reader and woman as writer. In the first instance, feminist criticism took the form of a critique of literature written by men, exposing the ideology behind such writings and the stereotyped way in which women had been portrayed. In the second instance, which Showalter terms "gynocritics," feminist criticism began to explore women writers, along with questions of female language and the psychodynamics of female creativity (Showalter, 130). Showalter signals the future direction of feminist criticism, examining women's writing as "double-voiced discourse" that embodies the words and perspectives of both dominant and marginalized sectors of society (261). Showalter also anticipates postmodern discourse through the focus on black and

third-world women and the concept of distinct feminisms based on differences of race, class, age, and ethnicity (244). The most contemporary
discussions of feminism have gone so far as to include articles that discuss
how the current existence of feminism in the 2000s has been questioned
(the concept of postfeminism), such as Toril Moi's " 'I Am Not a Feminist, but . . . ' How Feminism Became the F-Word" (Moi, 1735–1741), and
those that represent a move away from the notion of feminism in favor of
the concept of gender theory. Gender theory is a more postmodern ter-
minology because it abandons the binary dichotomy implied by feminism
(female versus male), in favor of the concept of a continuum referring to
gender. This concept has been espoused by such critics as Judith Butler in
Gender Trouble (1990) and *Undoing Gender* (2004). Thus, in general, feminism is concerned not only with women's rights, but also with recovering
the work of women writers, analyzing the portrayal of female characters,
and any general issues concerning women.

The term *postcolonialism*, like feminism, merits definition and clarification. Once again, Linda Hutcheon is at the forefront of providing just such
a definition. According to Hutcheon,

> The twentieth century has seen the end of official colonial rule in much
> of the non-European world and, as many have argued, the simultaneous
> recolonization or neocolonization of the globe by multinational economic
> forces. Such a general statement, however, risks downplaying the signif-
> icant differences between the historical, political, and cultural effects of
> empire in settler colonies . . . and in the diverse nonsettler colonies. . . . The
> "structural domination" that empire represents . . . can take many diverse
> forms in each of its political, economic, military, intellectual and cultural
> manifestations. . . . According to both its theorists and its cultural activists,
> postcolonial criticism has positioned itself as a broad, anti-imperialist eman-
> cipatory project. . . .
>
> (Hutcheon, 7–8)

Neil Lazarus points out that in the 1970s, postcolonial studies was a peri-
odizing term rather than an ideological concept, but has now evolved
in the manner indicated by Hutcheon. In general, postcolonial criticism
"evinces an undifferentiated disavowal of all forms of nationalism and a
corresponding exaltation of . . . hybridity and multiculturality . . . it refuses
an antagonistic or struggled based model of politics in favor of one that
emphasizes 'cultural difference' [and] 'ambivalence' " (Lazarus, 2). While
Edward Said emphasizes the postcolonial critique of Eurocentrism and the
manner in which Eurocentrist discourse constitutes society, critics such as
Homi Bhabha focus on what Richard L. W. Clarke terms "the productive
ambiguity of the object of colonial discourse—its 'otherness' that is at once

the object of desire and scorn" (Clarke). For Bhabha, colonial discourse is based on this simultaneous acknowledgment and rejection of racial, cultural, and historical differences.

It is important to note here that postcolonial critics have emphasized the commonalities between feminism and postcolonial studies. Deepika Bahri points out:

> Feminist theory and postcolonial theory are occupied with similar questions of representation, voice, marginalization, and the relation between politics and literature. Given that both critical projections employ multi-disciplinary perspectives, they are each attentive, at least in principle, to historical context and the geopolitical coordinates of the subject in question. . . .
>
> [Fields such as women's studies and postcolonial studies have arisen in part in response to the absence or unavailability of the perspectives of women, racial minorities, and marginalized cultures or communities in historical accounts of literary annals. This lack of representation is paralleled in the political and economic and legal spheres. Those "other" to the dominant discourse have no voice or say in their portrayal: they are consigned to be "spoken for" by those who command authority and means to speak. (203–205)]

This drive to represent the previously silenced voice of women and racial minorities, the colonized and oppressed, began to take shape for women approximately 50 years ago, in the 1960s, during second-wave feminism, although this impetus did not reach its full peak in Latin America until the 1980s, when Isabel Allende published *The House of the Spirits*. This same decade also witnessed the gradual rise of postcolonial studies. Both of these ideological approaches have enormously impacted the development of the Latin American historical novel. As I will show in the following pages, through the analysis of a series of paradigmatic novels, the latest directions of historical fiction in Latin America have been shaped precisely by feminism and postcolonialism.[6]

National Identity and the Historical Novel

In order to facilitate my discussion of the influence of feminism and postcolonialism on the historical novel, I have identified four major categories of historical novels that attempt to redefine the historical novel and encompass the most recent developments in Latin American historical fiction. Although some of these categories dissent with the delimitation of the historical novel suggested by Pons and others, all of them subscribe to Pons's idea that the historical novel can be defined largely through its purpose. In the following pages I describe four major aims of contemporary Latin American historical fiction and how they build on previous categories of historical narrative.

The first purpose or category of historical fiction—search for national identity—has already been referred to by several of the critics whom I discussed in the first section of this chapter. Both de Groot and Pons discussed the importance of national identity in historical fiction. I propose to analyze the manner in which the concept of national identity in historical fiction has changed through the advent of feminism and postcolonialism through an analysis of two important Mexican novels: *La muerte de Artemio Cruz* (1962) [*The Death of Artemio Cruz*] by Carlos Fuentes and *Malinche* (2006) by Laura Esquivel.

La muerte de Artemio Cruz is a Latin American "Boom" novel based on the 1910 Mexican Revolution. Despite its experimental form, which has been extensively analyzed by critics, the novel in many ways conforms to the traditional idea of the historical novel as espoused by Lukács. The main character is not a major historical figure but rather an "average guy" who rises to wealth and power after the revolution. His trajectory reflects the historical forces and social trends in both pre- and post-revolutionary Mexico. Historical figures, namely, Pancho Villa, Venustiano Carranza, and Álvaro Obregón, among others, and events, such as Obregón's murder, are also mentioned, all of which affect the protagonist, Artemio Cruz. Although the novel provides a large dose of existentialism (in each episode the protagonist is faced with choices he must make and thus forges his own destiny), it is clear that the choices with which Cruz is presented have been shaped by the historical moment and that none of his options is very good in most instances. Consequently, history plays an important role in the protagonist's life, although critics such as Pons would not consider this a historical novel because time is not entirely presented in a linear fashion. The episodes are not narrated chronologically although one can reconstruct a linear time. Cyclical and mythical times are also incorporated through repetitions of oppressors and oppressed: The Menchaca family (who rose to power under Santa Anna/Maximillian) is displaced by people like Gonzalo Bernal (who gained his land through Juárez's appropriation of church territory and maintained power under Porfirio Díaz's landed oligarchy), who in turn is displaced by Artemio Cruz himself, who came to power through the Mexican Revolution. Nonetheless, history is the novel's major theme and catalyst, and therefore *La muerte de Artemio Cruz* should be considered a historical novel.

La muerte de Artemio Cruz goes beyond the title character's personal dilemmas to posit a theory of Mexican identity that owes a debt to Octavio Paz's *El laberinto de la soledad* (1950; augmented 1958) [*The Labyrinth*

of Solitude]. In this essay, Paz suggests a dichotomy of oppressors versus oppressed with its origins in the Conquest of America, to describe
Mexican identity. This dichotomy is then developed by Fuentes in his novel
to describe both how Cruz has sold out the Mexican revolution in which
he was a soldier, by becoming an "oppressor," and how essentially oppressors and oppressed are the only two options provided to all Mexicans
throughout history:

> Tú la pronunciarás: es tu palabra y tu palabra es la mía: ... blasón de la raza,
> salvavida [sic] de los límites, resumen de la historia: santo y seña de México:
> tu palabra: —Chingue a su madre.... Eres quien eres porque supiste chingar
> y no te dejaste chingar: cadena de la chingada que nos aprisiona a todos....
> (143–145)

> [You will utter it: it's your word, and your word is my word; ... coat of arms
> for the race, life preserver when you've reached your limits, summary of
> history: Mexico's password: your word: Motherfucker.... You are who you
> are because you knew how to fuck up other people and not let yourself get
> fucked over; you are who you are because you didn't know how to fuck up
> other people and you let yourself get fucked over. The chain of the fucked
> mother that binds all of us.... (136–137)]

Although *La muerte de Artemio Cruz* is an excellent novel that presents a
critical view of the corruption associated with the Mexican Revolution and
US imperialism, the novel's view of Mexican identity is schematic and traditional. The binary opposition suggested by the division of Mexicans into
oppressors versus the oppressed and the essentialism expressed through
this dichotomy are precisely the variety of typecasting that is decon-
structed, criticized, and rectified through feminist and postcolonial literary
studies, which evolve the novel from the singular search for a national
identity to the plural search for national identities.

We can observe the development of the Latin American historical novel
from the 1960s to the present through an analysis of another paradigmatic Mexican novel, Laura Esquivel's *Malinche* (2006). Esquivel bases her
novel on the figure of Malintzin (who was later baptized doña Marina),
the indigenous interpreter who aided Hernán Cortés in the conquest of
the Aztec Empire. Malintzin has generally been a reviled figure, considered by many Mexicans to have sold out the indigenous culture to the
Spaniards. In the aforementioned essay by Octavio Paz, the chapter that
views Mexican identity as a division between oppressors and oppressed is
titled "Los hijos de la Malinche" ["Malinche's Children"] and traces the origins of Mexican identity to Malinche's rape by Cortés. She is an ambiguous
figure, explored by Esquivel in terms of both her female and indigenous

identities, and is thus focused in the novel in terms of both feminism and postcolonialism.

Before entering into a discussion of Esquivel's portrayal of the Malinche figure, it is important to establish the historical character of the novel. Esquivel clearly indicates the novel's historical basis through a bibliography that refers to many of the historical sources used to create the novel. As I will show later in text, there is concrete intertextuality between the novel and some of the sources mentioned. Although much of what is written about Malintzin is conjecture, since she is only concretely referred to in Bernal Díaz's *Historia verdadera de la conquista de la Nueva España* (which was written toward the end of his life and published after his death in 1585) and in some of the indigenous codices, Esquivel has read and incorporated historical sources into the composition of the novel. This reliance on intertextuality places the novel within my third category of historical novels as well—novels that rely on historical intertextuality—but I prefer to discuss it here in terms of national identity, since La Malinche has played such an important role in the Mexican collective unconscious.

Through the main character, Malinalli (Malinztin/doña Marina), Esquivel fills in many historical gaps about the thoughts and motivations of this historical figure, both as an indigenous, colonized person and as a woman. These two perspectives are frequently intertwined. First, let us begin by discussing the elements of the novel that develop Malinalli's colonized perspective. The author establishes the indigenous viewpoint from the moment of Malinalli's birth, when the narrator states: "Y el cuerpo de esa criatura era como un bello recipiente en el que podían volcar las joyas más preciosas de la flor y el canto de sus antepasados" (3) ["and the body of that child was like a beautiful vessel that could be filled to overflowing with the most precious jewels—the flower and song of her ancestors" (5)]. Note that "flor y canto" is a direct reference to náhuatl poetry, and is thus a cultural reference specific to the indigenous people.

Malinalli is sold by her mother into slavery to the merchants of Xicalango, who eventually sell her to another indigenous tribe. Historically, the motivation for this action is unclear, although various theories have been espoused.[7] In the novel, Malinalli's father dies and her mother remarries, wishing to rid herself of Malinalli and start anew. This is the first step in Malinalli's transformation into a colonized and oppressed individual, which is completed later on when she is raped by Cortés and subjugated by the Spanish. Although she is granted the power of the word when she becomes Cortés's translator, we are told that

[e]lla tenía el poder de lograr que sus palabras incluyeran a los otros dentro de un mismo propósito . . . o los excluyeran . . . desamparados, tal como ella,

quien en su calidad de esclava por años había sentido lo que significaba vivir sin voz, sin ser tomada en cuenta e impedida para cualquier toma de decisiones. (64)

[for she had the power with her words to include others in a common purpose .... Or she could exclude them, making them into foes, separate beings with irreconcilable ideas, or into solitary beings who were isolated and destitute as she had been in her status as slave, feeling for so many years what it was like to live without a voice, without being taken into account and forbidden to make any decisions on her own. (66)]

Moreover, Esquivel, by giving voice to Malinalli in the novel, allows her to express her motivations for helping the Spanish. She articulates Malinalli's belief, first, that the Spaniards arrived to "restaurar el reino de Quetzalcoatl" (70) ["restore the kingdom of Quetzalcoatl" (68)], which would eliminate slavery and human sacrifice; this was one of Malinalli's principal incentives. Second, the reader learns of Malinalli's surprise and remorse, when she discovers the betrayal of the Spaniards through their massacre of the indigenous population in Cholula: "En cuanto asesinaron a todos los hombres que se encontraban allí reunidos, se abrieron las puertas del patio y Malinalli huyó horrorizada ... cargaba sobre sus espaldas cientos de muertos" (92) ["When all the men gathered there had been killed, the doors to the courtyard were opened and Malinalli fled in terror ... Malinalli ... ran until she reached the river, horrified by the hatred with which they slaughtered men, women, and children" (94)]. After the fall of Moctezuma, whom Malinalli wishes to warn against the Spanish, but is unable to do so, Malinalli perforates her tongue with a maguey thorn, which will destroy her ability to communicate effectively and thus impair her ability to assist in future conquests.

Another major way in which Esquivel's *Malinche* offers a postcolonial viewpoint is through its incorporation of an original codex at the beginning of each chapter. This codex, invented by Esquivel's nephew Jordi Castells, in imitation of the indigenous codices, suggests the presentation and importance of the indigenous, colonized viewpoint in the novel. Moreover, Malinalli repeatedly emphasizes her reliance on her own personal codex within the pages of the novel.

What makes the significance of the presence of the codices in the novel particularly interesting is the connection between this novelistic element and an intertextual source, Gordon Brotherston's article "La Malintzin de los codices," which appears in Margo Glantz's collection *La Malinche, sus padres y sus hijos*.[8] Brotherston insists on the importance of the little-cited codices in presenting accurate information about Malintzin and the indigenous viewpoint of the conquest:

Resulta sorprendente que hasta la fecha no se haya prestado más atención a las fuentes indígenas que se refieren a Malintzin, sobre todo a los códices que la presentan gráficamente....En el lenguaje visual tan elocuente de estas fuentes, la enigmática Malintzin adquiere rasgos reconocibles y altamente sugerentes que se leen por encima de diferencias políticas internas. Esclarecida, aun más mediante la comparación diacrónica, esta imagen suya corrige de todas formas excesos u omisiones de la historiografía occidental.

(Brotherston, 31)

[It is surprising that to date more attention has not been paid to the indigenous sources that refer to Malinztin, above all, the codices that graphically present her.... In the eloquent visual language of these sources, the enigmatic Malintzin acquires recognizable and highly suggestive characteristics that can be read between the lines of internal political differences. This image of her clarified to an even greater extent through diachronic comparison, in any case corrects the excesses and omissions of Occidental historiography.]

(my translation)

Brotherston emphasizes the fact that the codices present the viewpoint of the indigenous "other," the postcolonial approach to history that avoids the Eurocentric viewpoint. In Esquivel's novel, numerous passages emphasize the value of the codices, and images over words. For example, we are told about Malinalli's grandmother, the major influence in her life and the principal source of love and inspiration: "Desde muy temprana edad, se había encargado de enseñarle a Malinalli a dibujar códices mentales para que ejercitara el lenguaje y la memoria. 'La memoria' le dijo, 'es ver desde dentro. Es dar forma y calor a las palabras. Sin imágenes, no hay memoria. Luego le pedía a la niña que dibujara en papel un códice" ' (27) ["Very early on, she had taught Malinalli how to sketch out codices in her mind so that she could exercise both language and memory. 'Memory', she told the girl, 'is seeing things from the inside. It gives shape and color to words. Without images, there is no memory' " (31)].

In addition to Malinalli's experience as a slave of both indigenous tribes and the Spaniards, and her reliance on the traditional indigenous form of the codex, all of which provide the voice of the marginalized, indigenous people, Malinalli also offers the feminine viewpoint in the novel. Although we cannot exactly speak of Malinalli as a feminist in contemporary terms, the demonstration of the exploitation of women in the novel and the representation of female characters in a non-stereotyped way give a feminist bent to *Malinche*. The novel exposes many of the ways in which women are mistreated and misrepresented in society. For example, when she is sold to the merchants of Xicalango, "Le dolió recordar que ofrecieron mucho más por unas plumas de quetzal que por ella" (124) ["It hurt her to remember that they offered much more for quetzal feathers than they did for her" (20)], a memory that reveals how little women were valued in society. The criticism of the small worth of women is reiterated when Malinalli indicates her disagreement with the way in which the Mexica governed: "se oponía a un sistema que determinaba lo que una mujer valía, lo que los dioses querían .... Estaba convencida de que urgía un cambio social" (16) ["Malinalli was completely opposed to the way in which they (the Mexica) governed, could not agree with a system that determined what a woman was worth, what the gods wanted .... She was convinced that a political, social and spiritual change was urgently needed" (20)]. The lowly condition of women is reconfirmed when Malinalli is raped by Cortés: "Sintió alivio en recuperar su condición de sometimiento, pues le resultaba mucho más familiar la sensación de ser objeto al servicio de los hombres que ser creadora de su destino" (76) ["A woman who ... felt relief in reclaiming her condition of submission, for it was a much more familiar sensation to be an object at the service of men than to be a creator of destiny" (79)]. In other passages, Malinalli explains that she felt there must have been something bad inside of her "tal vez por el simple hecho de ser mujer" (96) ["perhaps the simple act of being a woman" (98)], obviously an idea preconditioned by the society in which she lived. Finally, toward the end of the novel, Malinalli dreams of "una mente femenina unificada," a positive image of a female unity in a world without pain, much of which has been caused by patriarchal society:

> En su sueño se vio como parte de una mente femenina unificada que tenía el mismo sueño. En él un grupo de mujeres descalzas ... fueron todas una sola mujer que se sostenía en el viento y que se alimentaba de la fe de todas las que querían liberarse de la pesadilla de sentir de tocar, de llorar, de amar, de sangre, de morir, de tener y dejar de tener. (113–114)

> [In her dream she saw herself as part of a united feminine mind that was having the same dream. In the dream, a group of barefoot women ... became one mind, one body, they were all one woman holding herself up in the wind, and nourished on the faith of all who want to free themselves from the nightmare of sensation, of touching, of weeping, of loving, of bleeding, of dying, of having and of letting go. (115)]

This idea of a universal feminine community suggests a feminine solidarity and perspective in the novel.[9] *Malinche* thus gives voice to both a female perspective and the women's societal condition throughout the text. Malinalli is revealed in the novel as a victim of both colonization and patriarchal society. Thus, these feminist and postcolonial elements evolve Fuentes's concept of Mexican identity as a division between oppressors and oppressed. Within the oppressed there are women and indigenous peoples who cannot be simply grouped with men and white or even mestizo society. These groups do not necessarily all share a single perspective. Esquivel's novel illustrates how such dichotomies as expressed in *La muerte de Artemio Cruz* have become obsolete and how identity in the historical novel needs to be re-imagined and redefined in terms of contemporary theories, notably those of postcolonialism and feminism. It is one of the many feminist and postcolonial historical novels that signal the fallacy of earlier historical novels to pinpoint a homogenous national identity and the new direction of the search for plural national identities in the Latin American historical novel.

In this volume, Chapter 2, "*Ashes of Izalco*: Female Narrative Strategies and the History of a Nation," by Patricia Varas, illustrates how Claribel Alegría's novel *Cenizas de Izalco* (1966) is an excellent example of the rejection of the concept of a singular national identity as promulgated through official historiography in El Salvador during the 1930s. According to Varas, the massacre at Izalco is constructed in the novel as a key moment in the formation of an alternative national identity to the one posited through official history. This alternative national identity is achieved through the use of feminist narrative strategies throughout the text. The protagonist, Carmen, a modern woman, returns to El Salvador for her mother's funeral. She is presented with her mother's lover's diary, a private document that also narrates the public event of *La Matanza*, the 1932 *campesino* massacre. Although the diary directly presents the voice of Isabel's lover, Frank, it is left to Carmen by her mother. It is through this diary that her mother's story and condition as a marginalized woman, with which Carmen identifies, is brought to the fore. Moreover, Carmen further mediates the version of history presented in the diary by constantly questioning its content. She takes control of its narrative by deciding which versions of national history to recover and accept, thus making Isabel, her mother, visible, and giving authority to the female voice in the narration. When, for example, Carmen accepts the Indian woman's narration of history as recounted in the diary, she is showing how the singular national identity postulated by official history becomes a series of national identities that include indigenous people as well as women. In this sense, Alegría's novel is an early example of how both feminism and postcolonialism have shaped the contemporary Latin American historical novel.

Chapter 5 of this volume, Elda Stanco's "Archaeologies of Identity: Revisions of the City and the Nation in Two Novels by Ana Teresa Torres," examines *El exilio del tiempo* (1990) [*The Exile of Time*] and *Doña Inés contra el olvido* (1992) [*Doña Inés Versus Oblivion*] as historical revisionist narratives that illustrate the importance of female identity within the

Venezuelan nation. Stanco constructs parallels between national history, Caracas, and the female protagonists of Torres's two novels. While Doña Inés searches for property titles that would legitimize her identity and becomes a metaphor for the city that is instrumental in redefining Caracas, in *El exilio del tiempo*, the female narrator gives her impressions of the city as she moves from the city center to the ultramodern and chic neighborhood on the east side of Caracas. Later on, her encounter with Paris on a trip to Europe is also crucial to the formation of her own critical, psychological, and social agency. Both of Torres's protagonists are new urban subjects who must read national history through the city and turn into archaeologists of Caracas. In both novels, the feminine subject manipulates the complicated historical image of the nation, thus disrupting the previous patriarchal mythology of the nation through her critical conscience. Torres's critical view in these fables of the Venezuelan national imaginary allows not only for historical revision and reconsideration, but also for the establishment of feminine voice and identity in historical Venezuela. The city comes to hold a cultural importance that is identified with the female perspective and ultimately illustrates how previous patriarchal conceptions of the nation were limited and have been negated by an equally valid feminine vision.

Chapter 6, "*Santa Evita*, History, Fiction, and Myth: A Narrative from Another Side," by Marcelo Coddou, is another good example of historical fiction that relates to national identity. Coddou analyzes Tomás Eloy Martínez's *Santa Evita* (1995) [*Saint Evita*] as a novel that employs historical sources and references to deconstruct and then reconstruct the myth of Eva Perón. According to Coddou, the novel can be considered a "true fiction" whose purpose is essentially to employ the reconstructed figure of Eva Perón as a symbol of multiple and distinct national identities, thus illustrating a postmodern concept of identity. In other words, Eva Perón is simultaneously seen as the voice of women (feminist), the anti-imperialist voice of the Argentine workers (postcolonial), and a symbol of a specific time period in Argentine politics. With regard to this last dimension, Martínez's construction of Evita's wandering corpse becomes a symbol of a wandering Argentina, whose "body" has also been disappeared and mistreated by military dictatorship. As Coddou points out, this politicized image is one of the ways in which Martínez seeks to "correct the future" by underscoring the historical minefields of the past. The fact that Martínez chooses a strong and influential female figure, Eva Perón, as the focus of his novel, further illustrates the shift toward feminism and the importance of women in the development of the contemporary historical novel.

Finally, in Chapter 9, "(In)submissive Imaginaries in the Contemporary Brazilian Historical Novel: A Reading of *Um defeito de cor* [*A Defect of Color*] by Ana Maria Gonçalves," Maria Josele Bucco Coelho examines both feminism and postcolonialism in Brazil through an analysis of Ana Maria Gonçalves's *Un defeito de cor* (2006). The novel traces the development of contemporary Brazilian hybrid identity by recounting the story of Luiza Mahin, mother of the first Brazilian black poet, Luiz Gama. The protagonist, Kehinde/Luiza, is an African woman who flees abuse in her country only to end up a slave in Brazil. The novel shows how Kehinde's identity is fragmented by her constant transit, the experience of which results in her simultaneous acceptance and rejection of elements from both African and Brazilian culture. Kehinde's hybridization is a good example of Homi Bhabha's postcolonial theorizing of this concept. However, in addition to its postcolonialism, the novel also brings to the fore what Bucco Coelho calls the "double oppression" of women of color that also constitutes Kehinde's identity. The novel criticizes the subaltern status accorded to women, and shows Kehinde's rebellion against this status through her desire to become a financially independent woman and her disposition to follow her sexual passion. Thus, Bucco Coelho's analysis emphasizes the manner in which novels such as *Um defeito de cor* undermine the hegemonic notion of national identity and serves as another good example of the influence of postcolonialism and feminism on the contemporary Latin American historical novel.

Magical Realism and the Historical Novel

The second category of contemporary historical novel is one that largely coincides with what Jacobs calls "recombinant fiction." These novels present a mixture of history and myth, and are akin to what has often been called "magical realism" in Latin American fiction. Magical realism, like feminism and postcolonialism, has been granted different meanings by different critics. Seymour Menton, in his article "Magic Realism: An Annotated International Chronology of the Term," provides an exhaustive catalogue of the different ways in which "magical realism" has been used. Menton distinguishes between two basic conceptualizations of magical realism: the Americanist and the Internationalist. The Americanists view Latin American culture as "clearly distinguishable from European and Untied States culture because of the mythological elements in its Indian and African substrata" (126), while the Internationalists do not see magical realism as a purely Latin American phenomenon. Another article useful for delimiting the concept of magical realism is Adalbert Dessau's "Realismo mágico y nueva novela latinoamerica: consideraciones metodológicas e históricas" ["Magical Realism and Latin American New Novel: Historical and Methodological Considerations"]. Dessau defines magical realism as the simultaneous representation of the characters' social and physical reality and the magical or mythic transformation that this reality undergoes in the popular imagination (Dessau, 354). Dessau is very adamant that the usage of this term must apply only with regard to realist novels or novels that try to reflect reality in a philosophically rational manner; it cannot refer to antirealist or nonrealist novels (351). As I have already noted, some critics, such as Pons, do not include these novels in the category of historical novels. However, if we consider the distinguishing characteristic of historical purpose, we can conclude that such novels should be incorporated into the category of historical fiction, because they ultimately seek to illustrate, through myth and fantasy, both how Latin American history at times seems more incredible than fiction[10] and how Latin American popular beliefs have influenced the perceptions of reality and history. In other words, history appears in these novels not as a mere secondary or decorative element, but as an essential part of the message and vision of the texts in question.

Two paradigmatic novels that illustrate the evolution of magical realism are Gabriel García Márquez's *Cien años de soledad* (1967) [*One Hundred Years of Solitude*] and Isabel Allende's *La casa de los espíritus* (1982) [*The House of the Spirits*]. García Márquez's text is the classic example of magical realism in Latin American fiction. Nonetheless, despite its association with exaggeration, hyperbole, and fantastic elements, such as Rebeca's levitations or the butterflies that follow Mauricio Babilonia, the novel concretely portrays a number of historical events and bases itself on historical chronicles. Indeed, the entire novel is ultimately a reflection upon the value of history and the ways in which history can teach us to avoid disaster.

In "One Hundred Years of Solitude as Chronicle of the Indies," Iris M. Zavala illustrates a close relationship between the novel and chronicles of the Indies. Of particular interest is the relationship that the foundation of Macondo bears to a Chronicle written by Gonzalo Jiménez de Quesada, the founder of Bogotá, who according to Zavala speaks of "a kind of prehistoric Macondo when, on arriving at Santa Marta in 1535, he finds four squalid houses and a miserable church" (Zavala, 113). Moreover, as Gene H. Bell-Villada shows in his article "Banana Strike and Military Massacre: One Hundred Years of Solitude and What Happened in 1928," the entire episode about the banana strikers is based on historical fact. According to Bell-Villada, "What we see happening in the banana fields of Macondo is narrative, is novel, is fiction; but it is also basically a true story, a piece of history carefully reconstructed, and then artfully exaggerated" (Bell-Vida, 129). The novel portrays many historical events, most notably the seemingly endless civil wars between liberals and conservatives in Colombia known as "La Violencia," which spanned the years 1948–1958. The "magical" techniques that García Márquez mixes into these historical events include a circular and mythic time, chronological anticipation of events, exaggerated or impossible occurrences, like the insomnia plague, Aureliano's 17 sons who are marked by a cross on the forehead and are eventually assassinated, Fernanda's invisible doctors, the appearance of death before Amaranta, Ursula bringing letters to the dead, and the rain that lasts for four years invoked by the banana company to avoid signing an armistice. These are just a few examples of fantasy, hyperbole, and popular belief in the novel. Nonetheless, it is important to emphasize that these elements are a literary technique with a specific aim, and in no way obscure the historical character of the novel.

García Márquez's *Cien años de soledad* to a large degree relies on irony and satire to achieve a portrait of Colombian history. The last Aureliano simultaneously deciphers and lives the apocalyptic ending of the Buendía family. As Brian Coniff points out, this ending illustrates the need to know and interpret history to avoid repeating its pitfalls (the birth of the child with a pig's tail):

> The novel's "apocalyptic closure" is a denial of progress, as conceived by either the scientist or the politician, and a momentary glimpse of the world that might have been, if the great patriarch had not been so carried away with his idea of the future—if he had tried, instead, to understand history.
>
> (Coniff, 144)

Thus, the novel ultimately provides a reflection on the value and importance of history through the narration of the story of the successive generations of the Buendía family.

Some 15 years later, Isabel Allende published *La casa de los espíritus*, a novel that has frequently been compared to *Cien años de soledad* and has occasionally been disparaged by critics as a poor imitation of García Márquez's landmark work. It is my intention to show in the following pages, quite the opposite: Allende's use of magical realism obeys different objectives and imperatives than those of her predecessor and clearly signals the movement of the magical realist historical novel toward a novel and important feminist perspective.

As various critics have noted, *Cien años de soledad* and *La casa de los espíritus* share many of the same characteristics. They are both based on historical events, the Colombian civil wars and the fall of Salvador Allende's Chilean socialist government in 1973 (followed by the Pinochet government), respectively. Both novels incorporate a series of "magical" events or popular beliefs. I have already mentioned several examples of this technique in García Márquez's work. Allende similarly employs a protagonist who can foresee the future, Clara del Valle; the appearance of the ghost of Férula, Esteban Trueba's sister, after her death; communication with spirits by Clara and the Mora sisters; and the magical healing powers of the first Pedro, who "recomposes" Esteban Trueba's broken bones after the earthquake, just to name a few examples. However, in my view, the exaggerations and employment of "magical" elements in *La casa de los espíritus* are scarce in comparison with those found in her predecessor's work. Consequently, the historical element in Allende's novel is much more apparent and prominent when compared to García Márquez's novel. Not only do specific, major historical figures, such as Allende and Pinochet, appear in the novel, but some of the fictionalized characters, such as Clara's brother Jaime, appear to have historical counterparts. Jaime, who accompanies Allende in the presidential palace on the day of the military coup, may well be based on Allende's doctor, Dr. Enrique París Roa, who was one of the last people to see Allende alive that day. Also, the citation of Allende's final address to the Chilean people adheres to historical fact and has been altered very minimally in the novel. The address appears thus in *La casa de los espíritus*:

> Siempre estaré junto a ustedes. Tengo fe en la patria y su destino. Otros hombres superarán este momento y mucho más temprano que tarde se abrirán las grandes alamedas por donde pasará el hombre libre, para construir una sociedad mejor. ¡Viva el pueblo!¡Vivan los trabajadores! Estas serán mis últimas palabras. Tengo la certeza de que mi sacrificio no será en vano. (387)

> [I will always be with you. I have faith in our nation and its destiny. Other men will prevail, and soon the great avenues will be open again, where free men will walk, to build a better society. Long live the people! Long live the workers! These are my last words. I know my sacrifice will not have been in vain. (368)]

This is an almost literal translation of Allende's actual speech, as can be observed in the following transcription of the radio broadcast:

> Siempre estaré junto a ustedes.... Trabajadores de mi Patria, tengo fe en Chile y su destino. Superarán otros hombres este momento gris y amargo en el que la traición pretende imponerse. Siga ustedes sabiendo que, mucho más temprano que tarde, de nuevo se abrirán las grandes alamedas por donde pase el hombre libre, para construir una sociedad mejor. ¡Viva Chile! ¡Viva el pueblo! ¡Vivan los trabajadores! Estas son mis últimas palabras y tengo la certeza de que mi sacrificio no será en vano.
>
> (Salvador Allende, "Último discurso")

[I will always be with you . . . . Workers of my Country, I have faith in Chile and its destiny. Other men will prevail over this gray and bitter moment in which betrayal attempts to impose itself. Continue to know that, sooner rather than later, the great avenues through which free men walk will be open again, in order to construct a better society. Long live Chile! Long live the people! Long live the workers! These are my last words and I am certain that my sacrifice will not be in vain.]

(my translation)

Thus, Isabel Allende also inscribes herself not only within the category of magical realist historical texts, but also within the category of texts that directly engage with historical documentation.

While Allende's focus on Chile's historical governments is of great interest, and her criticism of the Pinochet dictatorship and the complicity of the Chilean bourgeoisie, which partially enabled it, is clearly the novel's main topic, Allende subtly inscribes a second history within this first, political theme. Throughout the novel, different female characters enact key moments in the history of the feminist movement, and embody dilemmas inherent to the female gender. I will here briefly summarize how Allende gives a feminist twist to Chilean history.[11]

First, it is no coincidence that Nívea del Valle, the first generation of women in the del Valle family, is a spokesperson for women's suffrage. We are told that Nívea primarily supported her husband's political bid for the senate "en la esperanza de que si él ocupaba un puesto en el Congreso, ella podría obtener el voto femenino" (13) ["hoping that if he won a seat in Congress she would finally secure the vote for women" (3)]. Thus, Nívea incarnates first-wave feminism, which in Chile ends in 1949, when women finally earned the right to vote in all elections. Allende continues to trace the historical development of feminism through her other female characters. A good example is her narration of the March of the Empty Pots. Although this march was a protest against the Allende government by conservative women, it led to the formation of a group called Fem Power, which Lisa Baldez calls "The Chilean version of Women's Liberation" (Baldez, 82). Moreover, during the subsequent Pinochet dictatorship, the empty pots became an inverted symbol of protest against the dictatorship and an important symbol of female mobilization in Chile. This historical event is chronicled in *La casa de los espíritus*: "Las mujeres de la oposición . . . desfilaban por las calles aporreando sus cacerolas en protesta por el desabastecimiento" (380) ["The women of the opposition, paraded in the streets pounding their empty pans in protest against the shortages in the stores" (362)].

Similarly, Isabel Allende exemplifies the mobilization of working women under Salvador Allende's government through the character of

Clara's daughter, Blanca. Blanca is a sculptor who begins to teach her art to working-class women in the shantytowns where "comenzó a enseñar cerámica en las poblaciones marginales, donde se habían organizado las mujeres para aprender nuevos oficios y participar por primera vez en la actividad política y social del país" (365) ["the women had organized to learn new trades, and for the first time, she took an active role in the political and social life of the country" (347)]. Moreover, Blanca, who is a single mother, prefers not to marry her lover, Pedro Tercero, thus illustrating the women's liberation movement of the 1970s and her refusal to accept the traditional roles of wife and mother. Blanca's daughter, Alba, who becomes a true political activist, portrays the increasing independence and public voice of women in the 1970s and 1980s through her helping political dissidents into exile and freedom. Finally, Amanda, Nicolás's girlfriend, undergoes an illegal abortion, which further portrays the plight of women in Chile, where abortion is still illegal. Many more examples of Allende's focus on women's issues and feminism abound in the novel, but these suffice to illustrate my point: Allende portrays a specific time period and two concrete governments in Chile, not only to criticize dictatorship and US imperialism (through its support of Pinochet—an implicit postcolonial topic), but also to illustrate how this time period (and others prior to it in the del Valle family history) interfaced with women's historical condition. In the 1980s, this was a relatively novel element in Latin American fiction. Women writers, who had been totally excluded from the "Boom" and hence "magical realism" (and ultimately the literary canon), began to emerge as an important voice in fiction. Along with Isabel Allende, whose enormous success catapulted her to the forefront of women's fiction, the 1980s saw the rise of other important female novelists, such as Luisa Valenzuela in Argentina and, as we have already seen, Laura Esquivel in Mexico, just to give a few examples. Valenzuela's *Cola de lagartija* (1983) is also an important historical novel. It is based on the figure of Juan Perón's fascist minister, José López Rega, and employs magical elements that reflect Argentine superstitions associated with Juan and Eva Perón. López Rega is depicted as an evil sorcerer and precursor to the subsequent "Dirty War" (1976–1983) in Argentina. Esquivel's popular *Como agua para chocolate* (1989) takes place during the 1910 Mexican Revolution. Although *Como agua para chocolate* is not primarily a historical novel, it does contain historical elements mixed with hyperbolic magic to portray the condition of women during the early twentieth century in Mexico. Also noteworthy of mention is the Paraguayan writer Renée Ferrer's *Vagos sin tierra* (1999), a historical novel that focuses on the colonization of border territories by Paraguayan peasants during the eighteenth century. The novel mixes colonial history with several characters (Bernardita, Teodoro) and events that are associated with magic. Bernardita can foresee the future, while Teodoro, the orphaned man-boy, frequents the witch doctors and mysteriously disappears, allegedly to unearth "urnas funerarias a fin de tranformar en flautas los huesos de sus amigos" (107) [funereal urns in order to transform the bones of his friends into flutes]. The novel is peppered with a talking horse and various indigenous legends as well. However, all of these elements are employed within a historical context largely to expose the exploitation of the peasants, and in particular, the subjugated and abused condition of women in that society. Thus, as in the case of Allende's novel, magical realism is used as a feminist tool to underscore the inferior treatment of women. Similarly, Manlio Argueta's *Milagro de la Paz* (1994) simultaneously recalls the civil war violence in El Salvador during the 1980s while intermixing it with magical elements, like the sudden appearance of a young girl with butterflies in her hair who adopts Latina's (the protagonist's) family. Argueta's focus on the plight of a family of women at the end of the Salvadoran conflict in 1992 employs magical realism to reveal a female perspective of both the past and the present history of El Salvador.

Historical Intertextuality

The third category of contemporary historical novel is that of novels that employ historical intertextuality. This is perhaps the broadest of the four components of my definition of the historical novel. We have already discussed several novels from the categories of national identity and magical realism that also employ direct reference to historical documentation. Clearly, there is much overlap between this classification and the others. What is interesting about the topic of historical intertextuality is how its purpose has evolved through postmodernism. Novels prior to those of the Boom have undoubtedly referred to historical documents (albeit more indirectly or simply by engaging with historical facts in a more general way), but with a different goal: that of historical accuracy. The notion of capturing "historical reality" with a didactic purpose disappears in the postmodern novel, which negates any such concept in favor of historical realities or subjectivities. This idea is further developed through historical novels that are postcolonial and feminist in nature, because the versions and perspectives on history from these marginalized groups are often in dissent with that of "official history" of white, patriarchal society. Thus, while the earlier historical novel was concerned with teaching the reader about history and subscribed to the belief that there was a definable set of historical facts, the more recent historical novel recognizes the subjectivity of history and the existence of different versions of the same events linked to individual perspective.

Instead of examining a traditional historical novel that aims to capture historical accuracy and to adhere to so-called historical fact, I would like to compare two historical novels from the past 50 years that are both contestatory of official historiography but illustrate the subtle move from a postmodern to postcolonial focus. The first novel, *Yo el Supremo* (1974) [*I the Supreme*] by the Paraguayan writer Augusto Roa Bastos, is perhaps the Latin American novel most famous for its historical intertextuality. More than 30 historical documents and books are either directly or indirectly cited or referred to in *Yo el Supremo*, including Guillermo Cabanellas's *El dictador del Paraguay*, Marco Antonio Laconich's *El Dr. José Gaspar Rodríguez de Francia: Supremo Dictador de la República del Paraguay*, Bartolomé Mitre's *Historia de Belgrano y de la Independencia Argentina*, Rengger and Longchamp's *Ensayo histórico sobre la revolución del Paraguay y el gobierno dictatorio del Doctor Francia*, John and William Parish Robertson's *Letters on Paraguay*, José Antonio Vázquez's *El doctor Francia, visto y oído por sus contemporáneos*, and Enrique Wisner's *El Dictador del Paraguay Doctor José Gaspar Rodríguez de Francia*, just to name a few (Weldt-Basson, *Augusto Roa Bastos's I the Supreme*, 110–170). The novel's protagonist, the nineteenth-century dictator José Gaspar Rodríguez de Francia, as well as a series of footnotes organized by a compiler, constantly discuss, contradict, and supplement this historical discourse. The novel is an ambitious attempt to revisit and overturn the "black legend" surrounding Dr. Francia, in large part written by Paraguay's imperialistic enemies—Great Britain and Argentina. Roa Bastos, using as a departure point citations from the revisionist history written on Francia by the Paraguayan Julio César Chaves, *El Supremo Dictador* (1942), attempts to provide the reader with a more balanced view of the dictator, his internal struggle between the allure of absolute power and the desire to help the populace and maintain Paraguay's independence from its powerful neighbors, Brazil and Argentina. At the same time, Roa Bastos offers a criticism of dictatorship, and the novel has primarily been classified as a "dictator novel" although many critics, such as Ángel Rama, have recognized its heterogeneity of genres (Rama, *Los dictadores*, 20–21).

In *Yo el Supremo* there is a complex set of interactions between the novel and its historical intertexts.[12] As already noted, a postmodern dialogue occurs in which various viewpoints interact and contradict one another. The reader has to make connections and deductions in order to make sense of the novel and can never be entirely sure about which interpretation of events, if any, is correct. Below I have selected one or two examples to illustrate the novel's postmodern and dialogic technique.

A source that proves extremely important for understanding the genesis of *Yo el Supremo* is the nineteenth-century essay written by Thomas Carlyle on Dr. Francia. Carlyle states that Dr. Francia is regarded as a chimera in the following passage:

> Francia, Dictator of Paraguay, is, at present, to the European mind, little other than a chimera. . . . As the Paraguenos, though not a literary people can many of them spell and write, and are not without a discriminating sense of true and untrue, why should not some real Life of Francia from those parts, be still possible! If a writer of genius arise there, he is hereby invited to the enterprise.
>
> (Carlyle, 4: 216–217, cited in Weldt-Basson,
> *Augusto Roa Bastos's I the Supreme*, 117)

The character El Supremo states: "Si una quimera, bamboleándose en el vacío, puede comer segundas intenciones, según decía el compadre Rabelais, bien comido estoy. La quimera ha ocupado el lugar de mi persona. Tiendo a ser lo quimérico" (102) ["If a chimera, swaying back and forth in a vacuum, can eat ulterior motives, I've been well chewed and swallowed, as compadre Rabelais put it. The chimera has occupied the place of my person. I tend to be the very image of the chimerical" (10–11)]; in stating this, he is thus clearly responding to Carlyle's essay. This contestatory relationship is made even more interesting by the fact that Carlyle suggests that a writer of genius write the true life of Dr. Francia, perhaps thus serving as Roa Bastos's inspiration to become the brilliant writer who achieves this task with the novel *Yo el Supremo*.

A second good example is Dr. Francia's version of events surrounding the Robertson Brothers, two British travelers to Paraguay during the nineteenth century, who subsequently published their *Letters on Paraguay* that largely maligned Dr. Francia. In the letter cited below, Robertson attempts to make Francia look foolish and unworldly be serving him sour beer:

> I once sent him a dozen bottles of porter . . . and three days afterwards, on paying a visit to his Excellency, the first bottle which had been drawn, half full, and without a cork, was brought in, and a wineglass was filled with Meux's "entire sour," and presented to me. I told Francia that we drank porter from tumblers and that a bottle once opened must be finished. Francia smiled. "I thought" said he, "it was rather sour today, at dinner, but come, we shall drink a bottle English style."
>
> (Robertson 2: 209–210, cited in Weldt-Basson, *Augusto
> Roa Bastos's I the Supreme*, 116)

This comment by John Robertson is directly contradicted by the dictator in the novel who is careful to explain that he knew all along the correct way to serve the beer but simply did not want to waste a new bottle on the Robertson Brothers: "Los Robertson se bebieron durante cinco años mi fermentada cerveza. No iba a destapar una damajuana cada semana en homenaje a estos fementidos green-go-home" (245) ["The Robertsons came around for five years to drink my invidious fermented brew. I wasn't going to uncork a fresh demijohn each week in honor of those perfidious green-go-homes" (Roa Bastos, *I the Supreme*, 116)]. He also indicates that the beer was purchased by him, and was not a gift, as suggested by Robertson. El Supremo uses this episode to underscore his honesty and his thriftiness.

These two examples suffice to illustrate my main point: the dialogic, contestatory, postmodern nature of the new historical novel that was emerging in the 1960s and 1970s. However, it is also important to note that although *Yo el Supremo* is anti-imperialist and concerns itself with the repeated British intervention in Paraguay as well as the multiple attempts at annexation by Brazil and Argentina, these topics appear as sub-topics that somewhat justify the dictator's actions, but do not form the main purpose of this historical novel. In other words, there is an emerging, but not full-fledged, postcolonial element in *Yo el Supremo*. The main theme is rather the analysis of the hunger for absolute power, the ways in which governments deviate from their initial ideals and become corrupt, and the re-evaluation of Dr. Francia in terms of the pros and cons of his government. Consequently, while the topic of colonialism is clearly present and important in *Yo el Supremo*, it can be said that is not yet the central purpose of the novel.

In contrast, as we start to enter the 1990s and beyond, the postcolonial perspective begins to dominate much of historical fiction as its primary focus. In 2001, the Puerto Rican writer Rosario Ferré published a novel titled *Flight of the Swan*, which first appeared in English, and then as *Vuelo del cisne* in Spanish in 2002[13]. Although Ferré is a renowned writer, this particular novel has received little critical attention. The novel is based on the life of the famous Russian ballerina, Anna Pavlova, who lived during the first half of the twentieth century. Two of the novel's principal historical sources are, first and foremost, the biography with the same name, *Flight of the Swan: A Memory of Pavlova* by André Oliveroff, a dancer in Pavlova's troupe; and second, a book titled *Pavlova: Portrait of a Dancer* by Margot Fonteyn. The novel blatantly calls attention to the first of its historical intertexts by sharing its title: This is an important element that initiates the dialogue between Oliveroff's account and the novel about Pavlova's life written by Ferré.

The way in which Ferré employs her intertexts differs from that of Roa Bastos. With perhaps one or two exceptions, Ferré does not actually quote from these texts. Nonetheless, there are several ways in which Ferré directly alludes to her sources and dialogues with them.

The first connection is almost identical to the connection established between *Yo el Supremo* and Carlyle's essay on Dr. Francia. As we saw in the analysis of *Yo el Supremo*, Carlyle suggested the idea of a "writer of genius" attempting to capture on paper the "true" life of Dr. Francia. Similarly, in Oliveroff's biography of Pavlova, he states: "Her ballet company formed an integral part of her theatre and since it was through and for her theatre that she lived, perhaps there is no more direct approach to this curiously inaccessible woman than through the eyes of those who shared with her, her life of the dance" (xi). In other words, just as Carlyle invites a more authentic biography to solve the mystery of the "chimerical" Dr. Francia, so does Oliveroff suggest that the only ones capable of writing a true biography of Pavlova, a "curiously inaccessible woman," are the members, such as himself, of her dance troupe. This statement and model clearly give rise to the narrative situation in *Vuelo del cisne*, since the narrator of Pavlova's life is a member of her troupe named Masha Mástova. Masha is not a historical character but appears to be based on another dancer described in Oliveroff's biography named Muriel, who, like Masha, eventually leaves the troupe to marry. The important point here is that Ferré follows the exact model of the biographical *Flight of the Swan*, which is the narration of the biography of Pavlova by one of her dancers.

Another way in which Ferré alludes to her intertextual source is by the constant reference to Pavlova as "Madame" in the novel. This is another element adopted from Oliveroff's biography in which he states: "I soon learned to refer to Pavlova as 'Madame'. She was nearly always called that by her company" (30). Many other details from Oliveroff's book suggest similar counterparts in Ferré's novel, such as the portrayal of Mr. Dandré, Pavlova's business manager as well as lover and possibly husband, as a vaguely shady and dislikable man, albeit attentive to Madame's needs. The presence of the character Juan, the shoemaker in Puerto Rico, appears to correspond to the fact that according to Oliveroff

> [s]he [Pavlova] had a real obsession about ballet shoes. They hardly ever suited her. She spent half her life fussing with them, trying on new ones, cutting them up, ripping out the inner soles and pasting in new soles so shaped that they would conform more closely to arch when she pointed her foot. As a rule she wore a new pair of slippers for every ballet. (40–41)

Oliveroff's comments also can be linked to Madame's desire toward the end of Ferré's novel to dance for the poor, thus following the goal suggested in Oliveroff's anecdote of a dialogue between Pavlova and her chambermaid: "But what have I done to evoke such enthusiasm? 'Madame' she replied 'You have made them happy in allowing them to forget for an hour the sadness of life'. I have never forgotten that answer. The simple girl . . . a Russian peasant she was, gave my art a new goal" (59–60). Similarly, the constant insistence that art comes before love, the idea that a true dancer cannot marry, is also documented in this historical source. Oliveroff quotes Pavlova thus: "People ask me why I do not marry. The answer is very simple. I believe that a true artist must sacrifice herself to her art— absolutely" (Oliveroff, 61). Finally, she also takes a direct quotation from the previously mentioned book by Fonteyn, who states regarding Pavlova's South American tour: "During the war we were kept almost as prisoners in South America for two years" (96)—a statement that is echoed by Masha when the troupe arrives in Puerto Rico in *Vuelo del cisne*: "Nuestra troupe se encontró varada aquí a comienzos de la Primera Guerra Mundial durante tres meses estuvimos prácticamente prisioneros" (5) ["Our ballet company was stranded here during the Great War. For three months we were virtual prisoners" (4)].

The adherence to these many details raises an important question: Is Ferré merely producing a traditional historical novel by obeying historical fact and adhering as closely as possible to the biographical accounts available on Pavlova? Despite Ferré's apparent imitation of historical sources and superficial appearance of historical accuracy, in reality, the Latin American tour did not actually stop in Puerto Rico, and the novel invents much material that takes it in a completely different direction than one of historical fact. Ferré artfully uses the life of Pavlova as a platform for criticizing colonization of Puerto Rico by the United States in the early twentieth century and also as a feminist motif, since Pavlova was a woman who broke many of the taboos established for women during that time period. Hence, the novel employs historical intertextuality with a postcolonial and secondarily feminist intent, as I will show in the following pages.

The fictive element in Ferré's appropriation of Pavlova is largely connected to her love affair with a Puerto Rican anti-imperialist activist, Diamantino Márquez. The relationship between these two characters causes tension between Madame and her dancers, who do not approve of Madame's breaking of her own rule: not to fall in love and to remain totally dedicated to dance. The figure of Márquez and the resetting of the dance troupe's tour from other parts of Latin America to Puerto Rico both allow Ferré to contradict the official historical record and to develop the novel in a postcolonial direction. The following extract describes one scene that illustrates well how Pavlova becomes a postcolonial prop; here Puerto

Ricans are being made into American citizens, incited to fight in World War I and to collect money to feed the US soldiers:

> Cerca del Puerto había mucha actividad, la multitud se aglomeraba en las aceras cantando el himno nacional norteamericano y agitando banderitas.... Nos preguntamos cuál sería la razón para aquel despliegue enloquecido del patriotismo... "Nos hicieron ciudadanos americanos hace poco y tenemos que defender nuestra ciudadanía con la vida." Madame lo fulminó con la Mirada. "Eso es imposible. Como puede uno convertirse ciudadano de un país que no es el suyo" preguntó. (58–59)

> [A line of uniformed recruits marched toward the wharf, knapsacks on their backs, carrying Winchester rifles. The column was headed by still more flags and a large band played a march by John Philip Sousa, the American composer.... Madame was amazed. "And why should they defend Panama? It's not their country, is it?" She asked.... "It is now, Madame! We were made American citizens only last month, and we have to defend our citizenship with our lives." (53)]

Madame is a vehicle in this passage for criticizing the colonialist actions of the United States. She equally denounces the linguistic colonization of Puerto Rico when she hears the students reciting their multiplication tables in English and their singing of the Star Spangled Banner. The imposition of the US "dry laws" in Puerto Rico is also criticized as the reason that many of the Puerto Ricans cannot afford to attend Madame's ballet: the Puerto Rican economy, in which rum is a principal item, was adversely affected by these laws (107).

Although the topic of colonialism is prominent in *Vuelo del cisne*, the novel does not often present the ambivalence associated with the colonial subject: the vacillation between desire and scorn that is discussed as central to postcolonialism by Homi Bhabha. A touch of this aspect is revealed through the character Juan, the black shoemaker, who is both esteemed and demeaned by colonial society. On the one hand, Juan is a skilled craftsman who services the ballet company and is the object of Masta's sexual desires; on the other, he is treated as a peon by racist members of society, such as doña Basilisa: "Juan era un hombre educado y nunca hacía estos trabajos meniales, pero cuando doña Basilisa vio que era negro, lo mandó derecho a la cocina" (155) ["Juan was an educated man, but because he was black, Doña Basilisa sent him straight to the kitchen" (138)]. Although Juan is a relatively minor character, he embodies the problems and viewpoints of racial minorities in Puerto Rico and enacts the postcolonial vision of giving voice to racial minorities. This discrimination is echoed by Diamantino

Márquez when he complains that "Somos ciudadanos americanos, pero no de la misma categoría.... En cuanto a los alimentos que nos están obligando a sembrar para los soldados, deberíamos dárselos a nuestra gente, que se está muriendo de hambre" (146–147) ["We're citizens, all right, but not like they are. We're second class.... And as to the food they're making us grow, we should give it to our starving population instead" (129)].

Nonetheless, despite a loose adherence to the strict definition of postcolonialism espoused by Bhabha, *Vuelo del cisne* specifically employs history (Pavlova's biography) to evolve a criticism of colonialism through the words and actions of the colonial subject. Pavlova's romance with Diamantino Márquez clearly serves as a plot element whose principal purpose is to function as a vehicle for giving voice to the colonial subject through Márquez's character. The following is a typical comment expressing the colonial subject's view of his situation as expressed by Márquez in the novel: "Nuestro caso es trágico. Somos la última vagoneta del tren; la única colonia latinoamericana que no llegó nunca a ser independiente. Las tropas norteamericanas se quedaron con nosotros al final de la guerra hispanoamericana, y en el 98, pasamos a ser botín de guerra" (76) ["Ours is a tragic case. We're the only Latin American country that never became independent: the little caboose at the end of the train, held up by the American troops at the close of the Spanish–American War" (68)].

Although *Vuelo del cisne* ultimately reads more as an anticolonial novel than as a feminist one, Ferré definitely includes the feminist theme in her novel. As previously mentioned, the mere selection of Pavlova as a topic for her book suggests a feminist orientation, since Pavlova was the ultimate career woman during a time period in which women were mostly confined to the home. Pavlova is portrayed as engaging in a sexual freedom that was largely condemned and unknown to the average Puerto Rican woman. We are told in the novel that when she was 16 she was simultaneously the lover of both Dandré and one of his friends, resulting in an early pregnancy and abortion. Later on, she also participates in a passionate affair with Diamantino, which although is non-historical, contributes to the overall feminist image of the character.

In another instance, Masha points to the feminist character of ballet, which is clearly a female-centered activity: "En estos instantes me sentía completamente colmada. No tenía que envidiarles nada a los hombres. Tenía todo lo que ellos tenían porque en el ballet las mujeres suelen ser protagonistas y bailan el papel principal" (100) ["At that moment I felt completely fulfilled. We didn't have to envy men anything; we had everything they had, only better, for in ballet, women always performed the leading roles" (88)]. Finally, the novel implicitly criticizes the professional limitations placed on women in Puerto Rico when Ronda is not allowed to

become a veterinarian: "Ronda ... quería estudiar en una facultad veterinaria ... pero don Pedro se rehusó a complacerla. La carrera veterinaria era
solo para los hombres por aquel entonces" (169) ["Ronda said she wanted
only two things: to be able to go on to veterinary school and to own a
pura sangre .... But Don Pedro ... refused both. There were no women
veterinarians on the island—it was a career for men" (151)].

Vuelo del cisne, like *Yo el Supremo*, relies heavily on historical
intertextuality but takes this intertextuality in a completely different direction. Although it does contest some historical facts, the postmodern,
counterhistorical aspect of the novel is not primary. Instead, the novel
employs its historical elements, the figure of Anna Pavlova, in both a
postcolonial and a feminist fashion. These are persistent themes in Ferré's
fiction, especially in novels like *Maldito amor* (1989) [*Sweet Diamond
Dust*] and *La casa en la laguna* (1995) [*The House on the Lagoon*], which
both reflect on Puerto Rico's colonial status and liken it to the exploited
situation of women. The contemporary Puerto Rican writer Mayra Santos-
Febres is another good example of the feminist and postcolonial emphases
of many newer historical novels. Her novel *Nuestra señora de la noche*
(2006) is based on the historical figure Isabel Luberza Oppenheimer, a
famous Puerto Rican prostitute during the first half of the twentieth century. Although few facts are known about Isabel's life, the novel attempts
to historically document the reality of black women and racial minorities
during that time period.

In Chapter 8, "The Plural History of Memory: A Polyphonic Novel by
Ángela Hernández," Ester Gimbernat González examines the Dominican
novel *Charamicos* (2003), based on the post-Trujillo time period known
as the "twelve years of Balaguer" (1966–1978). During this pseudo-
democratic era, thousands of citizens were tortured by the Antiterrorist
and Anticommunist Front. The novel concentrates on the early 1970s,
when this para-police group was first formed. Gimbernat González examines how the novel's first-person female narrator, Trinidad, who has been
reductively termed a "testimonial" and "bildungsroman" voice by many
critics, is connected to the complexity and collectivity of this historical experience, offering both a feminine time frame and perspective that
succeed in tracing the almost invisible process of women's participation
in the history of the Dominican Republic during those years. Thus, her
study establishes a connection between Dominican political liberation and
women's perspective and liberation at the end of the twentieth century,
once again confirming the importance of feminism and gender studies in
the development of the contemporary Latin American historical novel. The
dialogue with historical intertextuality is achieved through the novel's second protagonist, Ercira, whose name is inspired by the historical figure

Sagrario Ercira Díaz. Díaz was murdered by the military during the protests at the Universidad Autónoma de Santo Domingo. Through the novel's incorporation of Balaguer's historical speech praising Díaz, Gimbernat González illustrates how the female voice of her protagonist engages with historical intertextuality to present a counter-history to patriarchal official historiography and grant feminist agency to women.

In Chapter 7, "Movements and Simulations of History in *Mujer en traje de batalla* [*Woman in Battle Dress*] by Antonio Benítez Rojo," Fátima R. Nogueira studies this Cuban novel published in 2001, based on the life of Henriette Faber. Faber was the wife of an officer in the army of Napoleon Bonaparte, in the early nineteenth century. The novel traces her marriage, widowhood, and studies in the Faculty of Medicine in the University of Paris, disguised as a man, her participation as a surgeon in some of the Napoleonic campaigns and her settlement in Cuba where she practiced medicine, married Juana de León under the name Enrique Faber and finally revealed her identity and gender, with an ensuing judicial trial and expulsion from Cuba. Nogueira analyzes how the transvestitism of the main character reflects historical processes and interpretations and also impacts on the conception of writing in general, reducing everything to a constant farce. This chapter engages with historical intertexts (including a painting for which the novel is named) and facts through a focus on gender and identity that clearly illustrates the importance of the theoretical framework of feminism and gender studies within the contemporary postmodern historical novel. Moreover, Nogueira discusses the ways in which Faber's historical transvestism is employed in the novel as a means by which to confront and combat the social injustices committed against women throughout history.

The Symbolic Historical Novel

The last category of contemporary historical novel is that of symbolic historical fiction. This type of historical fiction is less common than that of the other categories but is very well exemplified by much of the historical fiction written by Mario Vargas Llosa. Seymour Menton indirectly alludes to this technique in Vargas Llosa's novel *La guerra del fin del mundo* (1981) [*The War at the End of the World*] when he discusses the role of fanaticism in the novel:

> Vargas Llosa's condemnation of fanaticism in late nineteenth-century Brazil is also aimed at the left-wing extremists who have excoriated him, particularly since 1971, for his criticism of the Cuban government's curtailment of freedom of artistic expression. Although the Peruvian Shining Path

guerrillas have also been a target of Vargas Llosa's campaign against fanaticism, they did not emerge until 1980, and therefore it is unlikely that they directly influenced the writing of the novel published in 1981.
(Menton, *The Latin American New Historical Novel*, 40)

In other words, Vargas Llosa employs an example from nineteenth-century Brazilian history to allude to fanaticism in twentieth-century Cuba. One country's history becomes a metaphor for another's. This is also the case in Vargas Llosa's important dictator novel, *La fiesta del chivo* (2000) [*The Feast of the Goat*]. The novel is simultaneously a fairly accurate portrayal of the dictatorship of Rafael Leonidas Trujillo in the Dominican Republic (1931–1960) and a reflection on the government of Alberto Fujimori (1990–2000) and his abuse of power in Peru. The way in which Vargas Llosa offers the reader a "clue" to this relationship is through the character Henry Chirinos. Chirinos is presented as a minister in the Trujillo government in the novel, but in reality is based on a congressman during the Fujimori government named Enrique Chirinos Soto (Weldt-Basson, *La fiesta del chivo*, 125). The real Enrique Chirinos was overweight and had a drinking problem, both of which are characteristics attributed to the fictional Chirinos in Vargas Llosa's novel (Conaghan, 130). Consequently, Vargas Llosa invites the reader to consider the many parallels between the Trujillo dictatorship and the Fujimori presidency. Both dictators employed unscrupulous men to head their intelligence agencies (Johnny Abbés in the Dominican Republic and Vladimiro Montesinos in Peru), their intelligence agencies had similar names (SIM in the Dominican Republic and SIN in Peru), they controlled the press, and were responsible for persecuting enemies and human rights violations (Weldt-Basson, "La fiesta del chivo," 126). Thus, in many ways, Vargas Llosa's portrayal of Trujillo becomes symbolic of the Fujimori government in Peru.

Although Vargas Llosa is perhaps the best example of the symbolic historical novel, he is clearly not the only writer to employ this technique. Another good example is the work *El invierno de Gunter* (1987) [*Gunther's Winter*] by the Paraguayan writer Juan Manuel Marcos. Although *El invierno de Gunter* takes place in Argentina and refers to many Argentine historical events of the 1980s, such as the War against Great Britain for the Malvinas (Falkland Islands) and the Argentine Dirty War, it is essentially a reflection on Paraguayan history.

Marcos alludes to the Argentine dictatorship to establish parallels with the dictatorship of Alfredo Stroessner (1954–1989) in Paraguay. The novel's action takes place in Corrientes, Argentina and directly refers to the last president of the Argentine "Proceso," General Leopoldo Galtieri (Marcos, 183). However, almost all of the characters are modeled on

Paraguayan counterparts: Gumersindo Larraín shares characteristics with Alfredo Stroessner, while General González is similar in nature to General Andrés Rodríguez, the man who eventually overthrew Stroessner; Archbishop Cáceres evokes the Archbishop Ismael Rolón Silvero, famous for his opposition to Stroessner, and the torture of Soledad and Verónica, two important protagonists, can easily be interpreted as the torture of many Paraguayan political prisoners. There is also a reflection on past (rather than contemporaneous) Paraguayan history through the main character, Eliza Lynch, who shares her name with the concubine of the nineteenth-century Paraguayan President Francisco Solano López, who ruled Paraguay from 1862 to 1870. Marcos's reflection on the character Eliza Lynch presents a postmodern counterhistory that engages with historical intertexts on the topic and thus overlaps with the third category of historical novel discussed in this chapter.

These examples serve as a prelude to Vargas Llosa's most recent novel, *El sueño del celta* (2010) [*The Dream of the Celt*], which is another example of symbolic historical fiction that is discussed in Chapter 10 of this volume. *El sueño del celta* is in many ways a biography of Roger Casement, an Irishman famous for his denunciation of human rights violations in the Congo and Putumayo regions in the early twentieth century. However, in *El sueño del celta*, Vargas Llosa exposes Casement's ambiguity as both a supporter of the colonized and a representative of the colonial authorities (the British Empire). My analysis illustrates how Casement views the colonial subject as both an object of sexual desire, exotic other, and as human being, the same as himself or any other European, who has been shamelessly victimized. At times the novel falls into the colonialist trap of conflating the colonial situations of Africa and the Amazonian regions with that of Ireland vis-á-vis Great Britain, a tendency often criticized by postcolonial critics who emphasize the specificity of each geographical region. However, this conflation, which largely occurs in the character Casement's narration, is a good example of how Vargas Llosa uses history symbolically in the novel, which ultimately reads as the story of Casement's evolution into an Irish patriot executed for treason against the British government for his alleged participation in the Irish rebellion in 1916. As we shall see, this conflation somewhat diminishes the force of Vargas Llosa's anti-colonialist criticism in the novel. Nonetheless, through *El sueño del celta*, the reader can observe how the symbolic historical novel evolves from a political novel (as in the cases of *La guerra del fin del mundo*, *La fiesta del chivo*, and *El invierno de Gunter*), into a postcolonial political novel in which issues surrounding colonization and the colonial subject are the principal focus.

Chapter 3, "The Invention of Past and Present: Identity and the Historical Novel in the Works of Edgardo Rodríguez Juliá" by Víctor Figueroa, also deals with postcolonial realities. This chapter examines the Puerto Rican author's novels: *La renuncia del héroe Baltasar* (1974) [*The Renunciation*] and *La noche oscura del niño Avilés* (1984) [*The Dark Night of the Child Avilés*] as attempts to portray how national identities are not simply the result of historical processes that historians record, but also textual fictions created in the very process of historical writing. Figueroa examines how Rodríguez Juliá invents an alternative history of slave rebellions for Puerto Rico, thus creating what Turner would call a "disguised historical novel." Figueroa illustrates how the Puerto Rican writer symbolically refers to the nineteenth-century Haitian Revolution in his works to highlight both its successes and flaws. Thus, *La renuncia del heroe Baltasar* and *La noche oscura del niño Avilés* serve as two excellent examples of symbolic historical fiction. This chapter also shows how Rodríguez Juliá collapses the distinctions between historiographical writing and historical fiction, thus highlighting the political and social structures that underlie the production of both kinds of texts as well as the postmodern nature of Rodríguez Juliá's writing. Moreover, these two Puerto Rican texts overlap with the category of national identity, since Rodríguez Juliá posits black leaders for his slave rebellions as part of repressed national history and identity, thus emphasizing the postcolonial focus on marginalized racial groups during the process of national independence.

Another excellent example of the symbolic historical novel, this time achieved through historical intertextuality, is found in Chapter 4, Fernando Burgos's "The Galleys of History: Mirages and Madness of a Journey." Burgos examines the revised version of the Cuban writer Reinaldo Arenas's *El mundo alucinante* (1982, originally written in 1969) [*Hallucinations*] and the Uruguayan writer Cristina Peri Rossi's *La nave de los locos* (1984) [*Ship of Fools*] as historical novels by political dissidents who both use historical referents (*Las Memorias,* written by the Mexican priest Fray Servando Teresa de Mier [*Memoirs*] about his life in the late eighteenth and early nineteenth centuries and the "Tapestry of Creation," embroidered in the seventeenth century, from the museum of the Cathedral in Genoa, respectively) as metaphors for history that are utilized in their respective novels to question the ideals of order and revolution and to create an alternative mode of historical interpretation and social installment. Burgos's analysis also intertwines with gender and postcolonial studies through its emphasis on the importance of the perspective of the marginal "other." This is illustrated in Peri Rossi's novel through the isolation of the protagonist Ecks and the other exiled subjects on the "ship of fools,"[14] as well as through Arenas's focus on persecuted and marginalized beings who have been erased from official history, as symbolized by the dissident colonial priest Friar Servando de Mier. Friar Servando had been ex-communicated from the church, imprisoned and exiled for a sermon in which he dissented about the date of the apparition of the Virgin of Guadalupe and thus his history becomes symbolic of thousands of other persecuted and marginalized beings during the colonial period and beyond in *El mundo alucinante*.

This introduction to the Latin American historical novel of the past 50 years is just that—an introduction to the new directions defined by feminism and postcolonialism. It does not purport to offer a comprehensive overview of all the historical novels written since the 1960s in Latin America, but rather to illustrate these two new and important trends through a discussion of several paradigmatic novels. This introduction also seeks to broaden the definition of the historical novel through its discussion of four key categories of contemporary historical fiction and the illustration of the evolution of the historical novel within each of these domains. Since, as many critics of the historical novel have pointed out, the novel has evolved in Latin America from a minor to major genre, it is important to bear in mind the need for further expansion of research on the topic, as the genre continues to grow and change.

Notes

1. See the chapters titled "The Historical Text as Literary Artifact" (81–100) and "The Fictions of Factual Representation" (121–134) in Hayden White's *Tropics of Discourse: Essays in Cultural Criticism* for a discussion of metahistory (history's reflection on its own construction) and the similarities between the constructions of fictional and historical discourses.

2. There are some important studies that due to space constraint cannot be included in my discussion here. See Fernando Aínsa's *Reescribir el pasado: Historia y ficcion en America Latina*, originally published in 1974, and Raymond D. Souza's *La historia en la novela hispanoamericana moderna*, published in 1988. Noé Jitrik subsequently wrote a book further expounding on his theory of the historical novel: *Historia e imaginación literaria. Las posibilidades de un género*, published in 1995.

3. See the following theoretical works by Mikhail Bakhtin in which he discusses his concept of dialogism and the polyphonic novel in which a series of voices are given equal weight and not subsumed by the monologic vision of a single, authoritative narrator: *Problems of Dostoevsky's Poetics* and *The Dialogic Imagination*.

4. On the topic of the political and testimonial nature of historical fiction, see respectively: María Mudrovcic, "En busca de dos décadas perdidas: la novela latinoamericana de los años 70 y 80," and Linda Craft, *Novels of Testimony and Resistance from Central America*. Gainesville: University Press of Florida, 1997.

5. Some other very recent studies on non–Latin American women's historical fiction include: *African American Women Writer's Historical Fiction* by Ana Nunes (Palgrave 2011) and *The Daughter's Return: African-American and Caribbean Women's Fiction of History* by Caroline Rody (Oxford Press, 2001). Also of interest is Rosemary Erickson's study of feminist historical crime fiction: *Contemporary Feminist Historical Crime Fiction* (Palgrave, 2006). There also exist a number of studies specifically focused on historical romance: *The Historical Romance* by Helen Hughes (Routledge 1993) and Lisa Fletcher's *Historical Romance Fiction* (Palgrave 2008).

6. Note that although some novels that may be considered postcolonial exist prior to the 1960s, such as the work by Alejo Carpentier, it is not until approximately the past 50 years that this type of fiction begins to obtain momentum and have a true impact on the historical novel genre. The same can be said of feminist historical fiction as illustrated by various chapters in this book.

7. See the articles in Margo Glantz's *La Malinche, sus padres y sus hijos* for different interpretations regarding Malinche's relinquishment into slavery.

8. Esquivel cites various other important sources in her bibliography that appear to have influenced to some degree the manner in which she shapes the character Malinalli in her novel. See for example: Bernal Día del Castillo, *Historia Verdadera de la Conquista de la Nueva España*; Anna Lanyon, *Malinche's Conquest*; and Fernanda Nuñez Becerra, *La Malinche: de la historia al mito*.

9. See Nina Auerbach's *Communities of Women: An Idea in Fiction* for a discussion of the formation of feminist communities in literature.

10. The Cuban novelist Alejo Carpentier has made an important distinction between what he terms "Lo real maravilloso" (the marvelous real) and "realismo mágico" (magical realism). According to Carpentier, the marvelous real refers to novels that depict a Latin American reality that appears to be fictitious and magical, when in fact all the events are real, while magical realism mixes historical events with the magical popular vision of the Latin American people. See his prologue to his novel *El reino de este mundo* for his discussion of the topic. For my purposes, I have conflated these two perspectives here, because both constitute the same category of historical novel.

11. See Helene Carol Weldt-Basson, *Subversive Silences: Nonverbal Expression and Implicit Narrative Strategies in the Works of Latin American Women Writers*, for a more extensive discussion of the tracing of the history of feminism in Allende's novels.

12. See Helene Carol Weldt-Basson, *Augusto Roa Bastos's I the Supreme: A Dialogic Perspective*, for an in-depth analysis of the novel's extensive intertextuality.

13. There is an ironic contradiction inherent in Ferré's choice to publish this novel first in English, as opposed to Spanish, when the novel criticizes US influence in Puerto Rico, an influence clearly reflected by use of the English language on the island. A similar ironic element may be found in the character Diamantino Márquez who serves as an anti-colonial mouthpiece, since the character is the son of a wealthy Spaniard who has clearly benefited from Puerto Rico's prior status as a colony of Spain.

14. Mary Beth Tierney-Tello asserts that parallels can also be drawn between the marginalized, exiled state of the protagonist in *La nave de los locos* and the sexuality/plight of the woman writer. According to Tierney-Tello, Peri-Rossi has explicitly made this connection in several interviews. Moreover, *La nave de los locos* "flirts with androgyny throughout, implying that such a defiance of a determined gender could function as a method of resistance to the rigid binary oppositions of the patriarchal sexual economy" (193).

Works Cited

Aísna, Fernando. *Reescribir el pasado en América Latina*. Mérida (Venezuela): Celarg, 2003. Print.

Allende, Isabel. *The House of the Spirits*. New York: Bantam Books, 1993. Print.

———. *La casa de los espíritus*. New York: Edición Rayo (Harper Collins), 2001. Print.

Allende, Salvador. "Último Discurso." www.ciudadseva.com/textos/otros/ultimodi.htm. Web.

Argueta, Manlio. *Milagro de la paz*. San Salvador: Istmo Editores, 1994. Print.

Auerbach, Nina. *Communities of Women: An Idea in Fiction*. Cambridge (MA): Harvard University Press, 1978. Print.

Bahri, Deepika. "Feminism and Postcolonialism," in *Postcolonial Literary Studies*. Ed. Neil Lazarus. Cambridge: Cambridge University Press, 2004. 191–220. Print.

Bakhtin, Mikhail. *The Dialogic Imagination*. Ed. Michael Holquist and Trans. Caryl Emerson. Austin: University of Texas Press, 1981.

———. *Problems of Dostoevsky's Poetics*. Ed. and Trans. Caryl Emerson. Minneapolis: University of Minnesota Press, 1984.

Balderston, Daniel, Ed. *The Historical Novel in Latin America: A Symposium*. Gaithersburg (MD): Ediciones Hispamérica, 1986. Print.

Baldez, Lisa. *Why Women Protest: Women's Movements in Chile*. Cambridge (MA): Cambridge University Press, 2002. Print.

Bell-Villada, Gene H. "Banana Strike and Military Massacre: One Hundred Years of Solitude and What Happened in 1928," in *Gabriel García Márquez's One Hundred Years of Solitude: A Casebook*. Ed. Gene H. Bell-Villada. Oxford: Oxford University Press, 2002. 127–138. Print.

Bermann, Sandra. "Introduction," in *On The Historical Novel by Alessandro Manzoni*. Trans. Sandra Bermann. Lincoln: University of Nebraska Press, 1984, 1–59. Print.

Bhabha, Homi K. *The Location of Culture*. London: Routledge, 1994. Print.

Brotherston, Gordon. "La Malinche de los códices," in *La Malinche, sus padres y sus hijos*. Ed. Margo Glantz. México: Taurus, 2001. 19–38. Print.

Butler, Judith. *Gender Trouble: Feminism and the Subversion of Identity*. London: Routledge, 1990. Print.

———. Undoing Gender. New York: Routledge, 2004.

Carlyle, Thomas. "Dr. Francia," in *Critical and Miscellaneous Essays, Carlyle's Complete Works*. Vol. 4, 205–63. Boston: Estes and Lauriat Publishers, 1885. Print.

Carpentier, Alejo. "Prólogo," in *El reino de este mundo: Obras completes de Alejo Carpentier*. Vol II. Ed. María Luisa Puga. México: Siglo veintiuno editores, 1983. Print.

Clarke, Richard L. W. www.rlwclarke.net/courses/LITS3304/2009-2010/08 ABhabhaTheOtherQuestion.pdf. Web.

Conaghan, Catherine M. *Fujimori's Peru*. Pittsburgh: University of Pittsburgh Press, 2005. Print.

Coniff, Brian. "The Dark Side of Magical Realism: Science, oppression, and Apocalypse in One Hundred Years of Solitude," in *Gabriel García Márquez's One Hundred Years of Solitude: A Casebook*. Ed. Gene H. Bell-Villada. Oxford: Oxford University Press, 2002. 139–152. Print.

Craft, Linda. *Novels of Testimony and Resistance from Central America*. Gainesville: University Press of Florida, 1997. Print.

De Groot, Jerome. *The Historical Novel: The New Critical Idiom*. London: Routledge, 2010. Print.

Dessau, Adalbert. "Realismo mágico y nueva novela latinoamericana: Consideraciones metodológicas e históricas," in *Actas del simposio internacional de estudios hispánicos*. Ed. Matyas Horanyi. Budapest: Akademai Kiadó, 1978. 351–358. Print.

Elmore, Peter. *La fábrica de la memoria: La crisis de la representación en la novela histórica latinoamericana*. México: Fondo de Cultura Económica, 1997. Print.

Erickson, Rosemary. *Contemporary Feminist Historical Crime Fiction*. New York: Palgrave Macmillan, 2006. Print.

Esquivel, Laura. *Como agua para chocolate*. New York: Anchor Books, 1989. Print.

———. *Malinche*. New York: Atria Books, 2006a. Print.

———. *Malinche*. Trans. Ernestro Mestre-Reed. New York: Washington Square Press, 2006b. Print.

Ferré, Rosario. *La casa de la laguna*. New York: Vintage Español, 1997. Print.

Ferrer, Renée. *Vagos sin tierra*. Asunción: Servilibro, 2007.

———. *Maldito amor y otros cuentos*. New York: Vintage Español, 1998. Print.

———. *Flight of the Swan*. New York: Farrar, Strauss, Giroux, 2001. Print.

———. *Vuelo del cisne*. New York: Vintage Español, 2002. Print.

Fletcher, Lisa. *Historical Romance Fiction*. New York: Palgrave Macmillan 2008. Print.

Fonteyn, Margot. *Pavlova: Portrait of a Dancer*. New York: Viking Press, 1984. Print.

Fuentes, Carlos. *The Death of Artemio Cruz*. Trans. Alfred Mac Adam. New York: The Noonday Press, 1991. Print.

———. *The Death of Artemio Cruz*. México: Fondo de Cultura Económica, 1962. Print.

Freedman, Jane. *Feminism*. Buckingham (England): Open University Press, 2001. Print.

García Márquez, Gabriel. *Cien años de soledad*. 19th ed. Madrid: Cátedra, 2009. Print.

Glantz, Margo, Ed. *La Malinche, sus padres y sus hijos*. México: Taurus, 2001. Print.

González Echeverría, Roberto. *Myth and Archive: A Theory of Latin American Narrative.* Cambridge: Cambridge University Press, 1990. Print.

Hernández, Mark A. *Figural Conquistadors: Rewriting the New World's Discovery and Conquest in Mexican and River Plate Novels of the 1980s and 1990s.* Lewisburg: Bucknell University Press, 2006. Print.

Hughes, Helen. *The Historical Romance.* New York: Routledge, 1993. Print.

Hutcheon, Linda. *A Poetics of Postmodernism: History, Theory, Fiction.* New York: Routledge, 1988. Print.

————. "Introduction: Colonialism and the Postcolonial Condition: Complexities Abounding." *PMLA* (January 1995): 7–16. Print.

Jacobs, Naomi. *The Character of Truth: Historical Figures in Contemporary Fiction.* Carbondale: Southern Illinois University Press, 1990. Print.

Jitrik, Noé. "De la historia a la escritura: predominios, disimetrías, acuerdos en la novela histórica latinoamericana," in *The Historical Novel in Latin America: A Symposium.* Ed. Daniel Balderston. Gaithersburg (MD): Ediciones Hispamérica, 1986. 13–30. Print.

————. *Historia e imaginación literaria. Las posibilidades de un género.* Buenos Aires: Biblos, 1995. Print.

Lanyon, Anna. *Malinche's Conquest.* Crows Nest NSW (Australia): Allen and Unwin, 1999.

Lazarus, Neil. "The Global Dispensation since 1945," in *Postcolonial Literary Studies.* Ed. Neil Lazarus. Cambridge: Cambridge University Press, 2004. 1–19. Print.

Lukács, Georg. *The Historical Novel.* Trans. Hannah and Stanley Mitchell. Lincoln: University of Nebraska Press, 1962.

Lyotard, Jean-Francois. *The Postmodern Condition: A Report on Knowledge.* Trans. Geoff Bennington and Brian Massumi. Minneapolis: University of Minnesota Press, 1984. Print.

Manzoni, Alessandro. *On the Historical Novel.* Trans. Sandra Bermann. Lincoln: University of Nebraska Press, 1984. Print.

Marcos, Juan Manuel. *El invierno de Gunter.* 3rd ed. Asunción: Criterio Ediciones, 2012. Print.

Menton, Seymour. *Latin America's New Historical Novel.* Austin: University of Texas Press, 1993. Print.

————. "Magical Realism: An Annotated International Chronology of the Term," in *Essays in Honor of Frank Dauster.* Eds. Kirsten F. Nigro and Sandra M. Cypess. Newark (Delaware): Juan de la Cuesta, Series Homenaje 9, 1995. 125–153. Print.

Moi, Toril. " 'I Am Not a Feminist, But . . . ' How Feminism Became the F-Word," *PMLA* (October 2006): 1735–1741. Print.

Mudrovcic, María. "En busca de dos décadas perdidas: la novela latinoamericana de los años 70 y 80," *Revista Iberoamericana* (1993): 443–468. Print.

Nunes, Ana. *African American Women Writer's Historical Fiction.* New York: Palgrave MacMillan, 2011. Print.

Nuñez Becerra, Fernanda. *La Malinche: De la historia al mito.* México DF: Instituto Nacional de Antropología e Historia, 1996. Print.

Oliveroff, André. *Flight of the Swan*. New York: E.P. Dutton and Company, 1935. Print.

Paz, Octavio. *El laberinto de la soledad. Posdata. Vuelta a El laberinto de la soledad.* México: Fondo de Cultura Económica, 2004. Print.

Perkowska, Magdalena. *Historias híbridas: La nueva novela histórica latinoamericana (1985–2000) ante las teorías posmodernas de la historia.* Frankfurt: Iberoamericana-Vervuert, 2008. Print.

Pons, María Cristina. *Memorias del olvido: La novela histórica de fines del siglo XX.* México: Siglo veintiuno editores, 1996. Print.

Prieto, Cecilia Fernández. *Historia y novela: poética de la novela histórica.* Pamplona: Ediciones Universidad de Navarra, 1998. Print.

Rama, Ángel. *Los dictadores latinoamericanos.* México: Fondo de Cultura Económica, 1976. Print.

Roa Bastos. *Yo el Supremo.* Madrid: Cátedra, 1983.

———, Augusto. *I the Supreme.* Trans. Helen Lane. New York: Alfred A. Knopf, 1986.

Robertson, John Parish and William Parish. *Letters on Paraguay: Comprising an Account of a Four Years' Residence in That Republic,* under the Government of the Dictator Francia. 3 vols. London: John Murray, 1839. Print.

Rody, Caroline. *The Daughter's Return: African-American and Caribbean Women's Fiction of History.* Oxford: Oxford University Press, 2001.

Rössner, Michael. "De la utopía histórica a la historia utópica: Reflexiones sobre la nueva novela histórica como re-escritura de textos históricos," in *La novela latinoamericana entre historia y utopia.* Ed. Sonja Steckbauer, Eichstätt (Germany): Katholische Universität Eichstätt, 1999, 68–78.

Said, Edward W., *Orientalism.* New York: Vintage, 1979. Print.

Santos-Febres, Mayra. *Nuestra señora de la noche.* New York: Ediciones Rayo, 2008. Print.

Showalter, Elaine. "Feminist Criticism in the Wilderness," in *The New Feminist Criticism: Essays on Women, Literature, Theory.* Ed. Elaine Showalter. New York: Pantheon, 1985, 243–270. Print.

Souza, Rayond D. *La historia en la novela hispanoamericana moderna.* Bogotá: Tercer Mundo Editores, 1988. Print.

Tierney-Tello, Mary Beth. *Allegories of Transgression and Transformation: Experimental Fiction by Women Writing Under Dictatorship.* Albany: State University of New York Press, 1996. Print.

Turner, Joseph. "The Kinds of Historical Fiction." *Genre* 12 (1979): 333–355. Print.

Valenzuela, Luisa. *Cola de lagartija.* México: Editorial Planeta, 1998. Print.

Vargas Llosa, Mario. *La fiesta del chivo.* Madrid: Grupo Santillana de Ediciones, S.A., 2000. Print.

Wallace, Diana. *The Woman's Historical Novel: British Women Writers, 1900–2000.* New York: Palgrave Macmillan, 2005. Print.

Weldt-Basson, Helene Carol. *Augusto Roa Bastos's I the Supreme: A Dialogic Perspective.* Columbia (MO): University of Missouri Press, 1993. Print.

————. "Mario Vargas Llosa's *La fiesta del chivo*: History, Fiction or Social Psychology?" *Hispanófila* 156 (2009): 113–131. Print.

————. *Subversive Silences: Nonverbal Expression and Implicit Narrative Strategies in the Works of Latin American Women Writers.* Madison: Farleigh Dickinson University Press, 2009. Print.

White, Hayden. *Tropics of Discourse: Essays in Cultural Criticism.* Baltimore: The Johns Hopkins University Press, 1978. Print.

Zavala, Iris M. "One Hundred Years of Solitude as Chronicle of the Indies," in *Gabriel García Márquez's One Hundred Years of Solitude: A Casebook.* Ed. Gene H. Bell-Villada. Oxford: Oxford University Press, 2002. 109–126. Print.

2

Ashes of Izalco: Female Narrative Strategies and the History of a Nation

Patricia Varas
Translated from Spanish by Bruce K. Fox

In Spanish America, the historical novel has a long tradition and has acquired well-deserved recognition. Both male and female authors have successfully written this genre of novels, albeit with different ideological objectives and aesthetic strategies. One of the most important challenges that women face in history is "to make themselves count," and the female authors take on this challenge in their works, mixing fiction with history in order to develop plots that intertwine public and private worlds, while undoing hierarchies imposed by patriarchal, colonial systems.

Claribel Alegría, in her novel *Cenizas de Izalco* (1966) [*Ashes of Izalco*, 1989], creates both fictitious voices and narratives and recovers a traumatic episode that has marked Salvadoran history: *la Matanza* (the Massacre). In 1932, more than 30,000 *campesinos* (impoverished rural people) and indigenous people were massacred by the army during an uprising that was led principally by Agustín Farabundo Martí against the government of General Maximiliano Hernández Martínez. In interviews, Alegría tells how the recovery and retelling of this largely undocumented event, almost unknown and even forgotten by traditional Salvadoran history, became an obsession for her that needed to be exorcised by writing about it together with her husband, Darwin (Bud) Flakoll. She managed to reconstruct this event in her novel by means of newspaper articles about the massacre that were left by her father (Saporta Sternbach, 64) and by the memories of her own childhood (Forché, 11).[1]

Undoubtedly, *Cenizas de Izalco* is the most-well-known and well-analyzed work by Alegría. This novel has been read by a wide audience, and due to its fortunate balance of political message and aesthetic complexity, it has earned critical attention. I am interested in concentrating my study on Alegría's decision to narrate the historical event of the *Matanza* by means of feminist narrative strategies that express ideological messages in which the two dichotomies, public versus private and real versus fictitious, are juxtaposed in the novel. This concern for narrating a national, historical event has been used by Gabriel García Márquez in *Cien años de soledad* [*One Hundred Years of Solitude*] when he describes the massacre in which some three thousand workers died as a result of the suppression of a strike at the banana plantations of the United Fruit Company in the province of Magdalena, Colombia, in 1928. Rosario Ferré does the same thing in *La casa de la laguna* [*The House on the Lagoon*] as her novel's narrator tells the story of the Ponce Massacre (Masacre de Ponce del Domingo de Ramos) in 1937 in Puerto Rico, where 17 civilians died and hundreds were wounded during a peaceful protest that was organized by the Nationalists. These massacres are characterized as emblematic moments in the formation of an alternative identity and national history. Their depiction also expresses both aesthetic and ideological decisions of the writers in a syncretistic manner. These episodes become decisive and representative in the development of the plot and in the manner of story-telling in the novels. In *Cien años de soledad*, the chapter about the strike faithfully captures the event through magical realism (*realismo mágico*); in *La casa de la laguna*, the chapter on the Ponce Massacre is framed by irony, parody, and anachronism, all features that according to Seymour Menton characterize the new historical narrative.

The re-creation in *Cenizas de Izalco* of one particular moment of violence that has left a traumatic mark on the nation has special relevance, not only because of the topic itself but also for the manner in which it is narrated. In the novel, it is one of the three instances of crises that occur simultaneously: the eruption of Volcano Izalco, a natural disaster; the infidelity of one of the protagonists, Isabel, a bourgeois mother, a social disruption; and the massacre of *campesinos*, a national conflict. The narrator Frank, a foreigner and eyewitness to the massacre, simultaneously remembers his relationship with his lover, Isabel, and tells what occurred with the authority bestowed upon him by his gender and by having been present at the event. The ambush of the *campesinos*, the bursts of gunfire from machine guns, the arbitrary violence against all presumed subversives, and some heroic gestures are welded together by the "convulsión ... que emitía el Izalco" (Alegría, 205) ["convulsion ... from Izalco" (Flakoll, 170)[2]] and the painful memories of an impossible love. All of this takes shape in the novel through Frank's diary, Isabel's bequest to her daughter Carmen after her death. The social and historic catastrophe of the *Matanza* is accompanied by the natural catastrophe of the volcano and the personal commotion of the central characters. In this manner, Alegría makes the private narrative of a bourgeois woman and her love count within the national history and public tragedy, effectively erasing the traditional historiographic dichotomies and exclusions.

The Debate Continues: Fiction and History

When we think that everything has been told or, at least, that there remains little to be said, the summer 2011 issue of the French magazine *Le Débat* [*The Debate*] appears, dedicated to the dispute between history and fiction. This topic is the object of fierce debate because fiction continues to push the limits and recreate its relationship with history (for example, with the appearance of autobiographies, memoirs, and hybrid genres like auto-fiction, chronicles, and intimate journalism). Moreover, the debate is fueled by the fact that the social, cultural, and economic conditions of literary and historiographic production are subject to fluctuations of great ideological importance. As Pierre Nora indicates, in Europe, for example, there is a progressive peak or upsurge of the individual as the main actor of history due to "la pression du présent, les tragédies de l'histoire qui ont mobilisé tous les individus, la poussée même de l'individualisme, la pénétration de la psychanalyse, la démocratisation de l'histoire" (Nora, 9) ["the pressure of the present, the tragedies of history that have mobilized all individuals, the same push and pressure of individualism, the penetration of psychoanalysis, the democratization of history"[3]].

This controversy continues and is based on the work of other European and American literary critics and historians, such as Michel de Certeau, Paul Ricoeur, and Hayden White, who have made us reflect about the narrative qualities of history that tie it to narratological laws close to those of the novel, and on the work carried out by Hispanic critics and Latin Americanists like Seymour Menton, María Cristina Pons, Fernando Aínsa, Noé Jitrik, and Juan José Barrientos, who tied the study of historical fiction (practiced in the region since the colonial period) to an analytical reflection that increased our comprehension of it. All of these efforts illustrate the task of shattering the myth of history and the deconstruction of myths and narratives with which a national and exclusivist imaginary has been constructed. They also create an imaginative opening for new questioning narratives that fill the age-old silences of Latin America.

Cenizas de Izalco occupies a unique position in the debate about the historical novels written by women in Latin America. Other than the female narratives that promoted independence, it is one of the first narrations of the historical genre by women (appearing in 1966), and it precedes by a few years the revolutionary movements in which the Central American nations would be involved.[4] Moreover, the raw political and ideological commitment in the work goes beyond the narrative tricks typical of the "nueva novela histórica" ("new historical novel"), excluding it from this postmodern praxis but not from important narrative experimentations that, studied from a feminist angle, offer promissory and novel forms of relating or telling.

Cenizas de Izalco and Its Liberating Narrative Strategies

Alegría has spoken in detail about the origins of *Cenizas de Izalco*. While she was living in Paris, Carlos Fuentes encouraged her to narrate this bloody, historical event that haunted her, especially after the Cuban Revolution, which opened new possibilities for her and so many other writers to imagine the Americas. Alegría affirms that she was "nada política" ("not at all political") as a youth, even though she detested dictators, coming as she did from an anti-Somoza family (Rodríguez Moya, 55–56). Her husband, Bud Flakoll, invited her to work with him; she the poet and he the journalist would write a novel (Huezo Mixco, 91), the first of many collaborations. Julio Cortázar was her first reader, and he encouraged her to send it to the Seix Barral contest, where it was awarded second place (Huezo Mixco, 92). The awakening of a revolutionary conscience made Alegría rummage through the memories of her youth and her father's press clippings, which confirms that the birth of the work is in the subjective and familial memory of the writer.

Carmen is a young Salvadoran mother, transplanted to Washington, where she lives with her boring American husband and her children. She returns to Santa Ana for the funeral of her mother, Isabel. This homecoming is a spatial and temporal return, given that in the bosom of her family home, Carmen can remember her childhood, and above all, her mother. Isabel has left her the diary of a "gringo," who was her lover and through whom Carmen reconstructs the unknown personality of her mother, her life, her dreams, and her disappointments, to conclude that she never knew who her mother really was. The period of Frank and Isabel's romance takes place during the military coup d'état that overthrew President Araujo; brought the tumultuous dictatorship of Maximiliano Hernández Martínez and the popular uprising, whose leader was Farabundo Martí; and ended with the massacre known as the *Matanza*. As Carmen gets to know Isabel, she is also learning the history of her country. In the end, Carmen realizes that her condition as a woman has much in common with that of her mother, despite the time and miles that separate them. What unites them is their shared condition of being marginalized women.

In the excellent chapter, "Awakening Women in Central America: Claribel Alegría's Fictions," from her book *Writing Women in Central America. Gender and the Fictionalization of History*, Laura Barbas-Rhoden clearly describes a constituent element of the Salvadoran author's work that has been emphasized by several critics and is inscribed in her aesthetic choices: the double contestatory labor of her writing. This double contestatory labor consists of a clear political agenda manifested through a questioning of the capitalist and imperialist forces that have plunged the Central American country into a situation of inequality and injustice, at the same time that the discrepancies of gender and the marginalization of women are criticized. Barbas-Rhoden states: "Though the stories uniformly sympathize with leftist struggles, the introduction of gender concerns, as well as the incorporation of numerous voices within a single text, highlights the contested nature of representations of both identity and history" (16).

Alegría is a writer who has expressed her political commitment through her literary work. Her work "letras de emergencia" ("emergency writing"), as George Yúdice so fittingly called it in his article,[5] proclaims an ideological and creative commitment that approaches what Susan Rubin Suleiman calls "authoritarian fiction" to refer to "a novelistic genre that proclaims its own status as both overtly ideological and as fictional" (2) without falling, however, into the didacticism that marks this genre. In *Cenizas de Izalco*, there is also a semi-autobiographical element that enriches the novel, by giving it a dimension of personal feminine growth.

Yúdice mentions the "casi autobiográfico" (956) [almost autobiographical] element present in the novel, and in interviews, Alegría confirms how in the novel her personal life is interwoven with that of the characters. Her mother was from a well-to-do family from Santa Ana, and was a great reader, especially of French literature, as was Isabel in the novel. Her father was a Nicaraguan doctor who was living in exile in El Salvador because of his political activities and support for Sandino, very similar to Alfonso in *Cenizas de Izalco*. Alegría herself lived in Washington, where she went to study, just as Carmen did.[6] There are characters and episodes in the novel that clearly refer to the author's life. The "indio" ("Indian") Luarca, for example, has his origin in the teacher don Francisco Luarca (Don Chico in the novel), Alegría's literature teacher (Huezo Mixco, 84) in a high school very similar to the one that Carmen attends. Carmen remembers an incident in which her father intervenes in the moment when a colonel is beating a *campesino* with "las manos atadas por detrás con un cordel alrededor de los pulgares" (35) ["his hands were tied behind his back by a cord bound around his paired thumbs" (28)]. Her father, a doctor, rebukes the military man: "A un hombre indefenso no se le pega, coronel" (36) ["You don't hit a man whose hands are tied!" (28)]. Alegría recounts this in the same way in her interview with Forché, as an incident that happened in her childhood (11).

The growing awareness of both Isabel and Carmen is very similar to that of the author. Alegría explains that "no me podía imaginar que con la poesía se podía hacer algo" (Rodríguez Moya, 56) [I couldn't imagine that with poetry you could do something], and she talks of her youthful fear that people would find out that she wrote poetry, because it was frowned upon ("te veían como una loca" [they looked at you as if you were crazy]) in her social class. She did not want to be rejected with the result "que mis amigos no me sacaran a bailar" (Huezo Mixco, 88) [that my friends would not take me out dancing]. Nevertheless, she recognizes a mark left by her father and his exile, and by her childhood teacher who talked to them about the *Matanza* (Huezo Mixco, 84) and how the consciousness resulting from the triumph of the Cuban Revolution wakes in the Salvadoran writer the impulse, obsession, and repressed childhood memories in a symbolic form of postmemory.[7] When Daniel Flores y Ascencio asks her about the trauma of the lost revolutionary wars and their deaths, he refers to a historical, genetic pain, to which Alegría responds with sorrow: "I was a child, seven years old, when the 1932 massacre began. I carried it with me as a terrible wound" (108). For Alegría, writing *Cenizas de Izalco* was not only a way to respond to the historical necessity of recovering the past, but rather it was a clear way to deal with and fight against the old, traumatic pain.[8]

Perhaps the problem of balancing a political message with the development of the female subject underlies what Yúdice writes about in his panoramic study of the author's work when he refers to "letras de emergencia" ("emergency writing") as a metaphor for the urgency of the message and its emergence. The critic explains that the developing feminine subject appears in *Cenizas de Izalco* in an incomplete manner (957), which is resolved only in *No me agarran viva* [*They Won't Take Me Alive*] when Eugenia, by means of an armed struggle, "se abre un espacio propio en la lucha por desenajenar su sociedad, construir nuevas formas de organización social, impulsar el desarrollo de un sujeto [femenino] emergente" (964) [opens up her own space in the fight to reverse the alienation of her society, construct new forms of social organization, and impel the development of an emergent (female) subject]. In other words, Alegría's work finds its maturity only when she organizes the trauma of the repressed memories of the Salvadoran past and when her female characters articulate their political commitment, projecting themselves toward a future of collective change.

The referential aspect of the historical novel has been the object of studies and debates. In the new Latin American historical novel, this element is eclipsed by "postmodern" textual strategies that question reality and its linguistic comprehension by means of parody, intertextuality, anachronism, and ludic elements, among others. However, in *Cenizas de Izalco*, Alegría prefers a mimetic narrative representative of reality, even though there are certain modernist characteristics that are important to point out.

Van Delden stresses that *Cenizas de Izalco* "is in many ways a highly accomplished example of modernist literature" in which one finds "links to international modernism" (47). Among the examples that he cites are the characters Frank (a Bohemian artist) and Isabel (a kind of Salvadoran Madame Bovary) and the themes of memory, desire, and identity developed by means of modernist strategies like the rejection of linear narrative (47). To these, I would add the highly symbolic elements in the narrative and the concern for investigating the female psyche's bonds that structure the mother–daughter relationship (see Galindo and Gandolfi). Nevertheless, as the critic recognizes, "it appears that the authors experimented with a modernist aesthetic not in order to escape from the pressures of history but rather as part of an effort to find new ways to criticize and denounce social and political injustice in El Salvador" (Van Delden, 47). This tenacity with which reality is presented in the novel emphasizes the importance of social criticism and the historical moment of the *Matanza*, which marks the characters and makes them conscious of the fact that their existence is historically conditioned—an essential requirement for a historical novel, according to Lukács.

This recovery of historical reality through an emblematic event, which has been distorted or repressed (many times it does not even appear in schoolbooks) to define the nation according to hegemonic patterns, is a fundamental characteristic of the historical novel in Latin America. By means of this fiction firmly rooted in reality, official history is rewritten and an alternative version is created that returns to it some verisimilitude. Of course, irony is part of the hybrid text of the historical novel: it is fiction that restores referential possibility to history.[9] In *Cenizas de Izalco*, the irony is double: the *Matanza* acquires a new importance, and the female characters establish their subjectivity by telling their own story from the intimacy of the domestic space, thanks to the intrahistory of a romance and a narrative familial legacy, Frank's diary.

The position of women in history and society has been one of subordination. From here arises the necessity of the writer to confront this reality by means of her work and language. Although readers let themselves be seduced by the narration, and they believe that they are in contact with reality, because of its apparent transparency, the realistic element of *Cenizas de Izalco* is not a mere reflection or copy, but rather a mediation. Luce Irigary writes about the relationship of women with the mimetic representation of reality that has been imposed upon them socially and artistically:

> To play with mimesis is thus, for a woman, to try to recover the place of exploitation by discourse, without allowing herself to simply be reduced to it. It means to resubmit herself... to "ideas," in particular ideas about herself, that are elaborated in/by masculine logic, but as to make "visible," by an effect of playful repetition, what was supposed to remain invisible: the cover-up of a possible operation of the feminine in language. (76)

Alegría carries out this imitation and representation of reality with her female characters, especially Isabel. The invisibility of Isabel is emphasized by Frank, beginning with the moment in which he meets her: "Tengo la impresión de que es una mujer alegre, pero que en presencia de su marido y de su padre, hace lo posible por borrarse" (50) ["She seems a gay and charming person, but I had the feeling that in the presence of her husband and father she was restraining herself" (41)]. This mother from the petite bourgeoisie of a small town does not try to change the state of things. She plays the role of conventional mother and wife well, adopting traditional behaviors deliberately, in order to later undermine them through her passion for reading, her travel fantasies, and her romance with Frank, or by maintaining a distance through her awareness of not belonging to that world: "a pesar de haber vivido aquí toda mi vida me siento como de paso, como si no perteneciese a este lugar" (63) ["I've lived here all my life, but I've always felt as if I'm only passing through Santa Ana, as if I don't really belong here at all" (52)]. However, that which should have remained invisible becomes visible throughout the novel, until we are presented with a new woman, the one who, as her daughter says, "nunca adiviné" (209) ["I never knew" (173)].

In *Cenizas de Izalco*, the following multitude of voices and narrative forms capture the complexity of reality: (1) a structuring female "I" of the narration, Carmen, who manipulates it with great authority and whose voice sometimes seems omniscient; (2) frequent dialogues among principal and minor characters that permit the contextualization of the local language and the reality of Santa Ana and of a bourgeois class marked by racism, sexism, and classism; (3) prolepses and analepses that permit the dead to talk and the memories and projections to occur, creating a mythical time; (4) a multiperspectivism that permits the reader to realize that there is not one sole way to interpret things; (5) Frank's diary, a male voice through which Isabel's romance and the *Matanza* are told with the authority of being a male witness; and (6) a symbolic richness, through which the relationship between mother and daughter is investigated and feminist concerns are expressed.

Carmen, by means of Frank's diary, regains her mother's past and tells her story, while at the same time recounting her own, a modern and liberated woman, who, nevertheless, suffers from the same silences and invisibility as her mother. The inclusion of the diary is "un recurso eficaz" (Yúdice, 957) [an efficient technique] that does not cease being problematic. As Dimo indicates, "vale cuestionar sin embargo, el uso de una voz masculina y ajena a la realidad salvadoreña para representar un punto de vista femenino y para dar testimonio de un evento tan importante en la historia de El Salvador" [it is worth questioning, however, the use of a male voice and one that is foreign to Salvadoran reality to represent a female point of view and to give testimony of such an important event in the history of El Salvador]. That the life of a woman is recovered and that another finds her identity through the diary of a man, and that a bloody historical episode of importance for national identity is told by means of a foreign voice, can bring with it a process of objectification that would go against the feminist and progressive premises that are advanced in *Cenizas de Izalco*. The effectiveness of Frank's diary, however, is in particular due to the fact that the narration in the diary is structured by a foreign, male voice, behind whose pseudo-objectivity lies Alegría's authorial voice as well as the female narrative "I" (Carmen). Frank is consciously elaborating the story that we read when "in 1964 it was revolutionary enough just to write about the Matanza, but to claim that women count enough so that their stories are really the stories of their countries allows us to examine women's roles in the formation of national states" (Saporta Sternbach, 63). Gandolfi suggests another explanation for the usefulness of this foreign male narrative: "el hecho de que Isabel haya decidido dejar a su hija el testimonio escrito por su amante, en vez de algo escrito por sí misma, subraya y denuncia la interiorización del estado de subalternidad de esta última y la falta de un lenguaje apropiado para poderse expresar" (Gandolfi) [the fact that Isabel has decided to leave the testimony written by her lover to her daughter, instead of something written by herself, emphasizes and denounces the mother's interiorizing of her subaltern state and the lack of an appropriate language for her to be able to express herself].[10] Finally, the diary as a central narrative offers diverse opportunities because of the nature and origin itself of this type of narration.

The diary and letters are considered minor genres, generally feminine because they reveal personal stories "of little value."[11] However, this is precisely the significance and implication of the diary in the novel, which as intimate writing, necessarily reveals the existence and historicity of the affectivity of its author and the other characters, at the same time as it situates them in Salvadoran history. A novel that deals with female and national identity finds in the diary the perfect manner of articulating this search. Frank writes for himself, while at the same time he writes for Isabel (and eventually he writes for Carmen also, because she becomes the guardian of the diary). The direct, oral, open, and honest tone, typical of the genre, permits a dialogue among the lovers, and because of this, their personal story and the national history are revealed. Although the diary feminizes the experiences of Frank, who, like Isabel, is carrying out a search, because he is a man, it also gives him the authority that moves his narrative away from sentimentality. Frank wants to escape from his reality; he is a sensitive and maladjusted artist. Carmen sees "en el candor de su diario... a un niño extraviado" (69) ["[in] Frank's candor... the wistful air of a lost child" (56)], and Isabel sees him like a man who "puede darse el gusto, sentir el hormigueo de la aventura" (113) ["is free to search for new experiences that give zest to living" (89)].

The diary is Frank's last attempt at being original, as a man and an artist. Perhaps it is born as a therapeutic exercise to establish his personal record of this rehabilitative trip and give expression to his impressions and vicissitudes, as he confesses: "he vuelto a leer las páginas escritas en estos días y lo único que encuentro en ellas es una pobre y narcisista introspección" (101) ["I've reread the pages of this notebook and have found in them nothing more than listless, narcissistic introspection" (81)]. The tone of the diary changes as Frank exposes himself to new situations, and the "niño extraviado" [lost child] becomes aware of himself and of the world. It seems as if nothing happens to Frank until he meets Isabel: the confessional and reflexive tone about his addiction and confusion gives way to a communicative tone in which the contrasts and violence surrounding him take on greater importance. What began as a private diary becomes a public one in which the writer (Frank), with full consciousness that it is going to be read, presents his opinions and directs himself to his public (Isabel) with the desire of convincing and contextualizing his observations through the authority that is conferred upon him because he is the author. In this manner, he persuasively writes:

> Para él, tú eres "esposa," "madre," "ama de casa," en la misma medida que una "maceta" es una maceta.... No te contentes con ser maceta el resto de tu vida, Isabel. En vez de eso te pido que seas mi mujer, mi camarada, mi compañera de aventuras, mi novia, mi amante. (179)

> [To him you're a wife, mother, housekeeper, much as a flower pot is a flower pot.... Don't remain a flower pot the rest of your days, Isabel. I ask you

instead to be my companion, partner, lover, fellow-adventurer, mistress, wife. (148)]

Frank is a lost man and an alcoholic who has been in a sanatorium and received psychoanalytic treatment. He does not represent the masculine qualities of a strong, formal, determined man, and exoticizes El Salvador "con ojos de extranjero" (117) ["with foreign eyes" (93)]. Despite his bias, his testimony about the *Matanza* and his observations of Santa Ana society and Isabel's family life count as the only existing written narrative, converting it into the sieve and axis of the novel, emphasizing the existence of multiple versions of reality. Carmen, however, questions it constantly by means of a series of chronological breaks and voices that require an attentive reader.

Gandolfi points out Carmen's vacillation and resistance, how the pages of Frank's diary alternate with Carmen's monologues and her questioning of what she reads, because "Carmen, habiendo crecido dentro de un sistema simbólico patriarcal, no se contenta únicamente con las palabras escritas por Frank, sino que empieza un tipo de indagación que ve como protagonistas a todos los miembros de la familia" (Gandolfi) [Carmen, having grown up within a symbolic patriarchal system, is not satisfied with only Frank's written words, but rather she begins a kind of inquiry that sees all of the members of the family as protagonists]. In fact, Carmen takes control of the narrative, and the female "I" dominates and decides which versions to recover or counterpoise, controlling the meaning of the novel and the reconstitution of her existence and that of Isabel, her mother, who without apparent voice establishes her complex identity as a bourgeois woman conscious of her limitations. As Carmen thinks, "recordándola me da la sensación de alguien que llevaba un bulto muy pesado y sólo se libraba de él cuando estaba fuera de casa o escondida entre sus libros" (19–20) ["remembering her, I have the sensation of someone carrying a heavy burden except when she was away from home or hidden behind a book" (16)].

Carmen, upon appropriating the narration, makes Isabel visible and makes the female voice take on authority. The feminist critic Joanne Frye maintains that the female narrative "I" permits the female characters to perhaps define themselves through their own premises without the necessity of falling into experimental forms, because it has "the capacity to engage the normative and simultaneously to elude and critique it, to evoke realities at the same time it interrogates our ways of defining them" (55).

In Carmen's contestatory and dialogic exercise, the marginalized identities of the female characters, of Frank, and the repressed history of the *Matanza* are inscribed. The female narrative "I" recreates the history of the event not by means of an epic account, but rather by means of the intrahistory of the family saga, through the personal perspective of an anonymous man (the *gringo* Frank) of which Carmen is the guardian, since she possesses the diary. The personal story of Isabel and her family crosses over to the background in the final part of the novel, when the massacre is presented and contextualized. It is because of Frank that Carmen will learn not only about her mother, but also about her country.

From the beginning, Frank contemplates the poverty in the country, and through Virgil, his missionary friend, he understands the ignorance and exploitation to which the poor are subjected. With his entrance into the bourgeois society of Santa Ana, he meets the Rojas family and their circle, who provide a multiplicity of points of view about Salvadoran reality, since, as Eduardo (one of Isabel's brothers) explains, in the family "hay de todo-se rió-; conservadores, católicos devotos, maestros, y revolucionarios parranderos como yo" (121) ["there was everything from schoolteachers, bank clerks, and devout Catholics, to atheistic, hard-drink revolutionaries like myself" (97)]. Thus, the *Matanza* is presented and described as both anarchy and a struggle for justice, depending upon who is talking. But, Frank's version, because it is a testimony, will have the irrefutable force of veracity and will silence the other versions.

Frank lives the violence in Izalco, the persecution of the *campesinos* and indigenous people, who are hunted "como a animales salvajes" (194) ["like animals" (161)], and he sees the preparations in the town plaza. He understands, together with Virgil, that the army is setting up an ambush of the *campesinos* who have been systematically disarmed in the region. Thousands of them are directed to the plaza where they will be mercilessly machine-gunned down in cold blood.

These historic events registered by Frank are inserted among the inquiries of Carmen, who asks questions within her inner circle in order to give us contradictory recollections. Her father remembers that "se cometieron muchos abusos" (91) ["there were many abuses" (74)] and that "en la famosa guardia cívica había muchos matones" (92) ["there were a lot of common murderers in your famous Civic Guard" (74)]. Dr. Selva remembers mournfully that the Luna and Zapata boys were shot together with Martí (93), while Celia and Meches praise the reestablished order since, "sin eso quién sabe, nos hubieran volado a todos la cabeza, igualito a Cuba estaríamos" (92) ["if he hadn't organized the Civic Guard, we might all have had our heads chopped off" (74)]. In a doubly marginalized effort because it is the testimony of an indigenous woman, Carmen prefers to end the polemical memory with one of her mother's recollections from that period: "Unitos quedaron en Izalco-le contaba a mamá la indita que venía a pedir limosna-. Unitos" (93) ["There's only a handful now in Izalco," the beggar woman tells Mother and me, "only a handful of us left" (75)].

Carmen, in a manner similar to that of Isabel, opts for the Indian woman's version, preferring to recover a repressed and forgotten memory, as the other versions demonstrate. This is part of her personal growth, of her becoming socially conscious. Isabel, in her questioning of the social parameters that are designed to control her, is transformed into another woman without openly breaking with her class or family. The woman who earlier did not think about politics and who feared a revolution because "esas gentes transpiran odio y teñirían con sangre el país" (50) ["those people are filled with hatred; they wouldn't stop chopping off heads until the country was running with blood" (41)] changes to be later remembered by Eduardo as follows: "de joven era conservadora [. . .]. Pero es curioso, con la edad se fue haciendo izquierdista. Tenía un gran corazón" (163) ["She was very conservative when she was young, but it's curious: the older she got, the more she turned to the left. She had a very generous heart" (133).] Isabel's ideological change is the result of a humanism that permits her to function within her social sphere where even religion is an acceptable consolation, where she can take refuge from the gossip and the prudish and hypocritical life in Santa Ana. Carmen shows her solidarity with her mother, demonstrating her impatience with gossip and visits: "Si no se van pronto voy a estallar. ¿Cómo pudo aguantar mamá? Todo está igual que antes y peor" (87) ["If they don't leave soon, I'll explode. How could Mother stand it? Everything is the same as it always was. Worse" (70).]

The Intrahistory and the "Silences of History"

The intention of recovering and restoring the silenced historic moment of the *Matanza*, through an intimate text as is Frank's diary, underscores the importance of the private and of the manuscript itself, in which the "páginas están gastadas de tanto manosearlas" (150) ["pages are dog-eared, worn with much handling" (121)]. At the same time, the message that is carried with it ends with Carmen because, once she carries out her apprenticeship as a female and historical subject, Isabel has ordered her to "destrúyelo" (181) ["throw it away or burn it" (149)]. This subjective origin of the recuperation of history has a moral value, as much for the characters (Isabel feels the need to leave this testimony to her daughter, and Frank must narrate what happened in Izalco), as for the author, who rejects neutrality, and openly exhibits her political commitment through her writing. Nevertheless, the private and public memory stays in the family. Carmen is the depository of the knowledge that confirms her growth as a subject of history.

Frank dedicates his final pages to the massacre in the Izalco plaza and its violence, even though his feelings toward Isabel are spread throughout the narration and determine many of his observations. His personal tragedy—he has begun to drink again—tinges the horrible moment in which he lives, which he only understands in a limited manner. His lack of knowledge serves as an example for Carmen (and the readers), of how this absence of consciousness limits us as actors and destroys the understanding that our experience is historically conditioned. For women, like Isabel and Carmen, to have a place in history, they must become aware that their subjectivity transforms them into participating citizens in a collective experience. The domesticity of the protagonists serves to situate them in the larger social context of the nation. As Saporta Sternbach asserts: "realizing the revolutionary struggle of their people helps them to recognize their own previous ignorance as well as to realize their own role in the struggle" (70–71).

Cenizas de Izalco confirms Alegría's effort to simultaneously accomplish two tasks. First, she creates a feminist novel in which the protagonists look for their female identity within a bourgeois society determined by *machista* values that by definition not only exclude but also oppress women. Second, she rescues Salvadoran history through an event in which the tragic and horrible magnitude makes fiction possibly the most appropriate form to capture the ineffability of the moment, because of its malleability and imaginative creativity. By preferring the domestic space of the family and home, by choosing a romantic plot about an impossible and prohibited love, Alegría suggests that the grand narratives are not necessarily the most suitable ones to recover the past, which is better revealed by the small narratives that fuse the private with the public in an honest and indisputable manner, by the fragments of memory, by the simple determination to tell it.

The female historical novel permits women to investigate the past in order to understand their present and make comparisons to see if there have been changes in their social and political condition. Alegría, making use of the historical novel and feminist narrative strategies, recovers Isabel's identity together with a silenced moment in Salvadoran history, the *Matanza*. The historical novel makes it possible to investigate the components of human historicity, at the same time as it dictates the organization of the plot, chronology, environment, place, and language. By means of the private narrative of Frank's diary and the authority of Carmen's female "I," the traditional separation of the domestic and the public is avoided. Carmen understands that she and Isabel have suffered the same inequalities and that her ideas of superiority because she belongs to a different time and lives in another culture are nothing other than false illusions. It is important to emphasize that despite this negative conclusion, there is a utopian impulse. Thus, as the past is inspected, the narrative, through Carmen, is projected toward the future in search of a break with the continuities of history and of its possibilities.

Cenizas de Izalco is the result of the persistence of memory, of Claribel Alegría's urgency to exorcize the painful recollection of an event that threatened to become a ghost, something nonexistent for having been repressed and denied by official history. The Salvadoran writer confirms the ability of fiction to recover the past and the importance of feminist narrative with its breaks with linearity, the preference for a multiplicity of voices, private genres, and the female "I," to narrate and make count the female experience in the national history. Alegría also illustrates the relevance of personal memory and intrahistory as opposed to the great narratives of epic character to create works that deal with collective traumas and recover the humble, small, forgotten actors who, nevertheless, also make history.

Acknowledgments

I would like to thank Rich Schmidt of the Hatfield Library for the help he gave me. I would also like to express my gratitude to the students in my Latin American Women Writers course for their comments and observations, especially Laura Gandolfi, whose keen analysis of *Cenizas de Izalco* in her master's thesis "Entre luz y sombra(s): Encuentro de discursos históricos, fantásticos y de género en algunas obras de Claribel Alegría" (unpublished) enriched my approach to the novel.

Notes

1. The work actually has two authors; however, in order not to encumber the essay, I principally refer to Alegría.
2. The English translations of passages from *Cenizas de Izalco* are taken from the version translated by Darwin J. Flakoll (*Ashes of Izalco*).
3. The English translations of all citations—other than those from *Cenizas de Izalco*—are Bruce K. Fox's.
4. This is important to emphasize, above all with respect to Central American literature in which there has been a tendency for text and context to coincide, as Julie Marchio suggests when citing Arturo Arias. Arias finds that it is impossible to extract literature ("manifestaciones sintomáticas" [symptomatic manifestations]) from its historical context (*Istmo*, 15 [2007]). Alegría's work is part of the search for an identity and a redefinition of nation, determining elements of Central American literature for Arias, but *Cenizas de Izalco* is a little ahead of its time with respect to certain thematic and aesthetic concerns.
5. Yúdice clarifies that the term comes from Claribel Alegría (957, note 8).
6. The author has revealed that the romance between Isabel and Frank is a product of her and Flakoll's imagination.

7. Marianne Hirsch uses the term to refer to the ability of reimagining memory: "postmemory is a powerful and very particular form of memory precisely because its connection to its object or source is mediated not through recollection but through an imaginative investment and creation" (22).

8. The open wound to which the author refers makes us think about studies about trauma and the necessity to deal with it. Allan Young explains that "fear is the memory of pain" (91) and that fear can be acquired ontogenetically (through one's own experience) or phylogenetically (inherited) (91). Following Dominick LaCapra and Cathy Caruth, among other scholars, we know that mourning is vital in order to close the wound and that to do a narration that can be told and shared, what Caruth calls a "narrative memory" (153), is part of the process of healing.

9. Carlos Fuentes maintains that fiction is the only way to uncover history's lies, and he states: "el arte da vida a lo que la historia ha asesinado. El arte da voz a lo que la historia ha negado, silenciado o perseguido. El arte rescata la verdad de las mentiras de la historia" (82) [art gives life to that which history has assassinated. Art gives voice to that which history has denied, silenced, or persecuted. Art rescues truth from the lies of history].

10. Because my study primarily concentrates on the narrative strategies utilized in order to create a female historical novel, I exclude the implications of the diary as a way to get to know the mother and to undermine the male symbolic order that has been studied convincingly by Galindo and Gandolfi.

11. Today, historians make use of these traditionally feminine genres as important sources of information that generally have been relegated to oblivion but that now serve to fill historical silences and gaps, and are fundamental in recreating social history with their details of daily life.

Works Cited

Alegría, Claribel y Darwin J. Flakoll. *Cenizas de Izalco*. 2nd edición. San José, Costa Rica: Educa, 1982. Print.

———. *Ashes of Izalco*. Trans. Darwin J. Flakoll. Willimantic: Curbstone, 1989. Print.

Barbas-Rhoden, Laura. *Writing Women in Central America. Gender and the Fictionalization of History*. Ohio: Center for International Studies, Ohio University, 2003. Print.

Caruth, Cathy. "Recapturing the Past: Introduction," in *Trauma. Explorations in Memory*. Ed. Cathy Caruth. Baltimore: The Johns Hopkins University Press, 1995. 151–157. Print.

Dimo, Edith. "Identidad y discurso en Cenizas de Izalco de Claribel Alegría." *Istmo* 3 (2002): http://istmo.denison.edu/n03/articulos/cenizas.html. Web.

Flores y Ascencio, Daniel. "Claribel Alegría." *Bomb* 70 (2000): 104–109. Print.

Forché, Carolyn. "Interview with Claribel Alegría." *Index on Censorship* 13.2 (1984): 11–14. Print.

Frye, Joanne. *Living Stories, Telling Lives: Women and the Novel in Contemporary Experience.* Ann Arbor: University of Michigan Press, 1986. Print.

Fuentes, Carlos. *Cervantes o la crítica de la lectura.* Alcalá de Henares: Centro de Estudios Cervantinos, 1994. Print.

Galindo, Rose Marie. "(Re)Escritura de la figura materna en *Cenizas de Izalco* de Claribel Alegría." *Cincinnati Romance Review* 13 (1994): 182–189. Print.

Gandolfi, Laura. "Entre luz y sombra(s): Encuentro de discursos históricos, fantásticos y de género en algunas obras de Claribel Alegría." Unpublished.

Hirsch, Marianne. *Family Frames: Photography, Narrative and Postmemory.* Cambridge: Harvard University Press, 1997. Print.

Huezo Mixco, Miguel. "La buena estrella. Entrevista con Claribel Alegría." *Cultura. Revista Bimestral del Ministerio de Cultura* 76–77 (1996): 81–95. Print.

Irigaray, Luce. *This Sex Which Is Not One.* Trad. Catherine Porter. Ithaca: Cornell University Press, 1985. Print.

Marchio, Julie. "De la libertad de la escritura a la libertad de las voces amordazadas: un diálogo entre Historia e historias en la novela femenina centroamericana reciente." *Istmo* 15 (2007). http://istmo.denison.edu/n15/proyectos/marchio.html. Web.

Nora, Pierre. "Histoire et roman: où passent les frontiers?" *Le Débat* 165 (2011): 6–12. Print.

Rodríguez Moya, Daniel. "Claribel Alegría: Nicaragua necesita otra revolución, pero al estilo de Gandhi, sin más sangre." *Cuadernos Hispanoamericanos* 708 (2009): 49–61. Print.

Saporta Sternbach, Nancy. "Engendering the Future: *Ashes of Izalco* and the Making of a Writer," in *En Claribel Alegría and Central American Literature: Critical Essays.* Eds Sandra Boschetto-Sandoval and Marcia Phillips McGowan, Athens, OH: Ohio University for International Studies, 1994. 61–74. Print.

Suleiman, Susan Rubin. *Authoritarian Fictions: The Ideological Novel as a Literary Genre.* New York: Columbia University Press, 1983. Print.

Van Delden, Maarten. "Claribel Alegría, the Neustadt Prize, and the World Republic of Letters." *World Literature* 81.3 (2007): 45–48. Print.

Young, Allan. "Bodily Memory and Traumatic Memory." *Tense Past. Cultural Essays on Trauma and Memory* 89–102. Print.

Yúdice, George. "Letras de emergencia: Claribel Alegría." *Revista Iberoamericana* 51. 132–133. (1985): 953–964. Print.

3

In Search of the Absent Revolution: Edgardo Rodríguez Juliá's Novels of Invented History

Víctor Figueroa

History-fiction

It would not be inaccurate to say that Edgardo Rodríguez Juliá has been for decades the Puerto Rican writer most deeply concerned with the island's colonial history, particularly the period marked by Spain's domination. His first published work, *La renuncia del héroe Baltasar* (1974), thoroughly re-imagined Puerto Rico's eighteenth century, and two other novels, *La noche oscura del niño Avilés* (1984) and *El camino de Iyaloide* (1994), returned to the same historical period.[1] However, much to the chagrin of some of Rodríguez Juliá's initial critics, his eighteenth-century novels do not follow the typical patterns of traditional historical fiction. As Aníbal González noticed not long after the publication of *La noche,* some of the novel's first reviewers were historians like Fernando Picó and José Curet, who complained: "¡Esto no es una novela histórica!" (583) [This is not a historical novel!]. Although one could accuse those initial critics of holding an excessively limited concept of what a historical novel is, they were in fact responding to peculiarities in Rodríguez Juliá's works that do set them apart from traditional historical fictions. As a matter of fact, these novels even go beyond the ludic, metafictional, parodic, and heteroglossic model that Seymour Menton proposes for what he calls "new" historical novels in Latin America. Although Menton adequately distinguishes those new historical novels from traditional ones, one implicit trait that they both seem to share in his account is the use of documented history as their point of departure, even if *new* historical novels often question the validity claims and paradigms of accepted historical accounts.

In contrast, Rodríguez Juliá does not simply alter or modify historical events (as all historical novelists do). Instead, he *invents* a whole alternative history for Puerto Rico—one that revolves around massive slave rebellions in the eighteenth century. Not surprisingly, even in his catalogue of non-conventional new historical novels, Menton himself has some difficulty ascertaining the right place for Rodríguez Juliá. Menton links Rodríguez Juliá to Carlos Fuentes, highlighting "the much more fanciful and pseudo-historical *Terra nostra*" and "the totally apocryphal *La renuncia del héroe Baltasar* and *La noche oscura del niño Avilés*" (Menton, 25). Such qualifications show how uncomfortably Rodríguez Juliá's novels fit within the "historical novel" genre, even in its "new" manifestations. One might even argue that, more than historical novels, Rodríguez Juliá almost writes "history-fiction," understanding this term in the same sense as "science-fiction," which creates fantastic but plausible scenarios for the future. Given the history of the Caribbean in the eighteenth century, Rodríguez Juliá creates a fantastic but plausible past for Puerto Rico.[2]

Evoking James Joyce, Rodríguez Juliá refers to his "invented narratives" as "nightmares of history," clearly stating: "No quise ir a la historiografía, tampoco a los documentos. Decidí inventarme un Siglo XVIII que fuera como una pesadilla de la historia puertorriqueña. Las pesadillas también hablan de la realidad" (Rodríguez de Laguna, 132) [I did not want to draw upon historiography or documents. I decided to invent an eighteenth century that would be like a nightmare of Puerto Rican history. Nightmares also speak about reality].[3] If we accept the author's claim that he did not rely on historical research or documents, even to subvert them, it becomes harder to classify his novels as historical fictions, except in the banal sense that they take place in the past. Revealingly, Rodríguez Juliá himself offers the parallel to science-fiction when describing the linguistic aspects of his novels: "Cuando emprendí en los años setenta la composición de mis novelas en torno al siglo XVIII puertorriqueño . . . me animaba la idea de lograr una adivinación descabellada, la invención paródica de un lenguaje y un habla para el siglo XVIII caribeño, aquel siglo distante; intenté una especie de ciencia-ficción lingüística al revés" (Rodríguez Juliá, *Mapa*, 112) [When I started the composition of my novels dealing with the Puerto Rican eighteenth century in the 1970s . . . . I was driven by the idea of achieving a mad divination, the parodic invention of a language and a speech for that distant Caribbean eighteenth century; I attempted a linguistically backward science-fiction].

As he frames his narratives, Rodríguez Juliá employs the same device in all three novels: the stories are presented as a series of talks delivered by a Puerto Rican historian, Alejandro Cadalso, in the late 1930s. Several critics have aptly pointed out that such a framing strategy allows Rodríguez Juliá to link his eighteenth-century stories to a period in Puerto Rico's twentieth-century history when the island, under Luis Muñoz Marín's leadership, was trying to consolidate narratives that would solidify its unique national identity while getting ready for accelerated industrial development fueled by US capital.[4] Thus, one could argue that Rodríguez Juliá's fiction (and this is certainly a trait he shares with Menton's new historical novelists) is interested not only in history but also in the *production* of historical accounts. Properly speaking, Rodríguez Juliá's novels are not historical fictions, but *historiographical* fictions.[5]

What, then, is the significance of Rodríguez Juliá's approach to history through his fiction? Why write *history-fiction* rather than historical fiction? If the objective is an exploration of Puerto Rico's history, or the effect of that history on the present, why not take that history as a point of departure, even if it needs to be transformed in order to reveal what official narratives have hidden? Are we dealing here with some idiosyncrasy of Rodríguez Juliá, or with some limitation in the very history of Puerto Rico (at least, as interpreted by Ródriguez Juliá)?

In order to approach these questions, we can depart from Rodríguez Juliá's own comments on the historical period that became the privileged object of his attention in his three novels. The writer has declared: "Pero, ¿qué me propuse con esta obra? Ni más ni menos ir a la semilla de nuestra nacionalidad, a ese siglo XVIII borroso donde se esconde el nacimiento de nuestra convivencia" (Rodríguez de Laguna, 131–132) [But what did I attempt in this work? Nothing less than reaching the seed of our nationality in that blurry eighteenth century, where the birth of our coexistence lies hidden]. When Rodríguez Juliá indicates that the eighteenth century contains the seed of Puerto Rico's national identity, he is in fact agreeing with the opinion of historians regarding not only the island but also the rest of Latin America. After all, it is during the eighteenth century that the cultural, political, and social conditions coalesce, which would lead to the independence movements at the beginning of the following century.[6] In addition to a heightened sense of difference from the colonial metropolis among *criollos* [creoles] and deepening discontent with colonial limitations on self-government and trade, the end of the eighteenth century brings to full force the ideas of the Enlightenment, which have as very concrete manifestations the American Revolution of 1776 and the French Revolution of 1789. In the Americas, another fundamental event is the Haitian Revolution of 1791, whose importance for Rodríguez Juliá's novels we will examine later in the text. In the case of Puerto Rico, the events in the rest of Latin America and the Caribbean had an undeniable economic, social, and cultural impact, but Puerto Rico did not follow the footsteps of its neighbors.

Puerto Rico's relation to that Age of Enlightenment is paradoxical at best. If the eighteenth century is, as it is all over Latin America, the period during which a national conscience coalesces, in Puerto Rico's case that process is compounded by the fact that the island lay relatively dormant, on the margins of Spain's dwindling empire. While Cuba and Santo Domingo retained some importance as ports for ships on their trips between Spain and the mainland colonies, Puerto Rico remained mostly (although never totally) outside of that circuit, surviving on local crops and smuggling. On the other hand, the island remained important from strategic geo-political perspective, and during the eighteenth century it was heavily fortified and militarized, a development that may have made internal resistance more difficult.[7] Cuba's nineteenth-century history coincides with its development as an important agricultural producer (sugarcane, tobacco, coffee), and it is not surprising that the nineteenth century is marked by numerous and extended attempts at obtaining independence from Spain. In Puerto Rico, other than the short-lived rebellion known as the "Grito de Lares" in 1868, one cannot find any comparable developments. In other words, if the Age of Enlightenment is in many ways the Age of Revolutions, in Puerto Rico it was paradoxically an age when no "important" events (at least in a dramatic sense) happened, no long-lasting revolutions, no game-changing affirmations of Puerto Rican national consciousness.[8]

It is important to highlight that this period in the development of Puerto Rican identity is characterized by a relative absence of dramatic or violent events, because it is precisely within the confines of that "absence," the "non-event" that was Puerto Rico's eighteenth century, that Rodríguez Juliá's fictions articulate their parallel, fictional, invented narratives. What his novels invent are precisely the revolts that never occurred in Puerto Rico, the *foundational violence* that traditionally engenders new nations or well-defined national identities.[9] Rodríguez Juliá's novels are fantasies or, more precisely, wish fulfillments—and here it is not coincidence that the novelist calls his fictions "nightmares of history," for they fulfill wishes much like Freud understood dreams to be wish fulfillments. The novels portray revolts against colonial masters—paternalistic and castrating authorities—invoking the kind of violence that is redeemed by its capacity to found a new national narrative. It is precisely this kind of violence that Puerto Rico lacks, in the view of some of its better known revolutionary visionaries, going back at least to Ramón Emeterio Betances in the nineteenth century.[10]

Filling the Void with Rebellion

Rodríguez Juliá's novels invent two similar albeit slightly different slave rebellions that, toward the end of the eighteenth century, manage to either temporarily topple or seriously threaten the control of colonial authorities in the city of San Juan, which constituted the stronghold of metropolitan authority in the otherwise half-forgotten island. In *La renuncia del héroe Baltasar*, a Machiavellian bishop, Obispo Larra, arranges the marriage between the daughter of one of the city's colonial officers and Baltasar Montañez, the son of the leader of a slave revolt who was executed by the authorities. The bishop's plan is to appease the black masses by providing them with the vicarious pleasure of witnessing one of them gain access to the hierarchies of white colonial power. However, that plan backfires when Baltasar, although willing to marry Josefina Prats, refuses to consummate his marriage to her. The bishop takes him prisoner, and this provokes a massive slave rebellion. Baltasar is an ambivalent figure: he refuses to stop the rebellion, but out of resentment for the way the black masses abandoned his father in his hour of defeat, he also refuses to become their leader.

La noche oscura del niño Avilés takes place in the same fictional universe as *La renuncia del héroe Baltasar*, although it is not technically a sequel. In this novel, Bishop Larra takes care of a deformed boy who was rescued from the waters, "el niño Avilés." The novel tells us that this boy will one day become the founder of "Nueva Venecia," a "free" city for maroon slaves and other marginal individuals built on the mangroves that surround San Juan. However, most of the narrative focuses on a massive slave revolt led by a black leader (later self-proclaimed king), Obatal. The slaves take over the city of San Juan and once in power, Obatal inaugurates a utopic "black kingdom" where African customs and beliefs reign free. Very soon a second war develops as Mitume, one of Obatal's generals, rebels against the king's excesses. Eventually, the city is taken back by the armies of Bishop Trespalacios, who exorcises the city and takes "el niño Avilés" under his protection.

From the previous summaries of the novels (which ignore numerous structural aspects and subplots of these dense, baroque texts), it should be clear that a decisive dimension of them is not only their invention of fictional rebellions in Puerto Rico, but also the fact that these rebellions are led by black leaders. Rodríguez Juliá has acknowledged his debt to the work not only of Luis Palés Matos, the first and most significant literary defender of the African dimension of Puerto Rico's identity, but also of José Luis González, whose groundbreaking *El país de cuatro pisos* (1980) provoked the island's intelligentsia by suggesting that not only conservative sectors of Puerto Rican society but also presumably revolutionary, pro-independence intellectuals had systematically identified Puerto Rico's culture with its Hispanic past, thereby minimizing the fundamental importance of Puerto Rico's African heritage.[11]

The critical consensus on Rodríguez Juliá's history-fictions alternates between two positions that, although seemingly at odds, in fact do not exclude each other. On the one hand, and precisely with regard to Puerto Rico's black identity, the novels are conceived of as recovering aspects of Puerto Rico's culture that have been denied or minimized in official histories. As Rubén González indicates: "Parodiar la historia es, en este caso, fondear el pasado y emerger con una imagen distinta. Cambiar la historia es buscar su reconquista" (Rubén González, 72) [To parody history is, in this case, to explore the depths of the past and to emerge with a different image. To alter history is an attempt to re-conquer it]. Julieta Novau further clarifies: "Rodríguez Juliá se apropia de conceptualizaciones provenientes de parámetros de pensamiento racistas ... para, simultáneamente a manera de oxímoron, revalorizar las bases culturales africanas como componentes insoslayables que hilvanan el tramado profundo de la condición puertorriqueña" (Novau, 7) [Rodríguez Juliá appropriates concepts that come from racist mind-frames ... in order to simultaneously renew the value, in an oxymoronic manner, of the African cultural foundations that are indispensable components of the deep fabric of the Puerto Rican condition]. In other words, the novels invent in order to better uncover and highlight the value of repressed histories.[12]

On the other hand, given the novels' ludic style, and their reliance on multiple voices, critics also point out that Rodríguez Juliá is not trying to provide an essentialist, albeit alternative, foundation for Puerto Rico's culture, but rather that he is attempting to show how such essential foundations are always fictional, always written into history by very partial actors in power struggles. As E. González Rodríguez states: "La novela adquiere así una sugerente ambigüedad que auto-referencialmente asume las identidades del discurso historiográfico y literario en la unicidad de su corpus (la novela) y deconstruye el mecanismo generador de ideología en dichos discursos" (González Rodríguez, 306) [Thus, the novel acquires a suggestive ambiguity, which, self-referentially, takes on the identities of both historiographical and literary discourses within its own text (the novel itself) and also deconstructs the ideology-producing mechanism of those discourses]. Rubén Ríos has aptly captured Rodríguez Juliá's precarious balance between the use of fiction to "recover" hidden truths and its use to parody and question the very aspiration to such truths:

> En Rodríguez Juliá el mito siempre descubre su factura precaria. Vivimos, nos dice en su crónica al músico Cortijo ... en un país donde el mito anda moribundo. Más que mito, hay en la novelística y en las crónicas de este

autor, una sed de mito, un intento de recuperar una memoria perdida por medio de una arqueología ficticia que le dé soporte, que la ancle en la densidad de un pasado. Por eso la parodia es siempre la cara final con que su escritura se acerca al pasado en busca de legitimidad. Se trata de una escritura correctiva, entregada a la melancolía incurable de una nostalgia falsa o ilegítima.

(Ríos Avila, Raza, 208)

[In Rodríguez Juliá myth always displays its precarious character. We live, he tells us in his chronicle on the musician Cortijo . . . in a country where myth is moribund. More than myth, what we have in the novels and chronicles of this author is a thirst for myth, an attempt to recover a lost memory through a fictitious archeology that may support it, that may anchor it in the density of a past. That is why, as it approaches the past in search of legitimacy, the final face his writing shows is always that of parody. It is a corrective kind of writing, clinging to the incurable melancholy of a false or illegitimate nostalgia].

While agreeing with Ríos's assessment, I would highlight that precisely because the melancholy is "incurable," parody is not always the final word in Rodríguez Juliá's fictions. Rather, the last word is precisely the undecidability between the parodic and the nostalgic stances.

We can rightly emphasize either (1) a desire to "correct" official versions of the past (by producing "truer" versions) or (2) a desire to parody the very attempt to produce "true" representations of the past, as fundamental thematic and stylistic concerns of Rodríguez Juliá's novels. However, I would add that both approaches treat these fictions mainly or merely as historical novels (or perhaps *new* historical novels), that is, texts that confront history as it happened or was recorded, and depart from there to correct or question those accounts. However, as I have suggested, Rodríguez Juliá's "history-fictions" operate in a slightly different manner. They point to events that never happened, but perhaps should have happened, and proceed to invent them, without ever grounding them in any documented historical context beyond the physical space of eighteenth-century San Juan.

Jean Franco clearly (although unintentionally) shows the subtle distinction I am pointing to when she states in her discussion of *La noche oscura:*

The period to which the documents supposedly refer dates from the end of the eighteenth century, that is, the period of the great slave rebellions that liberated Haiti from the French. Puerto Rican history records no such uprising, and its black culture was largely "hidden from history" by a ruling class that was mainly concerned with "whitening" the island.

(Franco, 135)

Again, there is no denying that the black dimension of Puerto Rico's culture has been denied by its white elites. To the extent that Rodríguez Juliá's fictions highlight the important presence and impact of that culture, it is accurate to say that his novels bring to light "hidden" histories. In Franco's reading, the slave rebellions in Rodríguez Juliá's novels may be regarded as *allegories* for the deep, and often denied, extended influence of black culture in Puerto Rico. However, I believe the novels also can be understood in a slightly more literal manner: they are novels about *concrete, specific slave revolts*. To the extent that the novels are not quite about cultural influence over long periods of time, but rather about *singular* events that forever shift the direction of the colony and violently found a new order (as the Haitian Revolution did), the texts are not about recovering a hidden past but about the *wishful* fantastic filling of a perceived historical hole or absence.[13]

To the extent that Rodríguez Juliá's novels attempt to fill the gaps of heroism in Puerto Rico's history, they cannot be considered merely ludic exercises that question essentialist narratives from the ironic perspective of radical undecidability. They also betray some nostalgia for the heroic, foundational sagas that they portray, a nostalgia that is unavoidably linked to the historical period when the novels were written: the 1970s (*La noche oscura* was written during that period even though it was not published until later). This was a period when the supposed material benefits brought to the island by Muñoz Marín's ideological compromises—his shift from a pro-independence position to a defense of the (colonial, for some) *Estado Libre Asociado* [Commonwealth]—were showing their underside of protracted economic dependence and persistent inequalities.[14]

In a revealing passage from *Caribeños,* a text that in many ways works as a multiform interpretive key for many aspects of Rodríguez Juliá's eighteenth-century novels, the novelist states:

> De la mera excentricidad me salva una tendencia notable de la literatura puertorriqueña. Nuestra tradición siempre ha vivido obcecada con la imagen de nosotros mismos, con esto que un tanto defensivamente se ha llamado el problema de la identidad; el esfuerzo de nuestra literatura ha sido fundar la imagen de nuestro pueblo. Pero el esclarecimiento de esa imagen, el intento por definir los modos de una colectividad y su convivencia, resulta asediada por el cambio social y la transformación del lenguaje. ¿Sobre qué puertorriqueñidad estamos hablando? . . . Mis novelas padecen el trasiego, la inquietud de una sociedad a medio hacer, que está por definirse.
> (Rodríguez Juliá, *Caribeños,* 69–70)

> [I am freed from sheer eccentricity by a notable tendency in Puerto Rican literature. Our tradition has always been obsessed with our own image, with what somewhat defensively has been called the problem of identity. The

effort of our literature has been to lay the foundations for the image of our people. But the clarification of that image, the attempt to define a group of people and their coexistence, has been threatened by social change and the transformation of language. What Puerto Ricanness are we talking about? My novels suffer from the agitation and the disquiet of a half-made society that still has to be defined.[15]]

Despite his awareness of the fact that there is not *one* "Puerto Ricanness" to be elucidated or defined in an essentialist manner, Rodríguez Juliá acknowledges that the identity question, the attempt to clarify that image, and above all the despair of writing in a "half made, undefined society" are key motors in his fiction.

In another passage from the same book, the author declares:

¿Caribeñizar a Puerto Rico o puertorriqueñizar el Caribe? Me temo que es lo segundo. Miro con preocupación un proceso que en nuestro país ha creado una fisura hiriente, destructiva. Me gustaría pensar que estamos alcanzando una idea más serena de nuestra identidad, una visión menos alienada de nuestra propia condición histórica; pero me temo que es todo lo contrario, que el Caribe nos alcanza en el tránsito por derroteros que sólo pueden conducir a un mayor distanciamiento de nosotros mismos.

(Rodríguez Juliá, *Caribeños,* 19–20)

[To Caribbeanize Puerto Rico, or to Puerto Ricanize the Caribbean? I am afraid it is the second option. I look with concern at a process that has created a wounding, destructive fissure in our country. I would like to think that we are reaching a more serene idea of our identity, a less alienated vision of our own historical condition. But I am afraid it is the opposite: it is the Caribbean that is approaching us through roads that can only lead to a greater distancing from ourselves.]

The mournful tone, the craving for a more "serene" idea of our identity, the concern with Puerto Rico's "alienation" from its own reality, and the concern that the rest of the Caribbean (traditionally regarded as more rebellious and faithful to its own unique destiny) is following Puerto Rico's example, all of those elements clearly indicate that, despite Rodríguez Juliá's astute ironic gaze, there is an undercurrent of sympathy for traditional discourses of identity, nationalism, and anticolonial resistance running through his work. We must regard his "history-fictions" then, in their attempts to create alternative historical scenarios, not only as mockeries of any attempt to find hidden historical certainties (although they are also that), but also as nostalgic gestures toward those absent certainties, particularly the ones that take daring, violent, revolutionary forms.

Aurea María Sotomayor has compellingly shown how Puerto Rico's nationalist discourse throughout the twentieth century relied heavily on the rhetoric and the myth of the "absent hero." In other words, Puerto Rican nationalism—particularly as incarnated in its most emblematic figure, Pedro Albizu Campos—presented its project in paradoxical terms: its struggle for a future independent Puerto Rico was articulated through a nostalgic evocation of the island's Hispanic past. In opposition to the industrial project of "modernization" set up by Muñoz Marín's US-backed "operation bootstrap," nationalist discourse presented an idyllic society of landowners and peasants, tied together by tradition and love of the land. Moreover, Albizu was fond of explaining the difficulties of the nationalist movement in terms of a lack of heroic spirit in Puerto Rico, the kind of spirit that produces martyrs who are willing to sacrifice themselves for the fatherland:

> Albizu es un reformador moral. La descripción que hace del pueblo puer-torriqueño como agobiado por una doctrina pesimista, su exhortación a crear un "espíritu público" confiado en el futuro, y el objetivo de transmi-tir una "infusión moral en nuestro pueblo para que vuelva a creer en su destino," son frases que van dibujando a trazos breves . . . *la imagen del héroe ausente.* Pedro Albizu Campos lamenta la ausencia de un relevo generacional y señala . . . a los "indignos sucesores de la memoria" que no están "a la altura moral de los héroes del 68." En su discurso, esta invalidez del heroísmo está marcada por una retórica fustigante que en lugar de alabar a su audiencia recrimina contra ella, la castiga, y le exige.
>
> (Sotomayor, 188–189)

> [Albizu is a moral reformer. His description of the Puerto Rican people as overwhelmed by a pessimistic doctrine; his admonition to create a "public spirit" with trust in the future; his goal of transmitting a "moral infusion into our people so that they will believe in their destiny again; all of those phrases gradually draw . . . *the image of the absent hero.* Albizu laments the absence of a new generation of heroes and he points out . . . " the unworthy inheritors of those memories' who are not at "the moral height of the heroes of 1868." In his discourse, that lack of heroism is highlighted by an aggres-sive rhetoric that instead of praising its audience reproaches, punishes, and makes demands of it.]

Thus, nationalist discourse revolves around an absence that its very rhetoric tries to fill: the absence of a hero and a heroic event that may found the new by returning to the legitimate roots of the old. Paradoxically, as we saw earlier, already in the nineteenth century Betances expressed concern and frustration over Puerto Rico's lack of revolutionary fervor.

Rodríguez Juliá draws upon this tradition when he invents precisely those absent heroes and events in his history-fictions. It is certainly true that the novels challenge the essentialist rhetoric of traditional national-ist discourse (in which Puerto Rico is a monolithic identity rooted in its Hispanic past). However, by taking as their implicit departure point the notion that Puerto Rico's history lacks such events and heroes, and that they must therefore be invented, the novels also follow the lead of one of Puerto Rican nationalism's most cherished tropes. Thus, one might argue that, although these novels do not follow a traditional nationalist agenda, they do not simply mock it either: they regard it with skepticism while betraying some nostalgia for those absent foundational figures and events.

If we are talking about foundational revolutionary violence and heroic figures, if on top of that we are talking about *black* heroes, if we are looking toward the end of the eighteenth century in the Caribbean, and if we link Puerto Rico (as Rodríguez Juliá certainly does, following the lead of Palés Matos and José Luis González) to its pan-Caribbean context, then we are most definitely circling around one fundamental event: the Haitian Revo-lution. Rodríguez Juliá himself suggests that interpretation when he states in a 1985 essay, regarding *La renuncia*: "Quien la lea superficialmente pen-sará que estoy hablando sobre Haití. Vuelva a leerla como una pesadilla, adivinando el anverso en el embuste" (Rodríguez de Laguna, 132) [Who-ever reads it at the surface level will think I am talking about Haiti. Let them read it again as a nightmare, trying to guess the underside of the invention]. Of course, the very structure of the author's negation, combined with his insistence on the *oneiric,* nightmarish quality of the text, bring to mind Freud's reflections on negation among neurotic patients:

> They say: "I've got a new compulsive idea. My immediate thought was: it could mean such and such. But no, surely that can't be true—otherwise, I couldn't have had that thought." The interpretation of the new com-pulsive idea that they reject with this argument . . . is, of course, the cor-rect one. The content of a repressed idea or thought can get through to consciousness . . . on condition that it is *negated.*
>
> (Freud, 96)

The Freudian commentary would not refer here to Rodríguez Juliá as an individual, but to the significance of his texts in the Puerto Rican cultural imaginary. The novels are definitely not about Haiti, they are about Puerto Rico. However, Haiti, or rather what Haiti represents in the Puerto Rican imaginary, is precisely an absence that can be imagined only as nightmarish fantasy. It is a country whose black masses took their destiny in their own hands and through an epic revolution of sometimes disturbing violence destroyed and expelled their colonial masters, without bothering to think about the consequences, focusing only on their thirst for freedom. From that perspective Puerto Rico is the *anti*-Haiti, the diametrical opposite in its historical trajectory. Rodríguez Juliá's novels, then, are about Haiti, not in the superficial sense that he rightly negates, but about Haiti as the best available symbolic incarnation, within a Caribbean context, of a possible content for that absence or hole that Puerto Rico's nationalism has long carried as a shameful burden.[16]

Thus, one could regard Rodríguez Juliá's novels as being "about" Haiti, or rather about the *absence* of Haiti (what Haiti represents) in Puerto Rican history. However, this does not mean what we get in the novels is a naive celebration of the Haiti that Puerto Rico should have been. What Haiti represents, from the perspective of the Puerto Rican cultural imaginary, is both an object of desire and loathing, of admiration and fear. And those conflicted affects spring, naturally, from the unavoidable reality that, if Haiti is Puerto Rico's "road not taken," then Puerto Rico works in a similar way for Haiti, and the resulting balance is by no means always negative for Puerto Rico. I will return to that issue in the final section of this chapter, but right now it might be useful to ask ourselves, do Rodríguez Juliá's invented slave revolts actually shed some light on the Haitian revolution? What image of "Haiti" emerges from the (distorting, desiring) mirror of Puerto Rican fear of, and desire for, the "absent hero?" Here we move to the other side of the novelist's approach, because although his novels betray some nostalgia for foundational revolutionary violence, they also show a keen, ironic eye for the many ways in which such violence can follow the wrong path or lose sight of its legitimate objectives. Consequently, *La renuncia* and *La noche oscura,* through their fantastic scenarios of a Haiti-like eighteenth-century Puerto Rico, actually illuminate with intense though often one-sided clarity many fault lines in the actual revolutionary events in Haiti. Among many issues we can identify several key ones.

First, let us consider the problem of revolutionary leadership. Do leaders guide revolutions and define their direction, or do they follow and obey the lead of the people? C. L. R. James addresses this issue in his classic text *The Black Jacobins: Toussaint L'Ouverture and the San Domingo Revolution* (1938; rev. ed. 1962). In this text he states: "Great men make history, but only such history as it is possible for them to make. Their freedom of achievement is limited by the necessities of their environment" (James, x). James's book is a brilliant exploration of how that dialectical relation between great men and their followers is in fact quite difficult to achieve. Despite his initial achievements, Toussaint gradually found himself increasingly alienated from his own followers, and "his error was his neglect of his own people. They did not understand what he was doing

or where he was going. He took no trouble to explain. It was dangerous to explain, but still more dangerous not to explain" (James, 240).
Toussaint had a lofty political vision, one that was in principle inspired by
the slaves' aspirations to freedom. However, his inability to communicate
effectively with them leads first to their mistrust, and then to his downfall.
This scenario opens the door to less "enlightened" leaders like Jean-Jacques
Dessalines, who in spite of his violent character, does speak the language of
the people, and leads the country to independence.[17]

In *La renuncia del héroe Baltasar*, the protagonist takes Toussaint's difficulties as a revolutionary leader to absurd extremes. Toussaint's inability to
convey his lofty vision to his people leads to their frustration and his downfall, and opens the door precisely to the violent forces that he was trying
to repress. In what seems like a perverse reading of the disconnect between
idealistic leaders like Toussaint and the masses, Baltasar refuses to subscribe
to any vision at all, and tries to make a virtue of that refusal. For Baltasar,
there is no "vision" that will not become, sooner or later, either a tool in
the hands of power or an object of resentment of the masses whom Baltasar
(as a "leader") condescendingly looks down upon. Thus, Baltasar eventually renounces the power and leadership that Bishop Larra has granted him.
In fact, he renounces his father first, by allying himself with Larra; then he
renounces Larra by refusing to consummate his marriage to Josefina Prats
and thereby pacify the black masses; finally, he renounces the black masses
by refusing to become their leader.

Baltasar is a hyper-deconstructionist of sorts: he cannot conceive of
any position of leadership or act of rebellion that does not end up surreptitiously subordinated to the very forces it rebels against. To oppose
power is still to be defined by power. Thus, Baltasar chooses not to choose:
he creates a radical nihilistic theology wherein all power is refuted (not
opposed): "Confío en que el hombre, como acto de libertad suprema,
preferirá destruirse y acabar con todo. Y así se corregirá el mayor error
de Dios, la creación" (*La renuncia,* 127) ["I trust that man, in an act of
supreme fiction, will prefer to destroy, to destroy everything. And thus we
will have corrected God's greatest error, creation" (*Renunciation,* 134)].
Although fictionally disguised as the expression of Baltasar's theological
musings, the novel points to the difficulty of every revolutionary leader:
the way in which revolutionary actions can be co-opted by authorities. This
includes the subtlest act of co-optation: the reduction of the revolution to
its purely oppositional stance, whereby it is defined only by that which it
opposes.

A very revealing example is Baltasar's position with regard to his
white wife. By choosing not to consummate his marriage with Josefina
Prats, Baltasar is in fact yielding to her father's racist opposition to their

marriage: "¿Quería decir aquella serpiente con mitra que yo, después de muchos sucesos, servía a los deseos de un hombre que me despreciaba a razón de mi raza, o en otras letras, que conservaba intacta la virginidad de su hija, honrando como fiel esclavo el deseo de amo?" (*La renuncia*, 83) ["Did that mitered serpent mean that I, after all that has occurred, served the desires of a man who despised me for my race, or in other words, that I preserved his daughter's virginity, honoring like the faithful slave his master's wishes?" (*Renunciation*, 63)]. On the other hand, were Baltasar to consummate the marriage, he is aware of the possible humiliating consequences: "En mí aúlla el deseo de toda una raza; pero he aquí que no es un deseo de placer, sino de humillación. Y es por ello que temo al treparla una muy glácida mirada de odio que me haga notar la debilidad de mi intento" (*La renuncia*, 83) ["Within me the desire of an entire race cries out, yet it is not a desire for pleasure, but rather a desire to humiliate. And it is for that reason that I fear that when I mount her I shall meet a glacial look of hatred, which will make me see the weakness of my attempt" (*Renunciation*, 63)]. The narrator comments: "Reconocía Baltasar la incapacidad del negro—depositario de las pasiones del esclavo y su sicología—para lograr la humillación del blanco" (*La renuncia*, 83–84) ["Baltasar recognized the inability of the black man—inheritor of the slave's passions and the slave's psychology—to truly humiliate the white" (*Renunciation*, 63)]. Baltasar is able to foresee that Josefina's contempt for him and his race, which is part of the epistemic logic of the colonial system in which both of them live, would preempt any attempt on his part to humiliate her.

Baltasar's "inability" to preserve his dignity whether he acts or not is a good example of what Walter Mignolo calls "the colonial difference." By "colonial difference" Mignolo understands a Eurocentric view of the world (indeed, the basis for the "modern/colonial world system," colonialism itself being nothing less than the underside of modernity, as the philosopher Enrique Dussel has aptly suggested) in which "others" are inherently subhuman and destined to occupy a subordinate (subaltern) position with regard to the European colonizer. Those colonial "others" perpetually aspire to "catch up," and achieve equality with the European (and later, North American) man that remains, by definition, impossible, thus eternally pursued and out of reach. Of course, the alternative is to reject that Eurocentric view and then retreat into a position or culture that colonialism has defined a priori as inherently inferior to that of Europe. Damned if he does and damned if he doesn't, Baltasar is trapped in that colonial double-bind.[18]

Evidently, Baltasar's option in the novel is not a real option. Not to choose is still to choose something, and in that regard, Baltasar's actions are the opposite of those of the leaders of the Haitian Revolution, with the possible exception of Toussaint in his hesitant relation to Napoleon and his refusal to push the revolution to its logical conclusion: a struggle for independence. However, even Toussaint was resolute in his stance against slavery. Baltasar's "theology" (all power must be renounced, therein lies the ultimate power, for there is no decision that ultimately does not become complicit with even more bondage) bears vague and unsettling resemblances to the position of Puerto Ricans and their commonwealth throughout the second half of the twentieth century: all the "definite" options have disadvantages, so it is perhaps better not to choose at all.

In *La noche oscura,* when Obatal takes possession of the city, the black masses rejoice in exuberant celebrations and dances that are rooted in African traditional beliefs. However, the narrator informs us: "Así se reconoció la autoridad de la tradición, y no la fuerza del poder, porque éste residía en el caudillo Obatal, quien estaba ausente de allí, de tan majestuosa ceremonia, por su condición plebeya" (*La noche oscura,* 53) [Thus, the authority of tradition was acknowledged, but not the strength of power, for the latter resided in the leader Obatal, who was absent from such a majestic ceremony, since it was a plebeian affair]. Obatal's unwillingness to join in "plebeian" festivities, his de facto distinction between "the strength of power" and "the authority of tradition," also has distinct echoes in the Haitian Revolution. First and foremost, we have the ambitions to royalty of both Jean-Jacques Dessalines and Henri Christophe. Dessalines was a self-proclaimed emperor, while Christophe was a king who created a court and nobility titles. One may also remember the attitude of the catholic Toussaint Louverture toward the popular, presumably ignorant beliefs of Voodoo. In fact, Toussaint energetically attempted to suppress Voodoo, as did Christophe.[19]

Another issue that Rodríguez Juliá's novels bring up is that of the vision and motives guiding the revolution. Was it a question of "universal emancipation," as critic Nick Nesbitt has argued for the Haitian Revolution, or revenge and the desire to occupy the position of the oppressor without changing the oppressive structure as such?[20] In *La renuncia,* Baltasar's actions stem from a deep resentment against the world itself that, as we saw, finds expression in a paradoxical nihilistic theology: "Para Baltasar el poder tenía un sentido lúdico, que consistía en incitar las pasiones y luego contemplar, con cínica sonrisa, como un dios que está por encima de los preciados motivos humanos, la inutilidad de todo esfuerzo" (*La renuncia,* 70) ["Power had a certain playful, ludic aspect for Baltasar, who was capable of inciting passions, setting the game in motion, and then standing back, with his cynical smile, like a god standing above vain human motives, to contemplate the futility of all effort" (*Renunciation,* 40)]. When Baltasar reflects on the slaves that rebel in his name, he comments: "algunos, los más ingenuos, piensan que matan por justicia" (*La renuncia,* 113) ["Some, the most ingenuous of them, believe that they kill for justice" (*Renunciation,* 113)]. Even though Baltasar does not share their naive, all-too-human view of justice, he welcomes their violence, as it ends up serving his appetite for destruction.

In *La noche oscura* we have a more traditional rebellion along the lines of the Haitian Revolution, but just as in Haiti, motives, ends, and means often lose their way. Obatal's men massacre whites at first, but then, when other black slaves run away, afraid to join Obatal's free city, "todos fueron perseguidos sin misericordia por la guardia brava. Los plantíos de caña recién quemados, todavía brumosos por el denso humo de la llamarada, desataron aquel nauseabundo olor a cuerpos descuartizados, vientres abiertos, cuellos cercenados por los incesantes machetes de los feroces guerreros de Obatal" (*La noche oscura,* 44) [They were all mercilessly pursued by the brave guards. The recently burnt sugar-cane fields, still clouded by the smoke of the flames, unleashed that nauseating smell of dismembered bodies, open bellies, throats slashed by the machetes of Obatal's fierce warriors]. Later on, when Mitume rebels against Obatal's excesses, Obatal's downfall begins "porque Obatal sólo reclamó venganza, humillación de su rival en vez de triunfo" (*La noche oscura,* 264) [because Obatal was only content with revenge, the humiliation of his rival, rather than simple victory]. Both the cruel treatment of a populace that does not adhere to the leader's wishes and the violence that does not stop at victory but continues into humiliation of the enemy can be found in the Haitian Revolution, particularly in the figure of Jean-Jacques Dessalines. When Toussaint sent Dessalines to "pacify" the mulatto population that had rebelled under the command of Rigaud, Dessalines's campaign was so violent that Toussaint had to put a stop to it, famously quipping: "I said to prune the tree, not to uproot it" (James, 236). Dessalines's "massacres" of whites after independence are also notorious.[21] It may be correctly argued that Rodríguez Juliá's approach is terribly lopsided, since he mainly portrays the vengeful, violent side of the revolution. What must be unfortunately acknowledged is that the revolution did show that violent face more often than not.[22]

It is not surprising that before long, Mitume, Obatal's main general, will rebel against his leader, appalled by his excesses. Dessalines and Christophe similarly abandoned Toussaint (due to the latter's hesitations, more than to his excesses), Christophe betrayed Dessalines, and Pétion rebelled against Christophe. Christophe's ambition, his megalomania that practically re-enslaved his people, and his tragic end (he shoots himself when all hope of victory against Pétion is lost) have inspired writers as diverse as Alejo Carpentier (*El reino de este mundo*), Aimé Césaire (*La tragédie du roi Christophe*), and Derek Walcott (*Henri Christophe*). Obatal also shoots himself in *La noche oscura,* and the discovery of this body in the throne room of his "tower," still with the gun lying on his chest, resembles Christophe's suicide scene in his "Citadel," in the works of these afore-mentioned Caribbean writers. As soon as he seizes power, Mitume has the body hanged from its genitals and tortured, in a clear indication that the emphasis on violence and revenge does not stop with Obatal (as it did not stop with Christophe in Haiti). However, Mitume's dominion will be short lived, as his forces will be soon defeated by those of Bishop Trespalacios.

Mitume's and Obatal's actions point to another unfortunate reality of the Haitian Revolution: the persistence of colonial structures and men-talities even after the colonizer has been defeated and expelled. This is what Peruvian sociologist Aníbal Quijano calls "the coloniality of power," that is, the survival after "independence" of Eurocentric social relations of inequality and domination that are racialized (that is, conceptualized as "inherent" or essential to the groups involved), and have their origin in, and served to justify, colonial domination.[23] Once such relations of domi-nation are conceptualized in such a Eurocentric racialized way, coloniality survives the defeat of colonialism, for "European culture became a seduc-tion; it gave access to power. Cultural Europeanization turned into an aspiration. It was a means of participating in colonial power" (qtd in Moraña et al., 282). The survival of such material *and* mental colonial structures is a sad historical reality in the case of Haiti, as shown in the rapid succession of despotic (and often racist) leaders after the indepen-dence, some of whom, like Christophe, went as far as recreating a royal court with its nobility.

While the survival of colonial structures is certainly due in part to the thirst for power of some leaders, it also has deeper causes rooted in global economic trends. Toussaint, for example, was quite interested in preserving the plantation system in Haiti, and several later leaders followed his exam-ple. The question for these leaders was: how was Haiti, until then a massive, monoculture sugar producer, going to survive economically? Understand-ably, the former slaves were not inclined to return to a system of production that they associated with their previous subjugation. In fact, most of them gravitated toward small-scale, subsistence agriculture in abandoned lots of land. This became a significant source of conflict between peasants and many Haitian governments. To this, of course, we must add the resistance of European countries and the United States to officially recognize Haiti's independence. The small, devastated country was quite isolated for many years after its revolution.[24]

The question of what happens after the revolution occupies a central but shadowy space in Rodríguez Juliá's novels. Naturally, since his novels work as "history-fictions" that must somehow tie in with Puerto Rico's current situation, the slave rebellions do not succeed. In fact, they are erased from collective history. However, the prospects for what would happen after possible victories are clearly indicated by the way the revolts are framed. In *La renuncia*, the slaves revolt in the name of a leader, Baltasar, who does not actually respect them. There is no vision of what the end result of the revolt might be other than freedom for slaves. In *La noche oscura*, the victorious slaves go on to create a *utopic city* in San Juan, a city full of celebrations, music, and African traditions. Although beautiful, those celebrations offer little in the way of practical planning, and one of the narrators comments: "Pero también toda aquella abundancia vista en el campamento de negros llenó mi alma de pena, porque pensaba yo que durante un largo asedio llegaría el momento en que las provisiones se acabarían, y entonces mostraría su negra cara el hambre cruel" (*La noche oscura*, 81) [But all that abundance in the encampment of blacks also filled my soul with pity, because I realized that during a long siege the moment would come when the supplies would run out, and then cruel hunger would show its dark face]. There are no clear plans, and no strategy, just the present joy of conquered freedom.

La noche oscura also points to the future city of Nueva Venecia, founded by Niño Avilés, where maroon slaves and others on the margins of society will live. The city is described as "aquella ciudad libertaria y utópica" (*La noche oscura*, xii) [that utopic and libertarian city]. That libertarian ethos avoids the controls and intromissions of official authorities as well as the imperative to plan a society in terms of the need to integrate a newly obtained freedom into the constraints and impositions of a global capitalist economy that ultimately developed as part of the long history of European colonialism. That libertarian vision certainly connects with the inclinations of those Haitian peasants who preferred humble survival in small-scale subsistence projects. Whether such attempts were ever realistic or not (given the brutal resistance of Europe and the United States to the new Haitian nation), one can certainly understand the fears and aspirations that guided these men. Similarly, Rodríguez Juliá's rebellious slaves do not attempt to plan beyond the utopic, libertarian space of their newly re-conquered freedom.[25]

"Caribbean Existential Anguish"

In the previous pages I have attempted to show how Rodríguez Juliá's eighteenth-century novels work as "wish fulfillment" fantasies of Puerto Rican history whose clear referent, in many ways, is the Haitian Revolution, precisely the kind of national-independence-achieving,

African-culture-affirming event that never happened (at least, not in such a definitive manner) in Puerto Rico. I have also tried to show how in the process of nostalgically looking at those events while also not losing an ironic perspective, the novels illustrate some of the more difficult dimensions of the Haitian Revolution: the frequent disconnect between leaders and masses, the spiraling out of control of violence and the difficulty of keeping truly emancipating ideals in sight, the sheer blind ambition of many of its leaders, and the difficulty of articulating a view for the future of the country that would not compromise the recently acquired independence. All of the above leads to one final question: given the historical destiny of Haiti so far, how has Puerto Rico, the non-Haiti, done by contrast? After all, that is another one of Rodríguez Juliá's fundamental preoccupations, namely the one that dominates his *crónicas* [chronicles] and his non-history-fiction novels.

A paradox of Rodríguez Juliá's "history-fictions," when contrasted with his chronicles of the contemporary Puerto Rico and the Caribbean, is that although there is an undeniable nostalgia for what I have called the foundational violence of revolution, by focusing not on the *real* great revolutions of Haiti (or Cuba), or on the many small *real* resistances of Puerto Rico, but rather on a great Puerto Rican revolution that is wholly fictional, that foundational violence can be kept safely at bay in an imaginary realm, for it may prove undesirable as a reality in the present. After all, if there is a void or lack in Puerto Rico's history, what could there be instead of it? One possible way to rephrase that question is: what is there in countries that did have their foundational epic sagas? Two examples come up in Rodríguez Juliá's writings: Haiti and Cuba, the latter with its socialist revolution.

Cuba, despite its successes, faces poverty and totalitarian repression. In a chronicle on Fidel Castro, Rodríguez Juliá, while still retaining some admiration for the man, cannot help but observe: "Fidel aún está en el proceso de ser juzgado por la historia; por voluntad de él, verdadero radical que lleva las cosas hasta sus últimas consecuencias, ese desenlace, posiblemente trágico, ensombrece la relación con el pueblo cubano y con el mundo. Hay algo de cimarrón libertario en él. Vive la paradoja de la inmovilidad revolucionaria" (Rodríguez Juliá, *Caribeños*, 312) [Fidel is still in the process of being judged by history. Since he is a true radical who takes things to their ultimate consequences, by his personal will that final outcome, which will possibly be tragic, darkens the relations between the Cuban people and the rest of the world. There is something of the libertarian maroon slave in him. He lives the paradox of revolutionary immobility]. One should notice the allusion to the "libertarian maroon slave" that brings distinct echoes of Rodríguez Juliá's own utopic black rebels: the goal is to obtain freedom, which contains its own dignity; beyond that, the practicalities of establishing a sustainable society that can preserve those freedoms on a long-term basis are not fully considered or assumed. The results, a paradoxical "revolutionary immobility" both in the novels and in Cuba, can be tragic. Haiti, on the other hand, is the poorest country in the Western Hemisphere. It has faced the rejection of other countries, the military occupation of the United States, several totalitarian regimes including the sinister rule of the Duvaliers, and horrific natural disasters (made worse by poor infrastructure) like the 2010 earthquake.

So it would seem that, in the company of such exalted examples of revolutionary transformation, Rodríguez Juliá's Puerto Rico, despite its less-than-heroic trajectory and undeniable inequalities that keep growing, is not doing so terribly badly—its problems and the standard of living of its population do not court abjection on a regular basis. Of course, how long such relative privilege can last in a political situation in which Puerto Ricans have no say in their own political future is anybody's guess, and undeniably a big part of what sociologist Arturo Torrecilla calls "la ansiedad de ser puertorriqueño" [the anxiety of being Puerto Rican]. It is possible to argue then that, if we examine Rodríguez Juliá's chronicles and his history-fictions, what emerges is an intellectual caught between nostalgia for a nonexistent past and fear of a precarious future, locked in a paradoxically comfortable but ideologically unacceptable, and possibly unsustainable, present. The position of that intellectual (by which I mean a composite of the narrative voices and strategies in the novels and the chronicles, not Rodríguez Juliá as an individual) closely resembles, not surprisingly, his island's political and cultural predicament throughout much of the twentieth century.

Nowhere is that paradoxical position as evident as in Rodríguez Juliá's moving chronicle on his visit to Martinican poet and politician Aimé Césaire. Martinique closely resembles Puerto Rico because Césaire, despite his literary fame as a fierce critic of colonialism and racism, decided *as a politician* that the best future for Martinique laid not in independence, but in permanent association with the colonial metropolis, France. Martinique has been a French "overseas department" since 1946, and Césaire was instrumental in that process. Not surprisingly, Martinique, like Puerto Rico, despite economic difficulties, has a relatively high standard of living for the Caribbean. Rodríguez Juliá reflects: "En Martinica existe una ansiedad parecida a la nuestra: ¿cuál sería la viabilidad económica de Martinica si Francia la independizara? La incertidumbre respecto del porvenir es una obsesión que Martinica comparte con Puerto Rico" (Rodríguez Juliá, *Caribeños*, 278) [In Martinique you find an anxiety similar to ours: how economically viable would Martinique be if France gave it its independence? Uncertainty about the future is an obsession that Martinique shares with Puerto Rico]. Curiously, in his conversation with Césaire, Rodríguez Juliá does not ask about the relationship between these two islands, but rather about Haiti, whose revolution looms large behind Césaire's *negritude.* Césaire avoids a direct answer, as he does with respect to Cuba (significantly, Ródriguez Juliá links both topics): "¿Hay alguna esperanza para Haití?, le pregunto al verlo esquivo respecto de Cuba... Césaire baja la voz, recoge las manos, coloca sobre el borde del escritorio sólo los dedos y se vuelve sombrío" (Rodríguez Juliá, *Caribeños,* 289) ["Is there any hope for Haiti?," I ask him when I see him avoid the topic of Cuba... Césaire lowers his voice, folds his hands, places only his fingers on the desk and turns somber]. Sadly, but realistically, Césaire points to racial divisions between mulattoes and blacks as one of the great sources of inequality on an island whose great claim to history lies in its successful slave rebellion. Thus, he justifies his political compromises, his rejection in real life of a great revolutionary tradition that his writings celebrate (in a manner, perhaps, not entirely foreign to Rodríguez Juliá's own fictional revolts).

Commenting on Martinique's political status, Rodríguez Juliá states:

> En el Caribe, por lo visto, todas las fórmulas complejas de relación con la metrópoli (Estado Libre Asociado, Estadidad Jíbara Federada, la autonomía integralista propuesta por Césaire) cobran un aura fantasmal, enrarecido y bizantino. Sólo la mención de una palabra—¡independencia!—vuelve más sobrio y terminante el discurso. Cuando le pregunto sobre la posibilidad de una independencia impuesta, vuelve a repetirme que Martinica no tiene fundamento económico alguno. Imposible competir con África y América Central en la venta del azúcar y el banano... además, los martinqueños le tienen miedo a la independencia.
>
> (Rodríguez Juliá, *Caribeños,* 287)
>
> [Seems that in the Caribbean all complex formulas of relation to the metropolis (the Commonwealth; a Federated Statehood that preserves Puerto Rican cultural identity; more autonomy within the frame of union with France as proposed by Césaire) acquire a ghostly, rarefied, overly complex aura. Only the mention of one word, "independence!," makes the discourse more sober and categorical. When I ask him about the possibility of an imposed independence, he repeats again that Martinique has no economic foundation. It is impossible to compete with Africa and Central America in the sale of sugar and bananas.... Besides, Martinicans are afraid of independence.]

Not surprisingly, earlier in the essay Rodríguez Juliá links Césaire to seminal figures in the mid-twentieth-century Caribbean, including one that greatly resembles, albeit in a most paradoxical way, Luis Muñoz Marín.

It is not possible, then, to read Rodríguez Juliá's "history-fictions" in only one key. They are wish-fulfilling fantasies of a writer with a strong nostalgia for heroic liberating narratives that never quite produced a ground shaking event in Puerto Rico. That explains why, rather than exploring Puerto Rico's actual history in order to correct or augment it through the creation of *historical novels,* the novelist follows the less familiar path of inventing an alternative history for the island. But as we have also seen, when regarded in the context of his other chronicles about Puerto Rico and the Caribbean, Rodríguez Juliá's history-fictions also betray a degree of relief about Puerto Rico's relatively comfortable position with regard to the rest of the Caribbean, particularly Haiti and Cuba. After all, *La renuncia* and *La noche oscura* dare to imagine their slave revolts, but they do not go as far as imagine the *success* of those revolts. They remain within the domain of utopic aspirations for a radical freedom that can never be fully actualized. This is, to a certain degree, how Puerto Rico looks at its Caribbean neighbors: they incarnate utopic projects that Puerto Ricans, with their mundane but practical caution, preferred to pass by. All of this, of course, does not deny the degree of anxiety that accompanies that position of relative privilege. Rodríguez Juliá makes the following comment toward the end of his chronicle on Césaire:

> Para Césaire existe una concepción trágica de lo antillano, porque nacimos de "la violencia histórica, del racismo, de la esclavitud" .... Se podría hablar, sin embargo, de cierto reencuentro con la esperanza, a pesar de esa *angustia existencial antillana* .... Me fascina esta última frase. La repito en español y él la repite en francés. Nos miramos en el desconsuelo de reconocernos como hijos de las mismas ilusiones, de los mismos fracasos.
>
> (Rodríguez Juliá, *Caribeños,* 289)

> [For Césaire, there is a tragic conception of the Caribbean, because we were born from "historical violence, racism, slavery" .... However, one could talk about a re-encounter of sorts with hope, in spite of that *Caribbean existential anguish* ... I am fascinated by that last phrase. I repeat it in Spanish and he repeats it in French. We look at each other with the sorrow of acknowledging ourselves as the children of the same illusions, the same defeats.]

It is that Caribbean existential anguish that Rodríguez Juliá's history-fictions attempt to exorcise like narrative charms. In doing so, they tragically illuminate the aspirations, successes, and failures of these islands: Puerto Rico's tremendous transformations and its stagnation, Haiti's glorious achievements and its heartbreaking defeats. Along the same lines of Césaire's "tragic concept of the Caribbean," it would not be inaccurate to say that Ródriguez Juliá's history-fictions could also be called "history-tragedies."

Notes

1. The last two novels are the first two installments of a trilogy whose third volume, *Pandemonium,* is supposedly written but has remained unpublished. Although *El camino de Yyaloide* is a continuation of *La noche oscura,* in this chapter I will focus on *La renuncia* and *La noche oscura,* since they portray the slave revolts that will be the main object of my analysis.
2. Carolina Sancholuz astutely adds Rodríguez Juliá's essay, *Campeche o los diablejos de la melancolía* (1986), to the cycle of the eighteenth-century narratives. The essay, which deals with the Puerto Rican eighteenth-century mulatto painter José Campeche, addresses, like the novels, the ethnic and colonial conflicts of that century "para leer y buscar en el pasado una explicación, casi siempre insatisfactoria, del presente colonial puertorriqueño" (Sancholuz, 233). I would go even farther. If Rodríguez Juliá's novels do not totally fit the model of "historical fiction," his essay, paradoxically, does. In his "readings" of Campeche's paintings, Rodríguez Juliá, as Aurea María Sotomoyar suggests, becomes a "ficcionalizador de imágenes" (one who fictionalizes images) (Duchesne, 127). He invents, interprets, and rearranges possible stories and contexts for the paintings, using the paintings as his historically grounded point of departure. Thus, he behaves more like a historical novelist in the essay than in the eighteenth-century novels.
3. Unless otherwise indicated, all translations from Spanish to English are my own.
4. See Santini (323) and Ríos's "La invención" (51).
5. That is the reading of César Salgado, who also offers an excellent summary of the critics' difficulties in classifying Rodríguez Juliá's novels.
6. For an overview of the gradual crystallization of national consciousnesses in Latin America throughout the colonial period, Keen and Halperin Donghi remain useful sources. For colonial Latin America, see also Burkholder and the excellent study by Stein.
7. See Silvestrini and Picó.
8. The fact that there were no dramatic events with the impact of Haiti's revolution or Cuba's Ten Year or 1895 Wars (both defeated for different reasons, but both an essential part of Cuba's national identity) does not mean there were no sporadic acts of violent rebellion, particularly with regard to slavery. For an overview of slave revolts in Puerto Rico during the late eighteenth and nineteenth centuries, see Baralt and Nistal Moret. The nationalists under the direction of Pedro Albizu Campos carried out violent acts in the 1930s and the 1950s, but they did not manage to ignite the revolutionary flame in the island.
9. Smith offers a compelling reading of the role of violence in *La renuncia.*
10. Betances's occasional impatience with what he perceived as Puerto Rican passivity is well known, and reached its climax at the island's inability to seize

the crisis of the Spanish American war in 1898 in order to claim its independence. He writes to Julio Henna: "¿Qué hacen los puertorriqueños? ¿Cómo no
aprovechan la oportunidad del bloqueo para levantarse en masa?" (Betances,
242–243) [What are Puerto Ricans doing? How come they do not take advantage of the blockade to massively revolt?]. He writes to Eugenio María de
Hostos in 1871: "Puerto Rico está en una borrachera completa. Allí están bor-
rachos con las reformas que no les han dado. . . . Es el espectáculo más raro
y triste el de todo un pueblo . . . celebrando las libertades que cree tener y que
no tiene" (Betances, 251) [Puerto Rico is in a state of total drunkenness. They
are totally drunk with the reforms that in fact they did not obtain. . . . It is a
rare and sad spectacle, to see a whole people . . . celebrating freedoms that it
believes it has, but does not have at all]. In 1887, he complains that even when
the right ideas for liberation are proposed, "todo queda en el aire; nada se pone
en práctica" (255) [everything remains in the air; nothing is put into practice].

11. For Rodríguez Juliá on his debt to José Luis González and Palés Matos, see
    Mapa and his interview in Hernández. For an overview of the ambivalent
    responses to Palés's defense of Afro-Puerto Rican culture, see Marzán.

12. For some critics, the task of uncovering and confronting "false" versions of
    Puerto Rican identity would link Rodríguez Juliá to a Latin American tra-
    dition of intellectuals trying to mold and gain access to positions of power
    through their writing. That approach to Rodríguez Juliá's writing (an author
    in search of a privileged locus of *authority* for himself as an intellectual) dom-
    inates in essays compiled in Juan Duchesne's important and influential *Las
    tribulaciones de Juliá*. Both Rubén González and Benjamín Torres Caballero
    strongly disagree with that approach, suggesting that Rodríguez Juliá's texts are
    much more ludic and "writerly" (in Roland Barthes's sense) than those critics
    give them credit for.

13. María Julia Daroqui suggests that in Rodríguez Juliá's novels "las historias
    apócrifas narradas . . . tienen la funcionalidad de llenar los vacíos del discurso
    historiográfico" (89). Again, the implication of that statement is that the novels
    rescue events that occurred but were not recorded, or long historical impacts
    (say, African culture in Puerto Rico) whose importance has not been recog-
    nized. Thus, we miss the important detail that the novels *invent* concrete events
    that never happened, and therefore were logically never recorded.

14. For a useful overview of this period in Puerto Rican history and culture, see
    Ayala.

15. For a lucid examination of the importance of *Caribeños* in Rodríguez Juliá's
    oeuvre and his vision of the Caribbean, see Franqui Rosario.

16. Haiti plays a similarly symbolic, yet ambiguous role in the poetry of Luis Palés
    Matos, see Figueroa.

17. Fick offers an important complement, or alternative, to better known accounts
    of the revolution such as James's, by focusing on autonomous forms of slave
    resistance that did not depend on the initiative of great "enlightened" leaders.

18. Fanon provides a keen illustration of that colonial/racist double-bind in *Black
    Skin, White Masks:* "When people like me, they tell me it is in spite of my color.

When they dislike me, they point out that it is not because of my color. Either way, I am locked into the infernal circle" (Fanon, 116).

19. See Dayan. Although Toussaint was opposed to the practice of Voodoo among the former slaves in Haiti, it may be the case that he also took advantage of those beliefs when he called himself "L'Ouverture"—the opening—an epithet that linked him to Legba, the Voodoo deity that opens all ceremonies. In the novel, we also see Obatal keeping his distance from traditional celebrations that he allows only because they consolidate his power.

20. Like James and Césaire (*Toussaint*) before him, Nesbitt compellingly argues for the impact of European enlightenment concepts on the vision that guided the slaves the Haitian Revolution:

> The abstract concepts of *liberté* and *egalité* that floated overseas to Saint-Domingue in August 1789 were not ossified universal precepts under which various empirical phenomena were to be subsumed, but just the opposite. The monstrous concepts were explosive destroyers of social customs and habits, whose meaning was quite unfixed and novel.... Only concerted acts of communitarian, inter-subjective political judgment, and not the forcible imposition of an ossified truth, could decide such questions and lead to the destruction of the abjection of the subjects of slavery, both Master and Slave.
>
> (Nesbitt, 30)

21. The issue of violence against the defeated *after* the revolution's victory does not play an important role in the novels, since the slave rebellions are defeated. However, in the case of Haiti, opinions have been divided on the justice and also the sheer practical wisdom of Dessalines's actions, and also on whether reports of the violence are accurate or not. James addresses the issue in the final chapter of *The Black Jacobins;* for a passionate defense of Dessalines's actions, see Dupont.

22. *La noche oscura* is the first installment of a trilogy whose third part would have shown the free city, Nueva Venecia, built by Niño Avilés. Would he have been a more "enlightened" leader than Obatal or Mitume? We will not know as long as the last part remains unpublished.

23. See Quijano.

24. See Nicholls, and also Dayan.

25. In his analysis of *La noche oscura,* A. Benítez Rojo regards that libertarian desire to escape toward unrestricted utopian freedom as recurring theme in Caribbean culture.

Works Cited

Ayala, César J., and Rafael Bernabe. *Puerto Rico in the American Century: A History Since 1898.* Chapel Hill: University of North Carolina Press, 2007. Print.

Baralt, Guillermo. *Esclavos rebeldes: conspiraciones y sublevaciones de esclavos en Puerto Rico 1795–1873.* Río Piedras: Huracán, 1981. Print.

Benítez Rojo, Antonio. *La isla que se repite: el Caribe y la perspectiva postmoderna.* Hanover (New Hampshire): Ediciones del Norte, 1989. Print.

Betances, Ramón Emeterio. *Las antillas para los antillanos.* San Juan: Instituto de Cultura Puertorriqueña, 2001. Print.

Burkholder, Mark, and Lyman L. Johnson. *Colonial Latin America.* London: Oxford University Press, 2004. Print.

Césaire, Aimé. *Toussaint Louverture: La révolution française et le problème colonial.* Paris: Présence Africaine, 1981. Print.

Daroqui, María Julia. *Las pesadillas de la historia en la narrativa puertorriqueña.* Caracas: Monte Ávila, 1993. Print.

Dayan, Joan. *Haiti, History and the Gods.* Berkeley: University of California Press, 1995. Print.

Duchesne, Juan, Ed. *Las tribulaciones de Juliá.* San Juan: Instituto de Cultura Puertorriqueña, 1992. Print.

Dupont, Berthony. *Jean Jacques Dessalines: Itinéraire d'un révolutionnaire.* Paris: L'Harmattan, 2006. Print.

Dussel, Enrique. *The Underside of Modernity: Apel, Ricoeur, Rorty, Taylor, and the Philosophy of Liberation.* Amherst, NY: Humanity Books, 2007. Print.

Fanon, Frantz. *Black Skin, White Masks.* New York: Grove Press, 1967. Print.

Fick, Carolyn. *The Making of Haiti: The Saint Domingue Revolution from Below.* Knoxville: University of Tennessee Press, 1990. Print.

Figueroa, Víctor. "Between Africa and Puerto Rico: Haiti and Lyric Self-Fashioning in the Poetry of Luis Palés Matos." *Latin American Literary Review* 35.70 (July–December 2007): 74–87. Print.

Franco, Jean. "The Nation as Imagined Community." *Dangerous Liaisons: Gender, Nation, and Postcolonial Perspectives.* Ed. Anne McClintock, Aamir Mufti and Ella Shohat. Minneapolis: University of Minnesota Press, 1997. Print.

Franqui Rosario, Rebeca. *Caribeños y la nostalgia de un Puerto Rico perdido.* San Juan: Instituto de Cultura Puertorriqueña, 2008. Print.

Freud, Sigmund. *The Penguin Freud Reader.* Ed. Adam Phillips. New York & London: Penguin, 2006. Print.

González, Aníbal. "Una alegoría de la cultura puertorriqueña: *La noche oscura del niño avilés* de Edgardo Rodríguez Juliá." *Revista Iberoamericana* 52 (Abril–septiembre 1986) 583–590.

González, José Luis. *El país de cuatro pisos.* Río Piedras: Huracán, 1980. Print.

González, Rubén. *La historia puertorriqueña de Rodríguez Juliá.* Río Piedras: Editorial de la Universidad de Puerto Rico, 1997. Print.

González Rodríguez, Eduardo. "Dos posesas (escritura e historia) en las obras de Edgardo Rodríguez Juliá." *Revista de estudios hispánicos, UPR* 27.2 (2000): 299–318. Print.

Halperin Donghi, Tulio. *The Contemporary History of Latin America.* Durham, NC: Duke University Press, 1993. Print.

Hernández, Carmen Dolores. *A viva voz: entrevistas a escritores puertorriqueños.* Bogotá: Norma, 2007. Print.

James, C. L. R. *The Black Jacobins: Toussaint L'Ouverture and the San Domingo Revolution*. New York: Vintage, 1963. Print.

Keen, Benjamin. *A History of Latin America*. Boston: Houghton Mifflin, 2009. Print.

Marzán, Julio. *The Numinous Site: The Poetry of Luis Palés Matos*. Madison: Fairleigh Dickinson University Press, 1995. Print.

Menton, Seymour. *Latin America's New Historical Novel*. Austin: University of Texas Press, 1993. Print.

Mignolo, Walter. *Local Histories/Global Designs: Coloniality, Subaltern Knowledges, and Border Thinking*. Princeton, NJ: Princeton University Press, 2000. Print.

Moraña, Mabel, Enrique Dussel, and Carlo A. Jáuregui, Eds. *Coloniality at Large: Latin American and the Postcolonial Debate*. Durham: Duke University Press, 2008. Print.

Nesbitt, Nick. *Universal Emancipation: The Haitian Revolution and the Radical Enlightenment*. Charlottesville: University of Virginia Press, 2008. Print.

Nicholls, David. *From Dessalines to Duvalier: Race, Colour, and National Independence in Haiti*. New Brunswick: Rutgers University Press, 1996. Print.

Nistal Moret, Benjamín. *Esclavos prófugos y cimarrones: Puerto Rico 1770–1870*. Río Piedras: Editorial de la Universidad de Puerto Rico, 1984. Print.

Novau, Julieta. "Presencia y significaciones de la afrocaribeñidad furtiva: Sobre *La noche oscura del Niño Avilés* de Edgardo Rodríguez Juliá." *Actas del II Congreso Internacional "Cuestiones Críticas," Rosario 2009*. Centro de Estudios de Literatura Argentina/Centro de Estudios de Teoría y Crítica Literaria. November 20, 2011. http://www.celarg.org/int/arch_publi/novau_acta.pdf. Web.

Picó, Fernando. *Historia general de Puerto Rico*. Río Piedras: Huracán, 1986. Print.

Quijano, Aníbal. "Colonialidad y Modernidad/Racionalidad." *Los conquistados: 1492 y la población indígena de las Américas*. Ed. Robin Blackburn and Heraclio Bonilla. Bogotá, Colombia: Tercer Mundo Editores, 1992. Print.

Ríos Ávila, Rubén. "La invención de un autor: escritura y poder." *Las tribulaciones de Juliá*. Ed. Juan Duchesne Winter. San Juan: Instituto de Cultura Puertorriqueña, 1992. Print.

———. *La raza cómica: del sujeto en Puerto Rico*. San Juan: Callejón, 2002. Print.

Rodríguez de Laguna, Asela, Ed. *Imágenes e identidades: el puertorriqueño en la literatura*. Río Piedras: Huracán, 1985. Print.

Rodríguez Juliá, Edgardo. *Campeche o los diablejos de la melancolía*. San Juan: Instituto de Cultura Puertorriqueña, 1986. Print.

———. *La noche oscura del niño Avilés*. 2nd ed. Río Piedras: Editorial de la Universidad de Puerto Rico, 1991. Print.

———. *El camino de Yyaloide*. Caracas: Grijalbo, 1994. Print.

———. *The Renunciation*. Trans. Andrew Hurley. New York: Four Walls Eight Windows, 1997.

———. *Caribeños*. San Juan: Instituto de Cultura Puertorriqueña, 2002. Print.

———. *Mapa de una pasión literaria*. Río Piedras: Editorial de la Universidad de Puerto Rico, 2003.

————. *La renuncia del héroe Baltasar*. México: Fondo de Cultura Económica, 2006.

Salgado, César. "Archivos encontrados: Edgardo Rodríguez Juliá o los diablejos de la historiografía criolla." *Cuadernos Americanos* 73 (1999): 153–203.

Sancholuz, Carolina. *Mapa de una pasión caribeña: lecturas sobre Edgardo rodríguez Juliá*. Buenos Aires: Editorial Dunken, 2010.

Santini, Carmen Hilda. "*La renuncia del héroe Baltasar* y la ficcionalización de la historia." *Revista de Estudios Hispánicos (U.P.R.)* 27.2 (2000): 319–331.

Silvestrini, Blanca, and María Luque de Sánchez. *Historia de Puerto Rico: Trayectoria de un pueblo*. San Juan: Editorial La Biblioteca, 1988.

Smith, Sara Ann. "*Violencia y heterotopía en La renuncia del héroe Baltasar*." *La Torre* 9.33 (1995): 71–88.

Sotomayor, Áurea María. *Hilo de Aracne: literatura puertorriqueña hoy*. Río Piedras: Editorial de la Universidad de Puerto Rico, 1995.

Stein, Stanley H., and Barbara H. Stein. *The Colonial Heritage of Latin America*. London: Oxford University Press, 1970.

Torrecilla, Arturo. *La ansiedad de ser puertorriqueño*. San Juan, PR: Vértigo, 2004.

Torres Caballero, Benjamín. *Para llegar a la isla verde de Edgardo Rodriguez Juliá*. Río Piedras: Editorial de la Universidad de Puerto Rico, 2007.

4

The Galleys of History: Mirages and Madness of a Journey

Fernando Burgos
Translated from Spanish by Tina Kosiorek

Do not believe a piece of historical writing if it does not spring out of the head of the rarest of spirits.

Friedrich Nietzsche

The term *galleys* crosses various semantic fields: nautical (a type of vessel used for centuries), culinary (the space in a boat or plane where food is prepared), and print (the printer's proof of a publication along with the metal plate displaying the composed type). This multiplicity of meanings is also appropriate to use with the metaphor *galleys of history* given that it conveys the symbols of taking a trip and the means of doing so in the first two fields, while conveying writing in the third. A dynamic image of history cannot be conceived without referring to a movement toward the past, and from there, toward the present and the future. Regarding this navigation and reflection, Nietzsche states:

> Thus, the person of experience and reflection writes history. Anyone who has not lived through something greater and higher than everyone else will not know how to interpret anything great and lofty from the past. The utterance of the past is always an oracular pronouncement. You will understand it only as a master builder of the future and as a person who knows about the present.
>
> (*On the Use and Abuse of History for Life*)

Of course, none of this would be possible without writing. A history without writing does not exist. It would be reduced to a condemned memory lost by the succession of generations. Eventually, a rapprochement of millenary cultures is unsustainable as a pure memory experience. However, in this case, the footnote about different writing types is a valuable consideration given that it deals with galley writing, which is never completely finished and is always subject to profound and continuous revisions. Those who write about history as a conclusive attempt tread closely to the arrogance exhibited by the powers of information and knowledge.

Without the existence of an art imbued with critical and transformational capacities (which is one of the most significant sources of discernment relative to history), the conceptualization of the historic would still be possible through philosophic discourse. This is true even though history's most intimate understanding (the constellation of webs, markings, and visions that allow for discourse about the dialectic nature of that entangled jungle named "history") would be limited to those constructs imparted by social institutions. This last scenario would be regrettable since it would occur on the horizon of what we understand as humanity, given that these determinations of history would have to correspond to what the current society would have deemed convenient, adaptable, and justifiable. Conceived as a set of events ordered by a social pact, history results in a woven web that is susceptible to manipulation through this complacent function loaned to it by that historic life. One of the few escapes from this comfortable and deceitful social hold on history is achieved by envisioning it as writing. This sets forth a broad scope of meanings in the realm of art, a perilous and sometimes even threatening plane for the historian when considering history's supposed reality, especially provided that its feigned concrete corporeality—in its artistic dimension—will involve chaos, an encounter with the incomprehensible, and it will reach and go beyond irrationality's doors and feel fantasy's drive as the only possible human power (a power whose fragile composition and overwhelming loneliness is compensated for by the unfettered activity of imagination). These are a few of the issues that I reflect upon while discussing the novels *La nave de los locos* [*Ship of Fools*] (1984) by the Uruguayan writer Cristina Peri Rossi and *El mundo alucinante* [*Hallucinations*] (1969) by the Cuban writer Reinaldo Arenas. This study revisits the critical positioning of postmodern works in order to both uncover the simulations of the social constructs of history and question the ideological parameters of institutional power that sponsor such manufactured concepts of history.

The vicissitudes of publication experienced by *Hallucinations* from its first attempts to be released to the public highlights the diverse and astonishing ways in which the Spanish title's adjective (*El mundo alucinante,* "alucinante" meaning "hallucinatory") might have had an impact on the reader. Before its Spanish edition in 1969, the novel first appeared in French under the title *Le Monde hallucinant* (1968) as a result of its prohibition in Cuba and its subsequent clandestine departure to Paris. Additionally, in 1982, a few years after Arenas went into exile, he managed to revise this work that appeared to have had a public history practically independent of what the author would have liked to have imparted in its final edition. The year of the novel's revision (1982) is chronologically close to the publication date of *Ship of Fools,* 1984. Both of these novels are Spanish–American works that had a huge impact in the 1980s because of their nonconformist tone regarding historic representations aspiring to canonize ideals like order and revolution. Yet more important than their chronological proximity is the fact that both authors approached the subject of history as dissidents of the totalitarian political regimes under which they had lived. The dictatorship during the 1970s in Uruguay caused Peri Rossi's exile in Barcelona, while Arenas's exile in the United States from Cuba resulted from the asphyxiating climate of infallible and dogmatic sanctity surrounding a stagnant concept of revolution that was indifferent to critical and creative undertaking.

Both *Ship of Fools* and *Hallucinations* are artistically configured by two principal referents, *The Tapestry of Creation* and *Memoirs,* respectively. The first is an embroidered panel from the eleventh century preserved in the Cathedral of Girona that projects a symbolic cosmology of earthly orders and their divine providence. The second corresponds to the work of Friar Servando Teresa de Mier, written in large part during his incarceration. De Mier's work was published posthumously under the title of *Memoirs* in 1917 and featured a prologue written by Alfonso Reyes. Reyes would clarify that the 1917 edition came from the *Biografía del Benemérito Mexicano D. Servando Teresa de Mier y Noriega y Guerra [Biography of the Distinguished Mexican D. Servando Teresa de Mier y Noriega y Guerra]*, which was published in Monterrey in 1876 and later appeared in increasingly more complete editions throughout the course of the twentieth century until it was finally published under the title *Memorias. Un fraile mexicano desterrado en Europa [Memoirs. A Mexican Monk Exiled in Europe]* (2006). While the iconographic saturation of *The Tapestry of Creation* demonstrates humankind's impossible attempts to understand its origin and place in the universe, *Memoirs*—also in a baroque manner— establishes yet another impossibility: specifically, the ability to express oneself without institutional restraints. This is captured by showing the consequences of contempt through the consecutive persecutions, exiles, imprisonments, and escapes of Friar Servando (1763–1827). *Memoirs* deals with referents that show an opposition to history in terms of its hermeneutic composition, which allows history to glide through multiple planes and concurrently include more than one seed of dissidence. The *Memoirs* is written as a means of refuting history's potentially dogmatic discourse and *The Tapestry of Creation* transcends its own realism by employing an excess of it. As a result, the history of creation flows forth from the work into a fictitious canvas. One of the central functions of these referents consists of undoing the notion of time as a measurement of progress and recreating it as a distinctly sensory understanding of temporality, or as a permanent image of the pure movement of exile in *Ship of Fools:* "Me llamo Equis—le dijo. Por circunstancias especiales, que tienen más que ver con la marcha del mundo que con mis propios deseos, desde hace años viajo de un lugar a otro, sin rumbo fijo" (78) [" 'Ecks is my name', he told her. 'For the past few years, due to special circumstances having more to do with the way the world turns than with my personal wishes, I have travelled from one place to another without any firm direction' " (76)].[1] In *Hallucinations,* these referents also deal with the resounding disintegration of any sort of order that would force the bells of history to toll: "Campanas, campanas alterando el tiempo; campanas, enloqueciendo a los pájaros . . . campanas, desatando la lujuria en los danzantes; campanas, campanas apagando el estruendo de la orgía que inunda la ciudad." (312–313) ["Bells, bells, unsettling the atmosphere; bells, driving the birds mad . . . bells, unleashing lust into the dancers; bells, bells, drowning the noise of the orgy which has now spread all over the city" (279–280)].[2]

I must clarify that what I have termed a *referent* constitutes an integral narrative substance in each of these novels. Thus, it is not a matter of works that merely refer to a background established as a purely allusive point for the text, but rather, in each case, the intertext's artistic dimension serves as the first plane of interpretation of the entire narrative. In the creation of a postmodern work, the function of correlates is to represent a web of artistic options so complex that it can even come to be seen as contradictory from analytic standpoints that attempt to cogently delimit its functionality and put in place a series of exact, mechanical congruencies between the work that is written and its correlate (which is perceived as background). An artistic postmodern discourse converts what superficially appears to be a backdrop, framework, scenery, correlate, or referent into just another vein of the narrative stream. By this, I affirm that a background that is conceived of as an independent statute—which is inscribed by the other work's birth—does not actually exist. This correlate cannot be registered nor can it feign any sort of coherence in terms of reciprocity. What this correlate grants is the privilege of its transgression: being transcended, corrected, and even stripped of its value. A work that is born before another in order to embody itself in a newly formed expression has arrived willing to give up its freedom, to extend the lack of conclusion that any artistic attempt assumes. In sum, it awards the posterior work its hermeneutical efficacy.

This is the reason why, when the sections exclusively dedicated to *The Tapestry of Creation* in Peri Rossi's novel are seemingly descriptive, they actually convene a reading of the text that considers individual arrangements and personal interpretations. It is also the reason why, when these same sections are decidedly exegetical, they propose both a rereading of *The Tapestry of Creation* as a connection with the worldview reconstructed in *Ship of Fools* as well as one that compares the scope of existential totality and affirmation encompassed by *The Tapestry of Creation* with the helpless wandering of the characters in Peri Rossi's novel: "En telas así sería posible vivir toda la vida, en medio de un discurso perfectamente inteligible, de cuyo sentido no se podría dudar porque es una metáfora donde todo universo está encerrado" (21) ["Immersed in such art, one could live one's life, engaged in a perfectly rational discourse whose meaning cannot be questioned because it resides in an image containing the whole universe" (14)].

Consequently, *El Tapiz* is not just a subtext or a source of allusions; rather, it is total and complete productivity inscribed in a new writing practice through which *The Tapestry of Creation* itself will be modified. As a result, the relationships that exist between the texts are double and are guided by their interconnections. It is not a question of one text interfering with the reading and production of another. Rather, both texts fuse together, for a variety of possible reasons: (1) because the metaphoric drive of a universe coded by symbolic signs may provoke the need to be read multivocally, given the uncertainty of *Ship of Fool*'s protagonists; (2) because of the chimerical geometric aspiration for a theory of creation; (3) because of the presence of motivations like those of the angels that move around in the murky waters announcing creation and history; (4) because of the unique position that each element of the tapestry occupies in this embroidery of the universe as if each represented a stratum of primordial meaning regarding the total displacement of *Ship of Fool*'s characters; or (5) because *Ship of Fools* questions the fact that a weaver is needed to make a tapestry of creation. In this last possibility, the weaver is none other than the production of textuality itself: "De este modo, el magnífico tejedor del tapiz ha completado la representación de los principios u Orígenes, ciñéndose a las Escrituras" (Peri Rossi, *La nave*, 150) ["Thus, the marvelous weaver completed his representation of the beginning of the world according to the Holy Scriptures" (Peri Rossi, *Ship of Fools*, 155)].

Besides *The Tapestry of Creation*, the writing of Peri Rossi's novel likewise makes possible many other iconic (Bosch, Brueghel) and textual (Brant, Erasmus) origins relating to the topics of *stultifera navis* and madness in their renaissance approach to satire, or as a deliriously tragic vision achieved by distinct exegetical formations, a mixed critical discourse with distinct artistic, sociological, literary, or philosophic stances. To this must be added real or fictitious journalistic paratexts, various texts whose designation as "unpublished" may be a false clue that would better be equated with "invention," humorist postmodern satires about Genesis, parodies about classical myths and chivalric romances, dream readings that seek to explore enigmas incapable of resolving anything in the empty time in which each character lives, and, notably, the accumulation of the references made to various writers, literary works, paintings, and actors. Peri Rossi's novel is a narrative loom so jam-packed it is almost as if its deliberate profusion could fill the hole of a history in which nations have disappeared.

There are two other essential components of *Hallucinations*'s postmodern artistic setting: its neo-baroque style and the exceptional treatment of its own foundational text, *Memoirs*. *Memoirs* serves as the central point of what Arenas warns is the scope of humanity's unrest: namely, history's authority to convert individual destiny into a forgetful wink that is practically indistinguishable within the depths of what is understood as civilization. In other words, the carrying out of a history to which contemporary institutions pay tribute (therefore guaranteeing their empire) is represented in *Hallucinations* as infamy's unfolding. In Arenas's artistic position, there are no positive histories for those who are objects—and not participants—of their construction. In the same vein, a benevolent view of history is either the most sordid manifestation of social alienation or a discourse that belongs to an imaginary utopia according to Arenas. *Hallucinations* is the creative and ideological development of *Memoirs*. It is a reading of its exegesis on an artistic plane where there is room for Friar Servando, Reinaldo Arenas, and any other anonymous being who has been abused, persecuted, marginalized, or eventually erased from history.

Thus, instead of paratexts, we are dealing with two works that are mutually absorbed in a fruitful postmodern and neo-baroque style. The wandering priest's future wager has found a countenance that not only understands and interprets him, but also makes him its own via the complete identification made in *Hallucinations* and in another one of Arenas's books published in 1992, *Antes que anochezca* [*Before Night Falls*]. In this last novel, Arenas writes about his own memories of persecution, incomprehension, and exile. Friar Servando Teresa de Mier's *Memoirs*, *Hallucinations*, and *Before Night Falls* are three books that all belong to each other and, by abandoning the traditional idolatry of chronology, they become instances of a measureless time that does not attempt to pigeonhole events. The author points out: "La Historia recoge la fecha de una batalla, los muertos que ilustran lo mismo, es decir, lo evidente. Estos temibles mamotretos resumen (y es bastante) lo fugaz. El efecto no la causa. Por eso, más que en la Historia busco en el tiempo" [History collects the date of a battle, the dead ones, everything that will illustrate the same, whatever is the evident thing. These fearsome, useless, hefty volumes summarize (quite well) what is fleeting. It is the effect, not the cause. Because of this, I look more at time than at History]. In these three texts, now grouped together, the subject who is dispossessed of history legitimizes his marginalization by employing a survival response whose distinct humanist universalization resides in its representation of destiny as a permanent state of exodus. However, it is not adequate to relegate *Hallucinations* to the category of mere metanarrative. In Reinaldo Arenas's case, one must also add the proliferation of neo-baroque devices to postmodernism's metafictional tendencies. The same is true of other Cuban authors like Lezama Lima, Alejo Carpentier, Severo Sarduy, and Guillermo Cabrera Infante: "No creo que mis novelas puedan leerse como una historia de acontecimientos concatenados, sino como un oleaje que se expande, vuelve, se ensancha." (*El mundo,* 88) [I don't think that my novels can be read as histories with chained-together events; rather, they should be read as a groundswell that expands, returns, widens].

In its postmodern configuration, neo-baroque is not just a style identified by its techniques, but also (and primarily) by a worldview, whose most extreme characteristic is its utilization of excessive disfigurement and dissolution as part of an unleashing process that culminates in individual liberation that is free from any social impact. This is one of the most significant dimensions of *Hallucinations.* It is a skeptical attitude about the construction of social statutes that permits the safeguarding of free will. The chapter that discusses Friar Servando's chaining (184–190 in the English edition) stands out as a central symbol of the novel and reveals how each of the semes utilized in his bondage comes together via the convergence of signifiers that are intent upon producing a deliberate ornateness of elements. This richness of elements, in turn, makes the metaphor's ideological planes even more obvious. Thus designed, the metaphor has an extraordinary composition. On the one hand, in this episode, the metaphoric dimension coincides with the total and absolute territorializing of a body that will be occupied, conquered, and dominated. However, on the other hand, this metaphoric dimension also recognizes the likelihood of the body becoming emancipated. Nothing belonging to the body is capable of escaping its moorings: extremities, head, testicles, teeth, tongue, hair, penis, abdomen, muscles, feet, nose, ears, everything until human flesh is turned into a mass of steel, an impregnable, ferrous web that silences voice and impedes movement. The successive disembarkments of ships carrying chains as cargo serve to augment the size of the chain's ball until it reaches enormous proportions. As a result, body and prison blur together into a single entity: "no fue más que una pelota gigante de plomo y acero, que ya engrosaba demasiado y llegaba casi al techo" (237) ["and the whole room was filled with an iron and lead ball of such excessive proportions which almost touched the ceiling" (187)]. Despite this expansive and asphyxiating shackling of the body, the body's condemnation by history is also seen here as an idea that cannot be chained. This is an important component of deterritorializing the body since the flow of the protagonist's thoughts is unstoppable, even when he is completely tied up, immobilized, and asphyxiated: "El pensamiento, emergiendo ligero de entre aquellas barras de acero, saltaba por sobre las mismas narices de los carceleros y llegaba, retrocediendo en el tiempo, hasta los campos de arena" (238) ["His thoughts would elude those bars of iron, sneak out right under the guards' noses and return, going back in time, to sandy fields" (188)]. The other element of deterritorialization has to do with the body and is evidenced when the chain's overwhelming weight ends up destroying the prison. The chain's ball, consisting of human flesh and of iron, rolls around blindly. It is in this violent freewheel that the marks of civilization will be destroyed:

Prosigue dando vueltas dentro de su armazón, destruyendo aldeas y sepultando poblaciones completas. Así cruzó toda Sevilla, desbordando el Guadalquivir y pulverizando juncos, ranas, pájaros y marismas. Luego continuó hasta Madrid, asolándolo. Y de allí retrocedió, pasando por El Escorial y reduciéndolo a un montón de piedras, sin dejar un árbol en pie. Asoló a las dos Castillas, y bajó luego por Cádiz, sumergiendo el puerto. (240)

[He rolled on, destroying villages and burying whole towns. He passed right through Seville in this fashion, causing the Guadalquivir to overflow, squashing reeds, frogs, birds, and meadows to pulp. Then he proceeded to Madrid and razed it to the ground. On his way back he took in the Escorial and reduced it to a pile of rubble, not leaving a single tree upright. He steamrolled his way over the two Castiles, and then went down to Cadiz and submerged the harbour. (190)]

In its final pilgrimage, the very sphere of the iron chain blows up, depositing the body's interior cargo into the sea. However, this liberation is only momentary. Knowing that the ocean is not its habitat, the body must return to the reality of the nation, where history will take upon itself the task of reterritorializing it.

The disfigured image of a human being converted into a mass of restraining chains and manacles also carries with it the signifier of history's oppressive weight. Man's liberation is transitory since, in the end, it is not possible to escape from history. Taken together with the eventual dissolution of the chains, the freely chosen fulfillment of a human being comes undone, regardless of where the being is located, even when history awards that territory the status of being a *nation*. In this postmodern, neo-baroque explosion within Arenas's novel, the narcissism and reflection on writing are not of as much interest as the process of its being ideologized along with writing's critical becoming. I am not referring to political condemnation, but to the fact that a belief in history and the foundation or maintenance of nations brings with it an accentuated scrutiny of these ideas. *Hallucinations* is a work in which the artistic plane leads to an epiphanous and philosophical construction that expresses the universal postulate that any truly historic work is ahistoric. In this ahistoric zone, all that is hallucinatory grants a marginal—but strong—voice to the silencing of dissidents. Unlike *Ship of Fools,* Arenas's novel is characterized by an abundance of nations instead of their absence. However, none of these nations harbors the individual or makes him feel like a citizen; instead, they reduce him to an entity devoid of history, or at least devoid of a history of his own. With this lack of alternatives, the act of hallucinating emanates from the only possible reaction one can have when faced with the realization that a history with humanist dimensions is an impossibility and that, consequently, history is a pure abstraction for the individual, a grotesque physiognomy only justified by its efficacy as a parameter of power.

In Peri Rossi's novel, *The Tapestry of Creation* is a work in need of being artistically examined. To carry out such a scrutiny, it is essential to assume an analytic position from which its creative, religious, and metaphysical dimensions regarding human destiny ramify. Among the diverse elements found in the tapestry from this analytic position, the Angel of Light and the Angel of Darkness stand out as two possible paths to history. As a result, we are in a zone of hermeneutical practice that mixes with the narrative trajectory of *Ship of Fools,* an issue that we cannot overlook given the presence of characters that prefer to reside in oceanic spaces that do not carry the stamp of nations. This is true although such nations do not hesitate to convert seas into human cemeteries in their constant persecutions of individuals by individuals. Both *Ship of Fools* and *Hallucinations* provide an ominous vision of history in two ways. First, their protagonists do not consider the ocean as salvation, but view the ocean voyage as a passage through time that is dispossessed of history. Second, history is presented as a permanently accumulating burden made of iron that shackles even the most miniscule human expression of freedom. This image of history as desolation in Peri Rossi's and Arenas's works was not created with the hope of modifying the social traps that cancel out the positive side of any tapestry of creation; rather, this image of history exposes the unseen surface of the iceberg of the mirages to which the social being turns for survival. This elucidation of social constructs could correspond with many aspects of the human experience, although in art they are profoundly distinctive insofar as art continues to be understood as a becoming of insights. This point is very opportunely illustrated in an essay about the artistic visions of history: Benjamin's exegesis on Klee's Angelus Novus. In many respects, this text is not just the formal discourse of a thinker, but also the painting of another artist:

> A Klee painting named "Angelus Novus" shows an angel looking as though he is about to move away from something he is fixedly contemplating. His eyes are staring, his mouth is open, his wings are spread. This is how one pictures the angel of history. His face is turned toward the past. Where we perceive a chain of events, he sees one single catastrophe which keeps piling wreckage upon wreckage and hurls it in front of his feet. The angel would like to stay, awaken the dead, and make whole what has been smashed. But a storm is blowing from Paradise; it has got caught in his wings with such violence that the angel can no longer close them. This storm irresistibly propels him into the future to which his back is turned, while the pile of debris before him grows skyward. This storm is what we call progress.
>
> (Benjamin, 257–258)

In Benjamin's critique of the idea of history as progress, Klee's angel (created through its artistic dissemination to be many kinds of angels at once) profoundly strikes Benjamin as being a symbol of history, thus constructing an indelible metaphor for the painting (which is but one of many). While it is possible that one cannot see exactly what Benjamin saw, even when one reads how Klee's angel revealed itself to him while simultaneously studying the painting, this is a moot point because within the reading of this German philosopher's text, there is something even more complex and unavoidable: how to explain the supernatural. This spectrality of history is also the magma in which the images of *Ship of Fools* and *Hallucinations* are buried.

Many narrative fluxes connect these two novels: exile, flight, the dissolution of borders, foreignness, a sense of not belonging, nomadism, transterritoriality, a nowhere protagonist, a wandering monk, betting on the probable, a distrust of dogma and infallibility, ships in unknown waters, arcane beings, the unknown, a destination-less trajectory through land and sea (or at least one with a risky path or forced direction), the person expatriated by others and by himself, the dissident who will be permanently divided, the rejected being who inhabits a border space, and the stateless individual: "Todos somos exiliados de algo o de alguien—contemporizó Equis. En realidad, ésa es la verdadera condición del hombre" (*La nave*, 106) ["'We have all been exiled from something or someone', urged Ecks in a conciliatory fashion. 'I think this is the human condition.'" (*Ship of Fools*, 106)]. Globetrotting is used as a metaphor for liberation. In this zone, land does not belong to anyone; it is not divided but is a place through which one may travel. A globetrotter is the representation of a possibly unreachable idea. A foreigner is never a citizen; he will always remain an outsider although *Ship of Fools* reclaims the biblical admonition for those who denigrate foreigners: "Ya que extranjeros fuisteis en la tierra de Egipto" (10) ["Seeing ye were strangers in the land of Egypt" (10)]. The idea of the foreigner is not a question of citizenship papers but of atavistic perceptions regarding other nations that are difficult to eradicate, like ownership, heritage, and superiority. The poet and the political idealist who, instead of imitating reality, interpret it in an attempt to communicate truths are both condemned *a priori*. They have no chance of belonging to anything:

> De nada sirve lo que hemos hecho si no danzamos al son de la última cornetilla. De nada sirve. Y si pretendes rectificar los errores no eres más que un traidor, y si pretendes modificar las bestialidades no eres más que un cínico revisionista, si luchas por la verdadera libertad estás a punto de dar con la misma muerte. (300, 302)

> [Nothing that we have done matters if we don't hop to the sound of the latest tune. It's no use. If you attempt to correct mistakes, you're just a traitor, and if you attempt to make life less bestial, you're just a cynical revisionist, and if you fight for real freedom, you pretty well condemn yourself to death. (267, 269)]

The condition of this exile is territorial and existential. There is no nation or destiny, no past or future. The present is the same as the wooden plank that is used for survival in the ocean. What sense can a project consumed by nothingness or resigned to persecution have? The semblance of an antihuman and absurd history may refer to what the consciousness of a specific period in history has deemed as being an important event, like the atrocities of the Inquisition, Nazism, or twentieth-century Latin American dictatorships. However, it also refers to what nobody wants to designate as history: a young, lonely girl to whom no one talks, who commits suicide in New York: "El diario dice que Kate se suicidó a las doce de la noche, en un banco de la plaza, ingiriendo una fuerte dosis de barbitúricos" (*La nave*, 71) ["The papers report that Kate killed herself around midnight on a bench in the square—an overdose of barbiturates" (*Ship of Fools*, 69)]. The same can also be said of an anonymous character like Ecks, a representative of any exiled individual, who is forgotten because of the insignificant routes of his own wanderings. In contrast, in *Hallucinations,* Friar Servando can be seen as an emblematic hero of freedom or as a poor monk whose absurd struggles are fruitless. What both texts underscore is the paradox that both a grandiose history and an unnoticed history are human constructs. Hence, the incomprehensible: history's setting is not something that has come down from the heavens.

Everything verges on uncertainty with regard to resolutions. The characters are recorded in time but are deprived of history because the time allotted to them has no chronology. There is only a sensation of being. Official histories—as well as unofficial ones—accentuate the idea of a nation. These two texts sail along in a manner diametrically opposed to history.

In *Ship of Fools*, Peri Rossi tells the story of the aimless wanderings of her protagonist, Ecks, whose political exile intersects with both his own existential banishment and an ancestral feeling of foreignness that has infiltrated the human race since our most remote relationship with religious foundational texts. The territories through which Peri Rossi's characters sail are ill-defined, and so mapping them is impossible: "En sus travesías, Equis llegó a una isla, en M., llena de vegetación tropical, caminos de piedras, grandes caracoles colgados de techos improvisados con ramas" (74) ["During his travels, Ecks came to an island in M., tropical in its vegetation. Its roads were cobbled, large seashells hung from the rooftops covered with branches" (72)]. Spatializations (like Germany or London) or a ship's port of origin (like Italy, Holland, or the Philippines) are more than inscriptions of belonging; they rather constitute passing mentions incapable of substantiating characters' origins or the territorial significance of places. When the novel focuses on or describes a detail in a place appearing to be a metropolis, it becomes a critique of the concept of cities. In this critique, the city is called the *Great Navel* and its citizens are referred to as *navelists* because of the absolutely alienating arrogance with which they overestimate their own importance. Additionally, this repetitive conceit reduces the city to the innards of a mine: "Atrapados como moscas, estiran en vano las patas, agitan las antenas, sacuden las membranas, pero los pliegues teguminosos del ombligo les impiden liberarse" (122) ["Trapped like flies, in vain they stretch their limbs or wave their antennae: the viscid folds impede their escape" (123)]. This mockery of human pride debunks the fallacy of society's insistence upon constructing a history based on society's development as if history were an abstract unfolding of the spirit. At the same time, the novel links to critical visions of art like Brueghel's painting *The Tower of Babel*, commented upon by Ecks. The painting refers to the tower's absurd ordering and series of social codings of the world vis-á-vis the complete lack of communication between its stories.

Inside these voyages from barely perceptible places to lands and seas belonging to nobody, Peri Rossi's novel gives shape to issues of social separation and muteness that go beyond a particular boundary of history. The course of history occupies a space of misfortune or forgetting. The eighth voyage found in her novel corresponds to her artistic representation of the motif of the *ship of fools*. It does not follow the moralizing tone of Brant's poem or Bosch's painting in which a critique is made of human options that are perceived as deviations from the institutionalism of certain ethical or religious values. Peri Rossi's novel is a representation that avoids the personalization of a single artist, turning instead to broader critical assessment of paintings, interpretations of traditions, pursuits of memory, and diverse inscriptions. The novel looks, thus, for a comprehensiveness of multiple points and foci that can even contradict themselves, annulling any possible historic reference since what they question is history's construction as truth. In this interpretation, the invention of a long literary tradition is not of as much interest as the criticism of a centuries-long social practice in which the current antisocial element is rejected and eventually eliminated. The novel is organized as a set of diverse trips during which its protagonists sail through remote oceans and nowhere places. This projects an image of a timeless and perpetual ship of fools full of abandoned prisoners.

Foucault illustrates the fact that the isolation of madmen, apart from its genesis of a literary tradition, was also an actual practice of social benefit and ritual efficacy toward the end of the Middle Ages:

> But among these satirical and novelistic ships, the *Narrenschiff* alone had a genuine existence, for they really did exist, these boats that drifted from one town to another with their senseless cargo. An itinerant existence was often the lot of the mad. It was a common practice for towns to banish them from inside the city walls, leaving them to run wild in the distant countryside or entrusting them to the care of travelling merchants or pilgrims . . . . This constant circulation of the insane, the gesture of banishment and enforced embarkation, was not merely aimed at social utility, or the safety of citizens. Its meanings were closer to rituals, and their trace is still discernible.
>
> (Foucault, *History of Madness*, 9, 10)

The madmen's ship that appears in Peri Rossi's novel navigates in a hallucinatory fashion through the canvas of time, and consequently through the folds of a history that cannot be circumscribed. As a part of the tragic vision of its representation, the course of history has been achieved by marginalizing any and all resistance to a univocal concept of social construction. It is in this context that Peri Rossi delivers the image of an embarkation that continues navigating until it arrives at the modern experience symbolized by the character of Vercingetorix, who is a victim of the "disappearing" practice used by dictatorships:

> De noche, recordaba la fábrica de cemento, y pensaba que del mismo modo que él había vivido en un pueblo fantasma, alejado del mundo,

donde camiones de prisioneros llegaban y se iban con su carga esperpéntica cubierta de polvo verde, era posible que en ese mismo momento... hubiera otro campo, otro infierno, separado del mundo, con su pueblo de fantasmas que morían violentamente y no dejaban rastros, porque eran lanzados al mar o enterrados en fosas comunes, sin nombre, sin memoria. (61)

[At night he remembered the cement factory and how he had lived in that ghostly place, banished from all the world, where truckloads of prisoners came or went covered in greenish dust. Perhaps at this very moment... there would be another camp, another hell, with its inmates dying without a trace, either thrown into the sea or buried in common graves, no name, no memory. (57)]

History's violence even includes the transgression of grammar. In the novel, intransitive verbs are reformulated: "*nos desaparecen, decía Vercingetórix*" (55) ["*We are being disappeared,* Vercingetorix had said...*" (51]). In the annals of historic events, a reflexive verb of primordial freedom changes according to history's new necessities, which unquestionably abrogate one of the few choices individuals have: people are "suicided." The folly of this modern sentiment of instituting *reparations* for history's injustices, as a farce for its own blindness, does not escape this critique. The attempt to show the strength of reason's empire is satirized in the chapter that is dedicated to the *stultifera navis.* In this chapter, the navigator Artemius Gudröm and the madman Glaucus Torrender appear as two indistinguishable characters: "Artemius y Glaucus se hicieron amigos, tan amigos como lo pueden ser, en definitiva, un hombre medio loco que parece cuerdo y un hombre medio cuerdo que parece loco" (51) ["One assumes that the two men became friends, as much as a half-madman, seemingly sane, and a half-sane man, seemingly mad, can ever be" (47)]. This suggests that if it is possible to trace a history of madness, the reverse, discovering the reason of history, may not necessarily follow. The issue of contamination between madness and reason is examined by Foucault on various levels beyond the scope of this work. However, besides the paths that connect madness and reason, Peri Rossi has created in her novel a unique dimension upon restoring the tragic vision of madness as a symbol for the social marginalization embodied by indefinite atemporal and directionless voyages.

Of the three methods for approaching history delineated by Nietzsche— Monumental, Antiquarian, and Critical—the prolonged dwelling on any one of them contradicts the balanced space that each of these methods should occupy and invalidates the dialectic resolution that should mediate between the historic, the ahistoric, and the supra-historic. An exaggerated emphasis upon a vision of the past as a collection of antiques in need of preservation is just as problematic as an excessive build-up of the historic by monumentalizing it:

> Monumental history deceives through its analogies. With its seductive similarities, it attracts the spirited man to daring acts and the enthusiastic man to fanaticism. If we imagine this history really in the hands and heads of talented egoists and wild crowds of evil rascals, then empires are destroyed, leaders assassinated, wars and revolutions instigated, and the number of historical "effects in themselves," that is, effects without adequate causes, increased once more. So much for the reminders of the injuries which monumental history can cause among great and active people, whether they were good or evil. But look at what it brings about when the impotent and inactive empower themselves with it and use it!
>
> (Nietzsche, *On the Use and Abuse of History for Life*)

The masks worn by history hold the incredible power to create sectors of belief that are similar to those of a cult. This is the alienating point of the monumentalizing of history. Here, one can behold art's fundamental role of removing these disguises, turning to the ahistoric in such a way that the active forgetting of the past allows us to critically return to it.

However, where can someone who occupies the opposite face of history go when all of the territories he has traveled through or will travel through are completely deterritorialized for him? This question is at the center of both novels' narrative. In *Hallucinations,* the distressing shift between prison and expulsion creates a narrative experience that confines multiple voices that do not have to agree among themselves. This lack of agreement is not because they are marginalized, but rather because they escape the orders of reason. Hence, what Friar Servando narrates can be taken as true, refuted as a product of his own fantasies, understood as a derivation of his own dreams, or situated in the gap that lies between invention and testimony. The horror of the history that he experiences should thus be represented by visions instead of by testimonies. An attempt to create a document based on veracity will only reveal history's fraudulence. It is only possible to reproduce the historic specter Friar Servando travels through by using a prodigious imagination cultivated by metaphoric superabundance. By means of such imagination, the most hidden narrative interstices convey signifiers. This last affirmation can be illustrated by three examples. First, the restricted space represented by the character's constant mobility can be thought of as a devastated country whose signifier unveils a critique of the becoming of a nation. This becoming is seen as the privileged supervision of a caste that transforms the participatory notion of a nation into a future state and, consequently, one under its control. Second, the justification of an anthropomorphic representation of nature lies in the creation of another being with whom Friar Servando can communicate and mitigate his solitude. It will also help him to find strength and to pray. The metaphoric sense of this union between nature and human beings consists of the reprobation of political power's extensive contamination, a contamination that has reached a level in which helping other human beings has become impossible. Third, any journey through territories that have been institutionally denominated as states is a journey through a zone of darkness. Here, the signifier carries with it a verbal attack against the ideas of development and the rise of history, whether this is called feudalism, the age of reason, capitalism, or the *ultimate* conquest of knowledge. In other words, the movement of history transpires as a time of gloom:

> Y así fue que, poco a poco, entramos en lo que yo llamé el *país de la desolación* .... Es así que *voy atravesando una oscuridad tremenda* a través de un pasillo tremendo, y llevo dentro un tremendo miedo, pues voy solo. (174, 179)

> [And so we gradually entered what I called the *land of desolation* .... And so *I go along this tremendously dark passage,* being tremendously afraid, because I'm on my own. (113, 120)]

The critique of a history that works via exclusion finds a plethora of signifiers in the motif of *stultifera navis* among which the following figure: First, there is the display of history's displacement in the parable of the blind guide who, upon falling, pulls all of the other blind men dependent upon him into the abyss. Second, there is the confirmation that history is an imposition of violence instead of the march of a spirit's ascension. Third, there is experience that a sojourn outside of history is a utopia, a narrative belonging to the kingdom of imagination. Fourth, there is the unmasking of the myth that the routes of history are a humanist endeavor. On the contrary, he who does not form a part of the operational mechanism of power is belittled as a social detriment and is immediately separated out. Fifth, there is the allegation that history's forced exclusion has many faces, including censorship, recrimination, isolation, identity elimination, annulation, exile, and extermination. When Foucault examines these ships' cargo as a practice from the end of the fifteenth century and places emphasis on the pragmatic function of cleaning the city and on the euphemism that the *undesirable* element was sent away on a trip instead of being expelled, he is likewise referring to the enormous symbolic weight deposited on these ships that have no final destination or return date:

> So the ship of fools was heavily loaded with meaning, and clearly carried a great social force. On the other hand, it had incontestably practical

functions, as entrusting a madman to the care of boatmen meant that he would no longer roam around the city walls, and ensured that he would travel far and be a prisoner of his own departure.

(Foucault, History of Madness, 11)

In the protagonist Ecks, just as in the mathematical variable implied by his name, one recognizes all of the people who are unknown as well as the individual who does not fit into history. Ecks is, therefore, a collateral piece of history, not a subject. Ecks is simply a surplus of history. If this historic excess were to become noticeable, it would constitute a disturbance in need of elimination. In Peri Rossi's novel, the trips represent an ignored pilgrimage to the deficient magma of history. It is the past and futureless destiny of the characters, not a project. Their habitat is the undefined present, as seen in the life experience of repeatedly crossing a sea with no coast. It is a present in elemental terms, making no reference to any kind of temporality whatsoever.

Arenas's and Peri Rossi's works transcend the conception of history as a tree of knowledge: "History, conceived as pure science, once it became sovereign, would be a kind of conclusion to living and a final reckoning for humanity" (Nietzsche, *On the Use and Abuse of History for Life*). Both artists thoroughly scrutinize within and behind history. They confront its dense veil of darkness. Foresight into the becoming of history is a fiction, although it may be necessary and preferable to the consigning of objectivity to a person claiming to have the key to the knowledge, reading, and direction of history. However, a hindsight of the past is a productive critical entrance into the chaotic matter, which a more simplistic position would sacredly maintain as arks of events or archives of knowledge. This discernment is an indispensable profanation of a record of history that is catalogued as studied and unchangeable. It is an incursion that is vital in order to understand present history. In an artistic interpretation, it should come as no surprise that art's dissent and iconoclastic perception are so aggressive.

However, for those who live trapped by history, destroying this mirage is an arduous task. Friar Servando's apocalyptic adventure is not a punishment for his civil and religious disobedience; instead, it is a moment of enlightenment. It is this apocalypse that leads to the critique of all social power and control. The state, as an expression of the elitist political body, justifies the necessity of history and puts it on a pedestal from which the important events of the past are revered, even if they are grotesque. This past that constitutes history does not allow its entrance to a veritable future of change. Rather, it allows for its entry into a chronological record of history as if it had already been made, meaning that its modification (though possible) would be a crime against an unchangeable statute. The symbolic figure of a woman who history presents as a witch (but who is actually just an irreverent voice with multiple possible countenances) warns Friar Servando about his naiveté:

> Yo te ayudaré a abrir los ojos, y a que no seas tan aldeano, tan provinciano, tan humano y tan campechano ... tan poco ocurrente, tan escaso vidente. Y a no tener imaginación. Y a que no te dejes llevar por la persuasión, y mucho menos por la emoción. Y aprendas que lo que más se debe ocultar es la razón, pues casi nunca nos sirve para nada, y solamente es arma de los vencidos, *fraile* ... irás a parar a la cárcel por muchos años *para que puedas aprender a través de este desengaño, fraile* .... *Y así fui, tanteando espejos, y rompiéndolos todos hasta que al fin hallé la puerta.* (183–184).

> [I'll help you to open your eyes, help you not to be so unsophisticated, so provincial ... so dull, so unperceptive. And to prune your fantasy a bit. And I'll help you be less susceptible to persuasion, and to be swayed much less by emotion. You must learn that honesty is the thing you must take most pains to hide, since it's hardly ever any use, and is a weapon used by losers, friar ... you're going to spend many years in prison *so that you can learn something from the sobering experience, friar .... And so I worked my way along the mirrors, breaking them all, until at last I found the door.* (124–125)]

The *stultifera navis* motif, projected with its ideological perspective and read as an encounter with the unsettling justifications of social constructions, is connected to the artistic vision of Peri Rossi's novel. This vision holds in contempt the privilege of reason and the unscrupulous proceedings elicited by the law of nations as undeniable principles of the construction of a model of history that has dominated the modern world since the sixteenth century. Faced with the emptiness of human existence that begins with both reason's undeserved prestige and the repudiation of an alternative dimension of madness, Peri Rossi's work turns to a complex hermeneutics that will expose a critical reading of history. Furnished with a significant ambivalence between history conceived as narrative and history conceptualized as the course of humanity, *Ship of Fools* refutes the fact that any of these writings can be seen as a linear, evolutionary progression in which human beings can transform themselves. At the same time, this would appear to justify the abysmal alternative of turning oneself over to time instead of to the illusion of cultural constructs: "En la historia no había ningún progreso, pero el hombre y Equis coincidieron en que la esencia de algunas historias es precisamente ésa: no modificarse, permanecer, como reductos estables, como faros, como ciudadelas, frente al irresistible deterioro en el tiempo" (45) ["A story without progress, but then again the two men agreed that the essence of some stories lies precisely in this: they do not change, but remain like citadels or lighthouses facing the irresistible assault of time" (45)].

One must ask: to whom does history belong, aside from the academy and the dominant political and religious powers? In Peri Rossi's and Arenas's interpretations, history relates to each individual's intrahistory (the insignificant account of anonymous people). This is art's humanistic response. In everyday social happenings, history should help us to live. On the contrary, both authors allege that history is destructive to human aspirations. Nietzsche affirms that this harsh and violent history has the potential to be transformed into art, although such a possibility will be socially rejected: "Only when history undertakes to be turned into an art work and thus to become a purely artistic picture can it perhaps maintain the instincts or even arouse them. Such historic writing, however, would go completely against the analytical and inartistic trends of our time; indeed, they would consider it counterfeit" (*On the Use and Abuse of History for Life*). In the novels written by Peri Rossi and Arenas, the true fraud resides in accepting a silence that imposes an overwhelming and totalizing vision of history as a motor of social progress. In these authors' artistic visions, facing history with social muteness is a regression, a double suppression of freedom and of human capability.

The critique of history found in *Ship of Fools* is artistically represented by references that might be situated in a determined geographic latitude and period. This is especially true for the historic memory of contemporary readings, but this narrative discourse is an ample tapestry that journeys through the universal seas of time no matter what incursions history may have made in it:

> Equis insiste en sostener que todos los tiempos han sido de desconcierto y penuria para los que no fueron tocados por el privilegio del poder y que nuestros días no se diferencian de los anteriores más que por en número de perseguidores, la sistematización de sus métodos y la fría lógica que aplican, cuyo resultado es el delirio. (101)

> [Ecks on the other hand maintains that all periods have been periods of poverty and uncertainty for those who have no power: our days are no different from the past, except in the number of tyrants, their systematic methods and the cold logic with which they lead the world to madness. (100)]

The matter of exclusion in *Ship of Fools* reveals a meaningful parallel with the Foucauldian attempt to delineate a history of madness since, in Peri Rossi's novel, the resolution of endless trips through places that are essentially gauges of temporality represents an invective against the disturbing necessity of creating the most diverse methods and institutions of isolation throughout history. This paranoid end seems to accentuate the arrogance of the idea of the infallibility of the most diverse social institutions and their foundation upon a supposed truth of reason. A boat separates the madman from society with the illusion of a trip; the insane asylum does the same with the illusion of a treatment or a cure. The arrival of reason and the implications of its medical and scientific manipulation have made the second illusion possible. Political prisoners are deposited in jails, common graves, jungles, and seas. They do not disappear; they are disappeared at the hands of a sacrosanct history. Exclusions made upon altars of social order escalate. Observing the grotesqueness in the renditions of art is no longer necessary since it has installed itself in the present reality of daily life. Thus, history remains unchangeable and unperturbable: "Hospitales militares para prisioneros políticos. Selvas apropiadas para arrojar opositores incómodos. Naves de locos. La nave sustituida por el manicomio" (176) ["Military hospitals housing political prisoners. Woods where troublesome opponents disappeared. Ships of fools, the ship as a substitute for the madhouse" (181)].

Although *Hallucinations* and *Ship of Fools* are very different narratives, they are located within the same tapestry that refutes history. The feeling of rejection regarding the ways in which history is constructed and, more particularly, regarding the apologetic rationalization of its harrowing course, leads Arenas to point out that the accident known as human being will inevitably be sacrificed by the course of history. As a result, the only thing he has left is a record of time without any notable events: "más que en la Historia busco en el tiempo ... porque el hombre es, en fin, la metáfora de la Historia, su víctima, aun cuando, aparentemente, intente modificarla, y, según algunos lo haga" (Arenas, *El mundo*, 87) ["I look more at a dimension of time than at History ... because man is, when all is said and done, a metaphor for History, its victim. This is apparently true even when he tries to modify it, which according to some, he is able to do." (Arenas, *Hallucinations*, 87)]. This anchorless human dimension of time will be reserved for those who march in complete opposition to history. Friar Servando Teresa de Mier is the symbol of this march in this novel. He is a character who represents all human beings who have been marginalized by history, whether for their deviation from the belief in the necessity of historic reason, for their mistrust of social hegemony, or simply for being considered the useless dregs of society for the so-called noble ends of history. What is dignified and progressive for history's servants is monstrous in Arenas's novel. Integrating oneself with history requires that one remain in the inner circle of determinations and decisions made by state institutionalization. Friar Servando is the essence of what is marginalized and, at the same time, is also emblematic of the eternal struggle against power, signifying all those who will never be recognized by or incorporated into the social contract. Friar Servando's nonconformist principle of freedom is not possible in the context of discourses concerning fatherland, nation, or common good and improvement. In the vision of Arenas's novel, history does not tolerate freedoms that involve its criticism. On the contrary, it is adept at subjecting others to pay tribute to its megalomania. Arena's novel narrates a world with absurd constrictions that gives rise to a critique of the grotesque political body. *Hallucinations* is characterized by an artistic, hallucinatory representation that exalts its protagonist's exaggerated attitudes, answers, and out-of-place nomadism.

In a scene from Peri Rossi's novel, just moments before a load of madmen are abandoned in a ship about to be set adrift in the ocean, the vessel's captain grants a special favor to one of the madmen with whom he sympathized. With his destructive and twisted compassion, he gives the madman command of the ship, only asking that he "la condujera suavemente en círculos para no modificar la trayectoria" (52) ["circle slowly, without stopping" (48)]. This form of exclusion unveils one of the key pretenses of history for those who live fraudulently separated from the social contract. History does not hesitate to produce illusions; those who are excluded may control their destiny as long as they do not abandon the circle designated for them. The fact that the ship's voyage cannot be altered is a clear allusion to the absolute power that history has reached, a unilateralism by which the social pact has been broken. This impropriety of history's absolutism is not presented in Peri Rossi's novel as a sudden awakening from ingenuousness, but as the disillusionment to be expected of a prolonged distrust of social agreements. This gives rise to the nomadism of Ecks and the other characters of *Ship of Fools*. It is preferable to travel through map-less spaces instead of turning oneself over to the jurisdiction of states, communities, nations, kingdoms, fatherlands, citizenships, and districts. In these demarcated territories, bodies are also circumscribed by agreements whose guarantee of respecting human rights is continuously violated by the subterfuge of protecting the common good over the individual. In this way, history is not an abstraction but a political body of power; history is both a constitution and its own potential violation. History is similarly both a social agreement and an infringement of that understanding. History is the building of nations based upon citizen participation and the arbitrary exclusion of the very same citizens. It is the institution and dissolution of slavery. History is a text that can be dismantled and whose principles are defended, diluted, and rewritten in accordance with the objectives of the political body that represents it. History is found in the antipodes of all that is human. It is as much a legal machine as it is a machine of war and destruction. History does not move in circles nor does it move in spirals.

It does not advance or turn back. It is a political construction of power that is sustained by a subtle machinery of illusions. In Arenas's and Peri Rossi's novels, the reverence held for historic beings and their establishment as citizens of nations is critically expressed as a stage set very close to deceitful conveniences of control. While Peri Rossi hurls her characters through seas of space and time instead of through history and nations, Arenas moves his suffering characters through a history that, for its hallucinatory levels, cannot be understood as anything else other than fiction.

Notes

1. Note that all translations of *La nave de los locos* are taken from *The Ship of Fools.* Trans. Psiche Hughes. Columbia, LA: Readers International, 1989.
2. Note that all translations of *El mundo alucinante* are from *Hallucinations*. Trans. Gordon Brotherson. London: Jonathon Cape Ltd., 1971.

Works Cited

Arenas, Reinaldo. *Hallucinations: Being an Account of the Life and Adventures of Friar Servando Teresa de Mier.* Trans. Gordon Brotherson. London: Jonathon Cape Ltd., 1971. Print.

———. *El mundo alucinante (Una novela de aventuras).* Ed. Enrico Mario Santí. Madrid: Cátedra, 2008. Print.

Benjamin, Walter. *Illuminations.* Trans. Harry Zohn. New York: Schocken Books, 1969. Print.

Deleuze, Gilles and Félix Guattari. *A Thousand Plateaus: Capitalism and Schizophrenia.* 12th ed. Trans. Brian Massumi. Minneapolis: University of Minnesota Press, 2007. Print.

Foucault, Michel. *Las palabras y las cosas: una arqueología de las ciencias humanas.* Trans. Elsa Cecilia Frost. México: Siglo Veintiuno Editores, 1968. Print.

———. *History of Madness.* Ed. Jean Khalfa and Trans. Jonathan Murphy and Jean Khalfa. London: Routledge, 2009. Print.

Invernizzi Santa Cruz, Lucía. "Entre el tapiz de la expulsión del paraíso y el tapiz de la creación: múltiples sentidos del viaje a bordo de *La nave de los locos* de Cristina Peri Rossi." *Revista Chilena de Literatura* 30 (1987): 29–53. Print.

Lyotard, Jean-François. *The Inhuman. Reflections on Time.* Trans. Geoffrey Bennington and Rachel Bowlby. Stanford, California: Stanford University Press, 1991. Print.

Nietzsche, Friedrich. *On the Use and Abuse of History for Life.* Trans. Ian Johnston. British Columbia (Canada): Vancouver Island University, Nanaimo. http://records.viu.ca/~ johnstoi/nietzsche/history.htm. 2010. Web.

———. *The Will to Power.* Trans. Walter Kaufmann y R. J. Hollingdale. New York: Vintage Books, 1968. Print.

Peri Rossi, Cristina. *La nave de los locos*. Barcelona: Seix Barral, 1989.

Peri Rossi, Cristina. *The Ship of Fools*. Trans. Psiche Hughes. Columbia, LA: Readers International, 1989. Print.

Ricoeur, Paul. *Tiempo y narración. Configuración del tiempo en el relato histórico.* Vol. I, 4th ed. Trans. Agustín Neira. México: Siglo Veintiuno, 2003. Print.

Rousseau, Juan Jacobo. *El Contrato Social o Principios De Derecho Político.* http://www.enxarxa.com/biblioteca/ROUSSEAU%20El%20Contrato%20Social. pdf. Web.

Verani, Hugo. "La historia como metáfora: *La nave de los locos* de Cristina Peri Rossi." *La Torre. Revista de la Universidad de Puerto Rico* 4.13 (1990): 79–92.

Archaeologies of Identity: Revisions of the City and the Nation in Two Novels by Ana Teresa Torres

Elda Stanco

In *El exilio del tiempo* [*The Exile of Time*, 1990],[1] Ana Teresa Torres (b. 1945)[2] establishes the historical revisionist narrative model that reappears in her following novel, *Doña Inés contra el olvido* [*Doña Inés Versus Oblivion*, 1992].[3] Together these novels constitute a practical encyclopedia of urban memory in Caracas and national memory in Venezuela. Upon reading them, it is evident that if the edifices and costumes of past epochs have slowly disappeared from the quotidian city, the work of literary urban history is to find voices that cut through time and space to reveal the indecent and ambiguous transformation of the capital city, and in turn, in the case of Venezuela, of the nation. Torres's critical view in these fables of the Venezuelan national imaginary allows for not only historical revision and reconsideration, but also for the establishment of feminine voice and identity in historical Venezuela. *El exilio del tiempo* and *Doña Inés contra el olvido* reflect the particularities of their time, and invite the reader to decipher new national historical processes and urban culture histories. The novels attempt to chart an unknown territory of Caracas and hence of the nation: Venezuelan identity.

Torres's urban archaeology invites the reconsideration of the history and culture of the city through mental and urban excavations, in the quotidian and irrelevant gestures of the poem by the Venezuelan journalist and poet,

Blanca Elena Pantín. Thus, a new feminine subject is *mise-en-scène*, capable of integrating herself in the historical backdrop of the city and the nation, and of establishing herself in the labyrinth of the citizens' memories. The integration of this new feminine subject is simultaneously a challenge and a threat since it produces a new radical subjectivity of the city and the nation, reminding the reader of the instances that Frantz Fanon would call a new society.[4]

Torres notes in her article "Premisas de la escritura provisional" ["Provisional Writing Premises," 1995]:

> No existe una Caracas definitiva, no hay, por lo tanto, una nostalgia precisa; escribirla es más bien una necesidad de asegurarse que existe ... espacios, siempre destruidos, renovados, o habitados de un modo diferente al concebido, la hacen resistente a cualquier crónica de descripción fija.
>
> (Torres, "Premisas," 30)

> [A definitive Caracas does not exist, there is no, therefore, precise nostalgia; writing [Caracas] is more of a necessity to assure oneself that it exists ... spaces, always destroyed, renovated, or inhabited in a manner different than what they were conceived for, make [Caracas] resistant to any fixed descriptive chronicle.][5]

Torres seeks to write the city and the nation so as to demystify it. She revises pieces of national culture, she imagines the "spaciousness of existence"[6] of the nation, and she incorporates psychoanalysis as a popular tool for urban exploration. In *El exilio del tiempo* and *Doña Inés contra el olvido*, patriotic instances are analyzed and narrated through the psychological intimacy of the characters. These characters have, or are themselves, psychoanalysts who diagnose and decode the symptoms of the fragmented city subject.

When reading Torres's novels, the reader may ask, as does Donatella Mazzoleni in "The City and the Imaginary" (1993), "Why approach a subject which touches not only on levels of cultural consciousness but also on those of the collective unconsciousness?" (285). Why occupy ourselves with the "spaciousness of existence," or the urban quotidian—the existence that goes beyond the architectural habitat, that which occurs on the streets and the walls of the city in *El exilio del tiempo* and *Doña Inés contra el olvido*?

To establish the *pathos* of an urban archaeology and its possible decodings, it is imperative to understand "A Chronicle of Berlin" (1932), in which Walter Benjamin proposes the metaphor of the archaeological excavation to illustrate that memory is the theater of the past. Benjamin narrates his childhood memories within rather personal, particular, and photographic chronicles of Berlin and Paris. His narrative informs and simultaneously comments on his old and new impressions of the city.

Language is, Benjamin writes, "the medium of past experience, as the ground is the medium in which dead cities lie interred. He who seeks to approach his own buried past must conduct himself like a man digging" (25–26). The city is a labyrinth wherein the explorer can find artifacts and past dreams that have been displaced by the new fashions and developments. The urban explorer is also an archaeologist who discovers vistas of a premodern epoch, and in this manner breaks any evolutionary scheme that anticipates that there be some degree of progress that can make the present better than the past.

Through the urban experience, modernity is not progress but rather what Mike Savage classifies as "the latest episode of [Benjamin's] 'ever same'" (40). The postmodern urban culture of Caracas in the 1990s is the latest episode of the "ever same," since "postmodern developments take their place in a pre-existing urban setting which continues to confront the traveler and resident alike with uncertainties and unanticipated encounters" (49). In *El exilio del tiempo* and *Doña Inés contra el olvido*, there exists, precisely, a timeless uncertainty and a persistent anguish in each list of historical dates, each complaint, each personal narrative stolen by intruders, and each unfruitful search. In these novels, history is always about to be produced and the identity of the nation is always about to be established.

The unknown voice of Doña Inés provides the first clue for reading *Doña Inés contra el olvido*: the ephemerality of time appears to be an accomplice when in reality it prevents and mars any legibility of the city. The novel begins with Doña Inés Villegas y Solórzano searching among papers for property titles to her lost lands. Three centuries of history are pierced by a solitary voice that refuses to die and that lingers in order to tell her resentful and hasty litany. The property titles would legitimize Doña Inés's existence, and hence her lineage could outlive the novel, like the Buendía Family outlives Gabriel García Marquez's *Cien años de soledad* [*One Hundred Years of Solitude*, 1967]. Her search, her personal archaeology of identity, continues chronologically for three centuries to conclude in the uselessness of memory; by the end of the *oeuvre*, Doña Inés literally comes undone, falling to pieces like the papers she sought and the house she inhabited. Doña Inés's archaeology of identity is crucial for historical reconfigurations of the city and nation that potentially reconceptualize and recapture women's historical perspective of the self and history. In *Female Citizens, Patriarchs, and the Law in Venezuela, 1786–1904*, Arlene Díaz maintains:

> Due to their subordinate position, women's voices are not audible in the public transcripts of the [colonial] time [period]. The actions of most

women were believed to be not worth recording, because the ruling men did not consider them part of history. (25)

Based on Díaz's declaration, we can assert that historically women in Venezuela have been excluded from the public, plural national memory. A new and imagined literary voice, like Doña Inés's, becomes instrumental in redefining the city and the nation because Doña Inés herself is a metaphor for the city: seismic movements ("el terremoto de 1766, que aquí cuando cae una piedra se deja caída hasta el fin de los siglos, pero al menos teniéndolo escrito, podremos recordarlo" (35) [the 1766 earthquake, because anytime a stone falls here it is left for centuries; but at least by having it written down we can recall it]); new architecture ("Ubicada en una casa de doble planta, la tienda había quedado emparedada entre dos altos edificios" (178) [located in a two-story house, the store had been sandwiched in between two tall buildings]); changes in tastes or fashions ("se mudaron al Este; destruirán la pérgola afrancesada que ella hizo construir para que jugaran y merendaran sus sobrinos" (169) [they moved to the East Side; they will destroy the French pergola that she had someone build so that her nieces and nephews could play and snack in there]), all contribute to the protagonist's personal crisis and the surging illegibility of the city. Caracas in 1985—the last year of the dispute in the novel— is a lost and troubled city, where the papers that were never found in the novel underscore the importance of the quest, of the voyage in time, of the *revealing* that Alejo Carpentier describes thus:

> Muy pocas ciudades nuestras han sido *reveladas* hasta ahora—a menos que se crea que una mera enumeración de exterioridades, de apariencias, constituye la *revelación* de una ciudad. Difícil es *revelar* algo que no ofrece información libresca preliminar, un archivo de sensaciones, de contactos, de admiraciones epistolarias, de imágenes y enfoques personales.
>
> (Carpentier, 12)

> [Very few of our cities have been *revealed* until now—unless it is believed that a mere enumeration of exteriors, of appearances, constitutes the *revelation* of a city. It is difficult to *reveal* something that does not offer preliminary scholarly information, an archive of sensations, of contacts, of epistolary admirations, of personal images and focuses.]

The voice refuses to die, thus persevering with the rich archaeological and organic guide of an impoverished Caracas. Doña Inés's struggle is remarkably recounted throughout the novel, and in particular, during her last run through the space and place that have become a strange city to her. Doña Inés must, as Benjamin notes, excavate the archaeology of Caracas so as to reclaim her past and to insert herself in the literary urbanism that metatextually is the urban chronicle titled *Doña Inés contra el olvido*. Even when the book ends, Doña Inés's voice seems to echo, evoking the need for what Baudrillard calls "una memoria instantánea, una conexión inmediata, una especie de identidad publicitaria que pueda comprobarse al momento. Todo se dice, todo se expresa, todo adquiere fuerza o manera de signo" (22) [An instantaneous memory, an immediate connection, a kind of advertising identity that can be verified on the spot. Everything is said, everything is expressed, everything acquires force or manner of sign]. The new voice creates a textual space that opens the possibility of encountering a new history. As Cynthia Thompkins notes, the commentaries that Doña Inés directs at other characters—husband, page, slaves—create immediacy and actuality in the text. In her search for the titles, Doña Inés opens an unedited space of Caracas: its exploration at the hands of a *mantuana*.[7] This heretofore ignored urban experience converts itself into new annals of the history of Caracas in which we read the experience of the colony, the economic and gender structures in Venezuelan history, and the formation of the new Venezuelan feminine urban subject. The exploration at the hands of Doña Inés is a timeless and anxiety-ridden task in a city that changes daily, for if in Rome we can still see the layers of daily life and history with a quick stroll through the *Via dei Fori*, in Caracas the increasing rubble and new constructions never allow the accumulation of the history of the nation's capital and center.

Benjamin's dialectic perspective allows for the city to be the space of the antique and modern simultaneously; the relationship between architecture, memory (collective and individual), and history gives each city and each *flâneur* in the city unique perspectives, almost uncertain ones. The photographic chronicle, to cite Benjamin's thesis on the aura,[8] would suggest that the techniques of mechanical and mass reproduction destroy the sacred relationship between the *objet d'art* and its respective tradition. The absence of the luminous—or the aura—questions the tradition itself; at the same time, the absence of tradition and aura creates a modern desire for authenticity. Benjamin's fascination with the city simultaneously recalls the high forms of art that cannot be mechanically reproduced and the distant construction of objects that allows for uncertain *liaisons*. For Benjamin, the city can maintain its own aura and thus "the ability to look at us in return" (155–200), as the gaze in "Some Motifs in Baudelaire" details. Paradoxically, new technologies are not unappreciative of the aura; it is actually the modern that conjures prehistory. In order to represent the modern city, one must excavate the past of the city. Mike Savage concludes:

> Benjamin's insight is that the urban built environment has a number of qualities which allow meanings to be encoded and decoded in ways which

are specific to it [. . .] Cities cannot be incorporated easily into his account of mechanical reproduction, and this fact explains his fascination for their distinct properties and qualities. (47)

The argument regarding mechanical reproduction could actually be employed to discuss the city in crisis: reproducible, interchangeable, lacking marvelous surprises. According to Savage, the postmodern urban culture of the 1990s in Venezuela could be the latest episode of Benjamin's "ever same." In *Doña Inés contra el olvido*, Caracas is a city in crisis that, at the same time, as Savage proposes, presents uncertainties to its inhabitants and strollers. The 1766 earthquake destroys the city, but Doña Inés perseveres, constructing a chronicle of the streets that have been turned into cemeteries and appropriating the fallen rocks, the river, the valley, the fog, the perennial Monte Ávila, and the *negros*. The time for freedom arrives with the heroes of the so-called cosmic change that the Americas give Europe: the miserable village of Santiago de León de Caracas advances to a lead role in the independence movements when it "echa a volar el fantasma de la emancipación que recorrerá el mundo" (49) [unleashed the phantasm of independence that would travel the world]. However, the War of Independence destroys the city that had survived earthquakes. We read how Caracas goes from being "Tierra de Gracia" [Land of Grace] to "tierra de nadie" (54) [no man's land]. The women sell all their belongings and secure their money for the war, while the *mantuano* families perish. The cycle of horror closes with a rain that purifies the city as its few remaining citizens wait in uncertainty. Each city block and street corner of the new independent American city could confront Doña Inés with new clues to urban, national, and familial reading. Doña Inés, new American urban subject, must obtain new tools for reading; otherwise, *Doña Inés contra el olvido* would become inscribed in the alternate literary current of literature of failure. As a national novel, Torres's work, with respect to its disillusion, could be read in a negated archaeology of Caracas and a lack of collective national identity.

For the nation, the city represents a territory of freedom and exploration, a cultural space that is simultaneously individual and collective. We can think of the fugitive in Italo Calvino's *Le città invisibili* as the subject who strolls, escapes, runs, remembers, observes—all in a city that is exclusive, intimate, and that only she knows in her own way. One can configure the city as a space that, to quote Doreen Massey in *Space, Place, and Gender*, "must be conceptualized integrally with time," since space is not "some absolute independent dimension, but [it is] constructed out of social relations: that what is at issue is not social phenomena in space but both social phenomena and space as constituted out of social relations, that the spatial is social relations 'stretched out,'" (Massey, 2). This is how one begins to glimpse what occurs between houses and buildings, and what could have happened in places that have disappeared from the map of Caracas—that which is precisely at the base of the construction of identity. The city is, obviously, a problematic nexus in the narrative of the turbulent 1990s in Venezuela because each literary text presents a micro-history of the city, a problematic fragment of urban space that reveals processes and codes of cultural forms. The multiple perspectives of Caracas that Torres presents once again remind the reader that the city—as notion, space, place, or site—serves as microcosm of the nation.

As in *Doña Inés contra el olvido*, in *El exilio del tiempo* the historical episodes sketch vivid portraits of the postmodern urban subject of the 1990s, giving life and voice to a new timeless subjectivity and its apprehensive critical conscience. The writer shows how the new subject is produced and she underscores the radical transformations that Caracas as a space confronts. The most recent episode of Benjamin's "ever same" envelops the dynamic between the subject's labyrinth of memory and his position in the space of the reproducible city. Caracas in *El exilio del tiempo* is a synchronic space of the ancient and the modern, a reservoir of personal memories and recollections of other cities. The city is the nexus of European cities like Paris, Rome, Madrid, and London; of metropolises like New York; of the "Venezuelan way of life" (67); of the cultural invasion of the United States via automobiles and television sets; of the "Construir, construir, construir" (129) [Building, building, building], as an imperative of history. Its position as a cultural *locus* allows it to be a cosmopolitan city according to Anthony Appiah's definition: "Cosmopolitanism is, to reach a formula, universalism plus difference. It is thus one of the two possible poles of humanism: it thinks nothing human alien, but not because it imagines all humanity in its own image" (Appiah, 202). Caracas is unique in its American cosmopolitanism. A flood of transatlantic vessels transports passengers and immigrants between the various European points and Caracas. Yet besides transatlantic and global, the city is also a national place, the site of discreet surprises in family sagas, of trunks replete with photographs and books, of the "pasado acomodado y modesto" (129) [the well-off and modest past] that turns mythical in the move to modernity: "[La mudanza] Fue una exhumación del pasado en la que los cadáveres de la memoria se removían tan incómodos que ninguno parecía calzar en su tumba" (236) ([The house move] was an exhumation of the past, one in which the corpses of memory turned so uncomfortably, it seemed none of them fit in their tomb]. Upon entering modernity, the nation must maintain and protect its identity through myths of creation. The exhumation in this novel problematizes the foundational myths, and thus opens a new space that allows us to re-imagine the origin of the nation and its foundation.

The excavation in *El exilio del tiempo* begins with the move from the archaic family homestead in the city center to the ultramodern and chic neighborhood in the East Side of Caracas. The emergence from childhood, or its memory, is constructed parallel to the exit to the street and the city, like Benjamin does in "A Chronicle of Berlin." The narrator—fresh feminine urban subject—crosses life, the day, the space of the metropolis, in order to indicate her impressions of the city. Her body charts the city, since "the dimensionality of space follows from the directionality of the body" (Cassey, 205), in directions that specifically accentuate "the intimate and indissociable bond between the body and the places it inhabits" (Cassey, 206). Torres illustrates the dynamic between the feminine subject, space, and the urban psychology:

> Las múltiples alternativas de la calle se ensanchan ahora y aturden como los anuncios luminosos, las invitaciones de sus palabras, tomar cada una de ellas, una cualquiera, sería enredarse en un falso laberinto. Quizás más lógico es aceptar la confusión y preguntarse qué hago yo aquí.
>
> (Torres, 138)

> [The multiple perspectives from the street now widen themselves up and daze like the luminous signs, their words extending invitations, to take each one of them, any one, would be to get entangled in a false labyrinth. Perhaps it is more logical to accept the confusion and ask oneself what am I doing here.]

Although the feminine subject questions herself, she moves through space, appropriating it for herself. The feminine subject forges new social relationships as she "stretches," to quote Massey, the space where she finds herself according to her new subjectivity.

Upon crossing the Atlantic and becoming a global citizen, the Caracas subject struggles to find a possible reading of her surroundings in the European city. Her fear is comparable to Benjamin's when he confronts a new and unfamiliar Paris that offers unexpected surprises on each city corner. The unknown European city is dangerous and traumatizing, but it presses the subject to form her own critical agency and to handle herself physically, psychologically, and socially. We see the ambivalence between the fragmented self and the organized self in Paris, because it is there where the feminine subject affirms her individuality and asserts the *liaison* between space and subjectivity. One of the great and characteristic keys to Torres's work is this challenge between the pre-established urban medium (Paris) that confronts the visitor (the Caracas subject) with uncertainties and unanticipated encounters and the organized chaos that leads the subject to question her identity, her history, and her origin. The challenge itself becomes a new way that the feminine subject sees herself, even when something is lacking, when it appears that something "que no podemos definir" (100) [that we cannot define] escapes her. The Caracas subject reads the allegorical and iconic novel *Ifigenia: Diario de una señorita que escribió porque se fastidiaba* [*Iphigenia: The Diary of a Young Woman Who Wrote Because She Was Bored,* 1924] by Teresa de la Parra (1889– 1936), a story of transatlantic travels very similar to *El exilio del tiempo*, while in Paris. In both works the voyage out marks the awakening of the feminine subject. The voyage back symbolizes the beginning of the feminine subject's personal archaeology, and armed with new European and US urban experiences, she returns to her own Venezuelan city. The link between Caracas and Paris is never complete, and it is, perhaps interestingly or paradoxically, the father who demonstrates it when he reprimands his daughters by reminding them that they were not in Chacaito (an area of Caracas), but rather in "una ciudad civilizada" (102) [a civilized city].

The Chacao neighborhood was the epitome of the early cosmopolitan Caracas, filled with the newness and hope of immigrants—or the members of a new budding nation. But to understand the archaeology of Caracas, the feminine subject must manipulate the complicated historical image of the nation that the city presents in *El exilio del tiempo*. Caracas is presented as a small town with aspirations to be a great metropolis, not just in its urbanism, but also in its daily idiosyncrasy. The ungrateful nation slowly neglects the jewel box that is the capital city, forgetting it along with its architectural catalogue, and thus wrecking its theater of past memories to which Benjamin refers. Architectural monuments like *El Calvario* and *El Capitolio* evoke former generations' outdated dreams of grandeur. In the Caracas of the twentieth century, the European architectural grandeur of temples and museums has been replaced by a new national treasure: oil.

It is quite impossible to overlook the almost leading role that oil has in the Venezuelan imaginary of the nation, especially as represented in the Venezuelan urban novel of the 1930s. The riches of oil augment the incoherency and illegibility of the Venezuelan capital, displacing countless peoples and excessively fragmenting the subjects who remain in the city. The Caracas of the "Saudi Venezuela" is splendor and shadow in *El exilio del tiempo*, as the inevitable exodus to the East Side of the city becomes an excursion, almost an exploration because the East Side is a blank canvas about to be constructed with the help of a handy architect. The move implies a disruption of memory, family history, the culture of the historical city, and the mythology of the nation. The city center of Caracas (the disloyal historical focal point of the city) is converted into an alien space for the narrator; her family forbids her to visit the area, but her cousin tells her how—in the new modernity—the city center is a crowded, extravagant, unknown, and almost dangerous space. The chaotic descriptions of the modern Caracas city center remind the reader of the consecutive images casually and fleetingly seen from an automobile: concrete, yet brief and transient. Even though these portraits could stun, like the famous and dizzying urban voyage of the emblematic Andrés Barazarte in Adriano González León's *País portátil* [*Portable Country*, 1969], it is rather a strange curiosity and a sense of the marvelous that they awaken in the reader. Businesses with international names like *Cataluña Book Shop*, *The Star of David*, and *The Lusitanian* detail the process of redefinition of a Venezuela that is understood as a Latin American allegory of modernity. The city subject enumerates the business signs of her space and appropriates the external so as to erect one last episode of Benjamin's "ever same" in her new cosmopolitan and global city.

In *El exilio del tiempo* and in *Doña Inés contra el olvido*, Torres informs about the uncertain national history while critically commenting on real and fictitious events. Each feminine subject in Torres's work is a portrait of the city; each subject gives voice and life to the critical conscience and illustrates the correspondence between the individual (psyche and soma) and the city (polis). It is the same analogy between the mind and the city as made by Freud in *Civilization and Its Discontents* (1929). Freud compares the idea that "in mental life nothing which has once been formed can perish—that everything is somehow preserved and that in suitable circumstances (when, for instance, regression goes back far enough) it can once more be brought to light" (16–17) with the Eternal City:

> It is hardly necessary to remark that all these remains of ancient Rome are found dovetailed into the jumble of a great metropolis which has grown up in the last few centuries since the Renaissance. There is certainly not a little that is ancient still buried in the soil of the city or beneath its modern buildings. This is the manner in which the past is preserved in historical sites like Rome.
>
> (Freud, 7–8)

The relationship between human habitat and the entity of the psyche would presuppose that the ancient and the new share a same space (perhaps an echo of Benjamin?) and that by changing the view angle, one could observe today's church constructed above yesterday's temple: "the same piece of ground would be supporting the church of *Santa Maria sopra Minerva* and the ancient temple over which it was built" (Freud, 18). Even though Freud eventually discarded the affinity between mental and city archaeologies as fantastic and absurd, the metaphor would be useful if we considered it in conjunction with Benjamin's proposal. The changes in the city must be material (of architecture, for example) or mental (of the perception of the architecture, for example); mental changes can also occur with or without physical alterations. Steve Pile suggests in *The Body and the City* that "the analogy would have held better had Freud thought about the struggles and conflicts within the urban which are traced through its fabric, through the production of space" (241), because the city changes not only through its material reconstructions, but also in response to the very same anxiety and threat that mold the psyche. We could even read the ancient structures as unfulfilled gestures of faith or hope, thus focusing on an architectural aura that may change without altering the architectural façade of the buildings. A capital city such as Caracas is a reflection of the nation; any urban metamorphosis is a reflection or echo of national changes.

If *El exilio del tiempo* presents a polyphony of voices that detail the new feminine urban subject, *Doña Inés contra el olvido* is a beyond-the-grave commemorative essential to the "production of space" (Pile, 241), in the urban history of Caracas. The posthumous maneuver stands out and opens new spaces in Torres's writing. Julio Ortega proposes that in some fashion, Torres's characters do not illustrate identity issues because they know who they are—they are conscious of their national identity, history, and class. While this is an interesting proposal, it must also be added that the conspicuous descriptions in the novel circulate around, precisely, what it means for the urban subject to express, demand, and reclaim her agency. The psychological subject exposes not only the cultural conscience, but also the collective unconscious.

The centrality of Caracas in every sphere—legal, administrative, cultural, and labor related—converges in each chapter of the novel. The first part of *Doña Inés contra el olvido* describes the years 1715–1835: times of foundations, placid contemplations, rebellion, and destruction for Caracas. The colonial period presents a village of Santiago de León de Caracas that is tranquil and insignificant in comparison to the great colonial centers like Lima or Potosí: a "pobre provincia olvidada" (38) [a poor forgotten province], and that did not have the riches of Perú nor the grandeurs of the New Spain. The community was a diagram of the Spanish city, with the pealing of the church bells reminding people of the Angelus prayer at noon and at dusk, calling for attendance to the rite of the mass, and announcing the birth or death of the inhabitants. It is the transplant of a strict and measured organization from Europe to the Americas:

El damero a partir de su idea primera centralizadora [. . .] a partir de un cuadrilátero vacío, la presencia fuerte de los volúmenes institucionales dominantes (catedral, cabildo, aduana) de donde parten vías y construcciones uniformes que pueden repetirse al infinito. La insistencia en la repetición no puede sino reforzar, hasta la exasperación, lo excepcional: la sede, el centro del poder.

(Altamirano, 21)

[The checkerboard, starting from its primary centralizing idea [...] going forth on an empty four square, the strong presence of the dominant institutions (cathedral, town council, customs office) from which began the streets and the uniform constructions that can be repeated *ad infinitum*. The insistence on repetition cannot but reinforce, to the point of exasperation, the exceptional: the seat, the center of power.]

Doña Inés's colonial life is just as schematic, monotonous, and repetitive, with her house at the center of her world and her husband at the center of power of that world. The afternoons and nights pass away in the same schematic fashion, a *mantuana* routine centered round the home, the husband, and the Catholic Church. Venturing out to the streets was for Catholic festivities or parties offered by the Governor, or to go to the Cathedral. Doña Inés does not perceive the miserable margins of her society because she has never left her quadrilateral dwelling space; the colonial urban subject represents the confined and omitted voice that in historical retrospective demands her space and agency in the urban history of Caracas and in the nation's fabled and outlandish history.

In *Doña Inés contra el olvido*, Paris enters triumphantly in the imaginary of Caracas under the presidency of Antonio Guzmán Blanco (1870–1889). Besides the new street lighting, the streets are finally clean and are now adorned in French style; one may stroll in the plazas and over the bridges, there is a new center of power called *El Capitolio* [*The Capitol*], and there exist diverse markets and theaters. If in the colonial period the feminine subject was prisoner to the urban block, in the time of Guzmán Blanco the francophilism in Caracas marks the liberation of the feminine subject and the creation and production of her own urban and national spaces. The new commodity is the telephone, and women peruse the street freely without the train of slaves accompanying them, going out at night to enjoy music and dance, sporting their new wardrobes from Paris and Madrid. A few colonial architectural layers accumulate in Caracas, but the majority disappears under the new and *in vogue* French styles. The urban subject now explores the public spaces and notes her first public architectural impressions of Caracas.

Torres details the rise to power of the dictator Juan Vicente Gómez, adding a special emphasis to how Gómez destroys the European architectural and social foundations that Guzmán Blanco had established in Caracas. The French-inspired boulevards, theaters, and bridges of this small tropical Paris remain as Benjamin and Freud's unfulfilled gestures of faith or hope of the architectural aura. The country and the capital are turned into a great hacienda with a short *cacique* (political chief) at the center of the checkerboard. As in *El exilio del tiempo*, in *Doña Inés contra el olvido*, it becomes inevitable to narrate in Caracas without referencing the oil boom and its imminent disgrace, disguised as bonanza. Gómez's dictatorship paralyzes the nascent urban cosmopolitanism of Caracas, eliminating any architectural surprises and any public gestures that manifest personal archaeologies.

The death of Gómez in 1935 opens the last part of the novel, entailing the years 1935 through 1985. It is a time of jubilation that marks the entrance of the city to modernity. In her nostalgia and newly recuperated freedom, Doña Inés does not know whether to cry or celebrate: she confesses that "yo también estoy en el siglo XX" (167–168) [I, too, am in the twentieth century]. The precipitous modernity of the nation dazes the urban subjects and, once again, throws the fragile contemporary identity into turmoil. The reader again encounters echoes of *El exilio del tiempo* in the city that expands horizontally toward the East Side and vertically with new buildings. The center of Caracas resurfaces as the mythical space that betrays the nation's origins through an uncertain history that is slowly disappearing. Doña Inés, now a mere ghost, crosses the area of her former mansion, recognizing that there is nothing left in Caracas that is hers:

Tumbaron todas las casas que alguna vez visité [...] Una a una fueron cayendo las que habían resistido a los temblores, a las revoluciones y a Guzmán [...] Echaron cemento sobre las lajas y el empedrado [...] ensancharon las aceras [...] porque era necesario que cupiera en la ciudad todo el siglo XX. (168)

[They demolished all the houses that I once visited [...] One by one, the ones that withstood the earthquakes, the revolutions and Guzmán, all came down [...] They poured cement over the slabs and cobbled paving [...] they widened the sidewalks [...] because it was necessary that all of the twentieth century fit in the city.]

In the twentieth century, there is no accountability of any urban architecture in Caracas; to the contrary, "Cada cuadra se dividió en mil pedazos para servir de vivienda a tantas personas, se levantaron edificios, se abrieron comercios, y en suma, lo que tú pensabas era el centro del mundo se convirtió en un lugar inhóspito" (169) [Each block was divided into one thousand pieces to serve as housing to so many people, buildings were erected, shops were open, and in sum, what you thought was the center of the world became an inhospitable place]. Torres vividly recalls that the exodus to the East Side is inevitable, the next step in the uncertainty of the city, in the urban chaos, in the fragmentation of the feminine subject in Caracas. The feminine urban subjects in *Doña Inés contra el olvido* and *El exilio del tiempo* must again excavate through Benjamin's rubble to recuperate and continue inscribing their personal archaeologies in the urban history of Caracas and the national history of Venezuela. The feminine subjects in the works of Torres seek to establish their history so as to continuously underline their subjectivity. These are subjects who can strip the quotidian city in the way that Carpentier described would be the enormous task of *revealing*. The city may reveal itself when we perceive it as a space of social relations— to recall Massey—and Torres illustrates how the feminine subject crosses Caracas to forge new models of existence and challenge, yet again, the space of the city according to the new subjectivity of the "ever same."

Caracas in Torres's urban novels expands horizontally toward the East Side and vertically with new high rises. The city changes illogically in its architecture, façades, views, and the response that the feminine subject enunciates at these changes. In her new radicalness, the urban subject crisscrosses the city from the East Side to the West Side, from the peak of the Monte Ávila to the depths of the river that divides Caracas. Her act of revealing the city implies new models of an "ever same," and reminds the reader that answering Mazzoleni's question—"Why approach a subject which touches not only on levels of cultural consciousness but also on those of the collective unconsciousness?" (285)—unleashes the unknown voices of the city. If in *El exilio del tiempo* the urban expansion is simultaneously horizontal and vertical, in *Doña Inés contra el olvido* the historical events and family sagas dictate the urban metamorphoses. The birth of Doña Inés's granddaughter mirrors the health of the city and the nation. Just as the city is reborn, the "criatura pequeña y amoratada" (56) [small and blue with cold newborn], lives. Caracas, destroyed and dusty when the granddaughter is born, is a city of debris and ghosts. Doña Inés cries over her family corpses, hears the voices in the empty streets, feels the former life of a city via its destroyed architecture. The city will be rebuilt, the nation will rise again, but it is the world of Doña Inés and her lineage that quietly disappear without leaving much trace or hints about its existence. In the abandoned mansion the spirit reminisces how "vivíamos nuestra pequeña aristocracia y tejíamos un mundo que nos parecía eterno" (73) [we used to live out our small aristocracy and weaved a world that seemed eternal]. Alone in Caracas, Doña Inés waits. Filled with rage and desolation she roams the city attempting to capture memories of her own small grandeur. If Doña Inés writes her family tales, these will serve as a city guide or a walking map; through her writings Doña Inés stretches the space of subjectivity and identity, and she marks a new American literary urbanism.

In *Doña Inés contra el olvido* the city's growth runs parallel to the narrator's aging. Doña Inés's descendants slowly begin to tell the micro-histories that Doña Inés had already narrated decades earlier. The very national history is the history of the family saga: Belén tells how Isabel—her grandmother and Doña Inés's great-granddaughter—flees Caracas in 1814 with Simón Bolívar in the Emigration to the Orient. Isabel is the strategic family link because "si se hubiera muerto también nuestra familia hubiera desaparecido" (175) [if she had died, our family would have also disappeared]. But Belén is also an anchor to the past: she exposes the impossibility of comprehending the present without knowing the past, or the aforementioned need that Benjamin notes: "He who seeks to approach his own buried past must conduct himself like a man digging" ("A Chronicle of Berlin," 25–26). In order to construct new myths of the nation it is necessary to imagine the past in new forms. If the city *flâneur* does not carefully observe the city architecture, she will miss the vague residues of the past: "La casa estaba en La Pastora, en una hilera de construcciones que conservaban el estilo antiguo del barrio, emparedadas entre altos edificios; el zaguán mostraba retazos del enlosado, el piso de mosaicos roto y humedecido" (*Doña Inés*, 190) [The house was in the Pastora [neighborhood], in a row of constructions that maintained the neighborhood's old style; the entrance hall showed remnants of the flagstone pavement, the broken and dampen mosaic floor]. Urban history does not seem to matter in the turbulent Caracas of the 1990s. But it is precisely in this restless decade that the foundational papers Doña Inés seeks throughout the novel are found; the foundational papers are the family property titles, now mere collectible items and memory cues that serve as communicating vessels to access the past.

Doña Inés concludes her search, closes her cycle with a last visit to the city, and confirms that her past is a mythical world, cut by nostalgia and bitterness toward what Arturo Almandoz refers to as the *atmósfera artificial* [the artificial atmosphere], that envelops the questionable historic city center in which now-English-speaking women take photographs of the sloths hanging from trees in the sacred Plaza Bolívar.[9] In one of the many nostalgic moments of the *oeuvre*, Doña Inés reflects upon the false illusion that the colonial province of Caracas offered: "Porque esta tierra, Alejandro, ha sido la invención de una promesa" (91) [Because this land, Alejandro, has been the invention of a promise]. The ancestors had been attracted by the promise of richness and grandeur, of gold and glory. Now that promise agonizes in a damned and bedeviled land that never crystallized the fantasy of *El Dorado*—that great foundational myth of the nation. The latent anxiety in *Doña Inés contra el olvido* was already gestating in the earlier *El exilio del tiempo*:

Cómo arrancar de las paredes el moho de nuestros recuerdos, cómo despegar de los pisos nuestros pasos, cómo evitar que en la lluvia que caía sobre

los patios no se confundieran las gotas de otros cielos, cómo impedir que
en el humo de la cocina no se levantara una emanación de nuevas exis-
tencias, cómo hacer para que nuestros escenarios no fueran invadidos por
los gestos y parlamentos de otros actores, que retomaran nuestros textos
desfigurándolos a su antojo. (134)

[How does one tear down from the walls the rust of our memories, how
to detach our steps from the floors, how to avoid that in the rain that used
to fall over the patios the drops from other heavens not be confused, how to
prevent that in the smoke from the kitchen an emission of new existences did
not rise, how to stop the invasion of our stages by the gestures and speeches
of other actors, who will once again take up our texts and deform them at
their whim.]

Without a valid space in a city she no longer knows, Doña Inés, "estreme-
cida del tiempo" (239) [shaken up by time], falls apart like her property
titles. It is, finally, the voice of the feminine subject that runs parallel to the
construction of the city and of the nation as an historical allegory.

As previously mentioned, in 1969, Adriano González León published
his great novel *País portátil*, in which centuries of national history and segments of personal history are accumulated into one easy-to-read portable
tome. For Torres, it is the capital city—center of the nation—that must fit
in a pocket-sized tome. The historical layering and positioning seen from
the window of González León's novel illustrates the scenery that Torres
minutely develops in her work:

Una ventana a la ciudad. La vista hacia las azoteas y las antenas y los anun-
cios de neón. [. . .] La ciudad planeada. El país planificado. El gran brillo.
La nacionalidad fue construida con muchos desvelos de la generación inde-
pendentista. La gruesa lanza de Páez atravesando la sabana, clavada en el
anuncio de refrescos. El caballo de Bolívar pastando sobre las terrazas, con
montones de paja en el hocico.

(González León, 283)

[A window to the city. The view of the terrace rooftops and the antennas
and the neon signs. [. . .] The planned city. The planned country. The great
splendour. Nationality was constructed through the pro-independence generation's many sleepless nights. Paéz's thick spear going through the sheet,
nailed on the soda billboard. Bolívar's horse grazing on the terraces, with
heaps of hay in his snout.]

González León utilizes historical figures to create flashes of the nation's history, introducing that very precise history that is questioned and ridiculed
in architectural models of the current urban reality of the 1960s depicted
in the novel. Venezuela in *País portátil* is in continuous motion, in a

permanent house move from one part of the city to another. Andrés
Barazarte, the novel's terrified protagonist, is "víctima de los fantasmas de
sus ancestros que se valen de él para revivir sus testimonios y los de un país
de pena y llanto, brutal y errante, sin más asidero que el coraje, la renuncia,
el adiós" (Crespo, 9–10) [victim of his ancestors' ghosts, who take advantage of him to relive their testimonies and those of a pained and crying
country, brutal and lost in wanderings, with no handle other than courage,
relinquishing, the good-bye]. The anxiety-ridden pages of Barazarte's voyage from the East Side to the West Side of Caracas drown the reader in
infernal planes, sinking one in a stunning curtain of pollution and noise:

> A las seis de la tarde comenzaba el tráfico enloquecedor. La avenida San
> Martín cubierta de humo de escape, papeles, cartones arrastrados, flejes
> y ronquidos. El pito de las fábricas tirando a empujones los obreros por el
> barrio de Artigas. Las pequeñas oficinas, las tiendas, los abastos, con gente
> entrecruzada y veloz. Los muchachos que voceaban el diario de tarde y no
> paraban de correr. Veinte uniformes escolares ocupaban por completo la
> acera de enfrente, se lanzaban a la calle con el semáforo en contra, cortaban
> el paso de automóviles. Se oían frenazos y mentadas de madre.
>
> (González León, 119)

> [At six in the afternoon the maddening traffic began. San Martín Avenue
> covered in car exhaust, papers, dragged boxes, metal bands and snores.
> The factory whistle pushing laborers through the Artigas district. The small
> offices, the shops, the markets, with interwoven and swift people. The boys
> who cried out the afternoon newspaper and did not stop running. Twenty
> school uniforms completely took up the opposite sidewalk, they threw them-
> selves on the street with the wrong traffic light, cutting the path of the cars.
> One could hear sudden braking and swearing.]

It is the same enumerated anxiety that appears in Torres's novels in the
form of lists of historical dates, urban catastrophes, lost documents, and
vain searches. The works of Torres and González León discuss historical
episodes while sketching vivid portraits of the urban postmodern subject of the second half of the century, giving life and voice to a new
subjectivity and its critical conscience. It is the creation of identity. Both
writers show how the new historical subject is produced and they underline the radical changes that confront Caracas as a space. The most recent
episode of Benjamin's "ever same" covers the dynamic between the subject's labyrinthic memory and her position in the space of the mechanically
reproduced city.

  In the popular imaginary Caracas is called "la ciudad que se nos fue"
[the city that we lost]; it is thus not difficult to understand why urban
novels of Caracas are overflowing with concrete or intimate exiles, with

emotional escapes to the evoked city, and with personal archaeologies that all together form the new literary urbanisms of Caracas. As novels of the nation, the works of Ana Teresa Torres unleash ignored or unknown voices so that these can fill with life the unjust enumeration of architectural exteriors in Caracas. Torres has expressed that the enemy of Caracas is neither time nor memory, but rather the little esteem toward the historical city and the absence of critical conscience. Under this lens, *El exilio del tiempo* and *Doña Inés contra el olvido* frame the most difficult exiles in Torres's writings. They remind the reader that the city is, ironically, a labyrinth of lack of communication and the only possible place for the writing and reflection of the personal archaeologies. These are the new archaeologies that form the literary urbanisms of Caracas and the collective and national history of Venezuela.

Notes

1. National Council of Culture Prize for Narrative, Venezuela, 1991.
2. Anna Seghers Prize, Berlin, 2001.
3. Mariano Picón-Salas Biennial Prize for Novel, Venezuela, 1991; Mobil Pegasus Prize for Literature, USA, 1998.
4. Fanon's work considers Algeria and the end of colonialism. See *A Dying Colonialism* (1965).
5. All translations, unless otherwise noted, are mine.
6. Minkowski derived the "spaciousness of existence" from his four-dimensional formula in which space and time are linked in one entity.
7. The *mantuanos* were "The creole elites [who] consisted of a group of whites with family lineages that had long enjoyed privileged status in the colony [...] These self-proclaimed 'familias antiguas, nobles, limpias y honradas' ['old, noble, clean and honorable families'] saw themselves as people of 'utmost distinction'. [...] Indeed, by the eighteenth century this group was known as the mantuanos for the distinctive *manto* (veil) that covered the faces and bodies of *mantuano* women in public places. Elite women's characteristic manner of dress signals the importance of control over women's bodies for *mantuano* honor and status. Such exterior signs of honor and status set the *mantuanos* apart from the common people. More importantly, the public display of the *mantuanos'* honor became a fundamental mechanism of social control that reaffirmed the social hierarchy and honor within the colony" (Díaz, 23–24).
8. For more on Benjamin's aura, see "The Work of Art in the Age of Mechanical Reproduction."
9. There is a Plaza Bolívar in most cities and large towns in Venezuela. This Plaza marks the city or town center and it usually has an equestrian statue of Simón

Bolívar at the center. In these Venezuelan cities and large towns the Plaza Bolívar is a bustling square where people gather on a daily basis.

Works Cited

Almandoz, Arturo. *Ensayos de cultura urbana.* Caracas: Fundarte/Alcaldía de Caracas, 2000.

Altamirano, Aldo José. "La selva en el damero: la evolución del espacio urbano latinoamericano." *La selva en el damero: Espacio literario y espacio urbano en América Latina.* Ed. Rosalba Campra. Pisa: Giardini, 1989. 17–26.

Appiah, Anthony. "Cosmopolitan Reading." *Cosmopolitan Geographies: New Locations in Literature and Culture.* Ed. Vinay Dharwadker. New York: Routledge, 2001. 197–227.

Baudrillard, Jean. *La transparencia del mal: Ensayo sobre los fenómenos extremos.* Barcelona: Anagrama, 1997.

Benjamin, Walter. "On Some Motifs in Baudelaire." *Illuminations.* Ed. Hannah Arendt. New York: Schoken, 1985. 155–200.

———. "A Berlin Chronicle." *Reflections.* Ed. Peter Demetz, Trans. Edmund Jephcott. New York: Schoken, 1986a. 3–60.

———. "The Work of Art in the Age of Mechanical Reproduction." *Illuminations.* Ed. Hannah Arendt. New York: Schoken, 1986b. 217–251.

Calvino, Italo. *Le città invisibili.* Torino: Einaudi, 1972.

Carpentier, Alejo. *Tientos y diferencias.* La Habana: Unión de Escritores y Artistas de Cuba, 1974.

Cassey, Edward. *The Fate of Place: A Philosophical History.* Berkeley: University of California Press, 1997.

Crespo, Luis Alberto. *Señores de la distancia.* Caracas: Editorial Mandoria, 1988.

de la Parra, Teresa. *Ifigenia: Diario de una señorita que escribió porque se aburría.* Caracas: Monte Ávila, 1989.

Díaz, Arlene. *Female Citizens, Patriarchs, and the Law in Venezuela, 1786–1904.* Lincoln: The University of Nebraska Press, 2004.

Fanon, Frantz. *A Dying Colonialism.* New York: Grove Press, 1965.

Freud, Sigmund. *Civilization and Its Discontents.* New York: Norton, 1961.

González León, Adriano. *País portátil.* Prol. Luis Alberto Crespo. Caracas: Monte Ávila, 1996.

Massey, Doreen. *Space, Place and Gender.* Minneapolis: University of Minnesota Press, 1994.

Mazzoleni, Donatella. "The City and the Imaginary." *Space and Place: Theories of identity and Location.* Ed. Erica Carter, James Donald and Judith Squires. London: Lawrence & Wishart, 1993. 285–301.

Minkowski, Hermann. "Space and Time." *The Principle of Relativity: A Collection of Original Memoirs on the Special and General Theory of Relativity.* Ed. Hendrik

A. Lorentz, Albert Eisntein, Hermann Minkowski and Herman Weyl. New York: Dover, 1952. 73–91.

Ortega, Julio. *El principio radical de lo nuevo: postmodernidad, identidad y novela en América Latina.* Lima: Fondo Editorial de Cultura, 1997.

Pantin, Blanca Elena. "En esta calle." *El hilo de la voz: Antología crítica de escritoras venezolanas del siglo XX.* Ed. Yolanda Pantin y Ana Teresa Torres. Caracas: Fundación Polar, 2003. 642.

Pile, Steve. *The Body and the City: Psychoanalysis, Space and Subjectivity.* London: Routledge, 1996.

Savage, Mike. "Walter Benjamin's Urban Thought: A Critical Analysis." *Thinking Space.* Ed. Mike Crang and Nigel Thrift. London: Routledge, 2000. 33–53.

Thompkins, Cynthia. "La re-escritura de la historia en *Doña Inés contra el olvido* de Ana Teresa Torres." *Escritura y desafío: Narradoras venezolanas del siglo XX.* Caracas: Monte Ávila, 1996. 103–120.

Torres, Ana Teresa. *El exilio del tiempo.* Caracas: Monte Ávila, 1990.

———. *Doña Inés contra el olvido.* Caracas: Monte Ávila, 1992.

———. "Premisas de la escritura provisional." Revista de literatura y artes venezolanas. 1.1 (1995): 27–40.

6

Santa Evita, History, Fiction, and Myth: A Narrative from Another Side

Marcelo Coddou

Introduction

If Tomás Eloy Martínez's intention is to encompass Argentina's reality, he does it by agreeing with what his admired friend Gabriel García Márquez has affirmed many times:"La realidad no sólo es los policías que llegan matando gente, sino también las mitologías, las leyendas, todo lo que forma parte de la vida de la gente, y todo eso hay que incorporlo" (González Bermejo, 23) [Reality is not only the policemen who arrive killing people, but also the mythologies, the legends, everything that forms a part of people's lives, and all of this must be incorporated.][1]

Through his incorporation of mythologies and legends surrounding Perón and Evita, which inalienably form a part of the lives of the Argentine people, Tomás Eloy Martínez situates himself in the sphere of narrative fiction that would come to be known as "The Latin American New Narrative,"[2] and which, with a wide variety of variables, undoubtedly continues to be one of the major literary expressions of our America. As Mario Vargas Llosa observes:

> Hoy nuestros novelistas ya no se esfuerzan por expresar *una* realidad, *sino* visiones y obsesiones personales: *su* realidad. Pero los mundos que crean sus ficciones y que valen ante todo por sí solos, son, también, versiones, calas a diferentes niveles (psicológicas, fantásticas o míticas) de América Latina.
>
> (Vargas Llosa, 31)

[Today our novelists no longer make an effort to express *a* reality, but rather visions and personal obsessions: *their* reality. But the worlds that their fictions create and that are valuable in and of themselves are also, versions, penetrations at different levels (psychological, fantastic, mythic) of Latin America.]

All of Tomás Eloy Martínez's novels point precisely to those levels. The psychological element plays a primordial role not only in his novels that are distanced from the prevailing political component (*Sagrado, La mano del amo*), but also in *La novela de Perón, Santa Evita*, and, without a doubt, *El vuelo de la reina* and *El cantor de tango*. The fantastic element, which must be understood in the sense that Vargas Llosa mentioned in the previous citation, is dominant in *Santa Evita*, a novel in which, nonetheless, the mythic element is what is offered as a decisive component of its narrative cosmos.

Privileging a specific sphere in an analytical reading is, without a doubt, valid. However, underestimating the total complex is obviously reductive. What I wish to propose, then, is that Tomás Eloy Martínez's work demands that we pay attention to its many levels. Any attempt to schematize is in conflict with the wealth of his proposals and expressive modes. It is not for naught that the Argentine writer has sought to escape limiting taxonomical labels. For example: Is his work "Peronist" or "anti-Peronist"? "No"! he has said. "They are works by a *Perontologist*." Historical novels? Of course, but with the need to be qualified because it is a category dangerously prone to being reduced to schemata. That is why he prefers to speak of novels about history. The mythic dimension, which this study will review, operates in directions that are not the same as those of Asturias, Carpentier, or Arguedas, because the world in which this mythic dimension manifests itself (so different from that of Guatemalan or Peruvian indigenism, or Cuban negritude) was constructed beyond the Latin American reality that had a very scarce presence (I do not speak of absence) in Argentina.

Historical Intertextuality and Myth

Gérard Genette designates the means of access to a text with the word "paratext," which he defines as a great indecisive zone somewhere in between the inside and outside of the text, where the social codes that govern the "outside" of the text are mixed with the productive codes that regulate the "inside" of the text. The French narratologist specifies that this mixture always implies and signifies a *transaction* in which the strategies and protocols of societal reception are decided (Genette, 7–8). Thus, the (social) appearance of the text is always realized in a preconditioned manner: its reading is always preceded by a pre-reading, realized with a more or less full cognizance that those familiar with the author or his complex literary, social, and political surroundings will interpret his writing precisely in function of its paratexts.

I would like to examine the paratexts of *Santa Evita*, the famous novel by Tomás Eloy Martínez, with the intention of achieving a critical reading of the novel. My reflections will go beyond the internal paratextual procedures (title, dedication, epigraphs, and acknowledgments) to encompass also part of the external paratexts. The external paratextual reception that might have preconditioned the reading of *Santa Evita* obeys many factors. The first—perhaps the most important—is the "serious" assumption that the novel was surely going to make of the discourse directed at a historical figure about whom only extreme attitudes seemed to predominate: scornful or praiseworthy: prostitute or saint. This was what led the author, according to his own declaration, to demand that his editors put under the book's title the genre indicator "novel." Tomás Eloy Martínez knew that everything that his text might say about Eva Duarte would have an already established sociopolitical and written context. That is why he insisted on demanding that the reception of what he wrote be what his authorial will had decided. The narrated world of *Santa Evita* is definitely *fictitious*.[3] This is true to such an extent that, as the novelist has testified, there is only one event narrated in his work that totally corresponds to its historical referent: it is the final chapter in which the novel narrates how the principal materials and information on the fate of Evita's cadaver came into the hands of the author (Mora).

This immediate genesis of the novel to which I refer (not the most profound, of course) was recounted by Tomás Eloy Martínez on more than one occasion in the many interviews that he granted. He relates that in the winter of 1989, three military men came before him affirming that they knew the truth about Evita's cadaver. Since at that same time there was a great controversy among the Argentine historians about his previous book, *La novela de Perón*, which caused a debate about the rights of novelists to modify official history,[4] before beginning *Santa Evita*, he wrote the lyrical novel *La mano del amo*, which demonstrated and convinced the author himself of his capacity for diversity so as not to be pigeonholed as a only a Perontologist. However, shortly after (*La mano del amo* was published in 1991), he says that his preoccupation with Evita, in whose official history he detected obscure points, returned, and it occurred to him that he might use journalistic strategies to narrate a fictitious history of Eva Perón. In order to write the novel, he took a year of sabbatical from Rutgers University, where he was a professor. He and his wife were heavily in debt and wondering how they would pay it off. They didn't know, they couldn't know, that the novel was going to become one of the greatest best sellers of Argentine literature, translated into 36 languages.

Let us return to the year 1989 in which Tomás Eloy Martínez finds out the truth about Evita's cadaver. I transcribe later in text the reconstruction of that which was narrated to Tomás Eloy Martínez, by the weekly newspaper *Noticias*, as it was published there:

> En una turbia medianoche...de 1989 sonó el teléfono en la casa de.... Tomás Eloy.... Era el Coronel Héctor A. Cabanillas...el hombre que había pivoteado, por expresa disposición de Pedro Eugenio Aramburu, el "Operativo Traslado" de los restos de Eva Perón a lugar seguro. Cabanillas había tenido un predecesor frustrado y demencialmente castigado por la obsesión de Evita: el teniente coronel Carlos Moori Koenig.... Esa noche...fue una noche de cita. Tomás Eloy fue al café Tabac.... Y allí se encontró con Cabanillas...[y] con Jorge Rojas Silveyra—embajador en España en los tiempos de Alejandro Agustín Lanusse.... Ellos le entregaron toda la documentación que tenían en sus manos, porque "el secreto los ahogaba." La historia del cuerpo de Evita empezaba a develarse.
>
> (Martínez, www.literatura.org/TEMartinez)[5]

> [In a tumultuous midnight of...1989 the telephone rang at Tomás Eloy's house.... It was Colonel Héctor A. Cabanillas...he was the man who had pivoted, by express orders of Pedro Eugenio Aramburu, "Operation Transfer" of Eva Perón's remains to a secure place. Cabanillas had had a frustrated predecessor who was crazily punished for his obsession with Evita: the lieutenant colonel Carlos Moori Koening.... That night...was the night of the meeting. Tomás Eloy went to the café Tabac... And there he met with Cabanillas...[and] with Jorge Rojas Silveyra—the ambassador to Spain during the times of Alejandro Agustín Lanusse.... They handed over all the documentation that they had in their hands because "the secret choked them." The story of the body of Evita was beginning to reveal itself.]

Now that the "external" genesis of the novel has been clarified, we can try to approach some of the problems that arise from a critical reading of the text. Tomás Eloy Martínez's novels definitely negate the distinction that, according to Hayden White, exists between historical "histories" and "fictional" histories. This distinction resides in the fact that the content of the former is based on real events, events that really *happened*, while the content of the latter are *imaginary events, invented by the narrator* (White, 67–68).

Tomás Eloy Martínez postulated and achieved in his work what Barthes has maintained with regard to the reality effect:

> Hay que descartar las afirmaciones relativas al *realismo de la narrativa* ... La función de la narrativa no es *representar*, es construir un espectáculo ... La

narrativa no muestra, no imita. "Lo que tiene lugar" en una narrativa desde
el punto referencial (realidad) es literalmente *nada*, "lo que sucede" es sólo
lenguaje.

(Barthes, *Análisis estructural*, 43)

[One must dismiss the affirmations relative to narrative realism . . . The function of the narrative is not to represent, it is to construct a spectacle . . . The
narrative does not show, does not imitate. "What takes place" in a narrative from the referential point (reality) is literally nothing, "what happens"
is only language.]

For Barthes the narrative structure reveals that historical discourse—that
of historiography, as a mode of narrative representation—is one of the
forms of ideological or imaginary elaboration and he calls attention to the
fact that the narrative structure that originally arose from the caldron of
fiction evolved into traditional historiography, both the sign and the proof
of reality.

Just like the French theorist, Tomás Eloy Martínez will question both the
unequivocal distinction between what is historical and fictional, as well as
the objectivity of historiography that is offered in modes of narrative representation. Needless to say, for the author, discourses are not mere vehicles
to transmit a content; they produce signifieds.

The narration achieves the transition from *occurrence* to *discourse*[6]
through a tropological procedure that Tomás Eloy Martínez called trans-
figuration and that White defines as "a displacement of the facts onto the
ground of literary fictions . . . the transition is effected through a process of
transcodification" (White, 47).

Tomás Eloy Martínez confronted the established idea that one arrives at
the truth only by means of scientific objectivity, subscribing to the thought
of those who sustain that the truth can also be transmitted through *figurative discourses,* those proper to literary fiction and that also constitute
historiographical and mythological narration. Just as Barthes, he thought
that fictions (not only true but all fictions) are more than a mere means
to provide information: they represent the meaning of events, what is
achieved through symbolization.[7] Martínez understands history as "historiography" and states the following regarding historiography's relationship
to literature:

la "nouvelle histoire" o "intellectual history" ha adoptado las herramientas,
técnicas y las tradiciones narrativas de la literatura para hacer a su modo la
historia tradicional [. . .] Cuando digo que la novela sobre la historia tiende a
reconstruir, estoy diciendo también que intenta recuperar el imaginario y las
tradiciones culturales de la comunidad y que, luego de apropiárselas, les da

vida de otro modo [...] La ficción crea otra realidad y, a la vez, renueva el mito. Forjamos imágenes, esas imágenes son modificadas por el tiempo y al final no importa ya si lo que creemos que fue es lo que de veras fue.

(Martínez, "Argentina entre la historia y la ficción," 18)

[The "nouvelle histoire" or "intellectual history" has adopted the technical tools and narrative traditions of literature in order to write in its own way traditional history... When I say that novels about history tend to reconstruct, I am also saying that they try to recover the imaginary and cultural traditions of a community and that, after appropriating them, they give life to them in a different manner... Fiction creates another reality, and, at the same time, renovates myth. We forge images, those images are modified by time, and in the end it doesn't matter anymore if what we believe happened was really what happened.]

It was not strange to him that the novel was the privileged genre, which is understandable if one takes into account Bakhtin's concept that the novel is a macro-genre in which the other genres are contained and which has the capacity to tell the truth by means of its figurative discourse.[8] Fiction thus conceived in its aptitude to show in all its complexity a reality that other discourses (historiography, novelistic biography, essay with a psychological, political or social orientation, traditional journalistic reporting) do not succeed in designing as definitively true, although they may programmatically postulate themselves as truthful discourse. The novelist, a writer with license to lie, as Tomás Eloy Martínez used to underscore, can make use of all these discourses and in their crisscrossing discover how to give life to the truth that one seeks to establish, and which is never definitive. In *La novela de Perón* we read: "esa pasión de los hombres por la verdad le ha parecido siempre insensata" (Martínez, *La novela de Perón*, 49) ["the passion people have for the truth has never made sense to me" (44)].[9] That is why, "[it] doesn't matter anymore if what we believe happened is really what happened" (Martínez, "Ficción, historia, periodismo").

Let us also remember what Tomás Eloy Martínez said about the historical novel ("about history," more precisely, in the writer's words). On the one hand, it reconstructs the recovery of the cultural imaginary and traditions; on the other, it gives them life in a different way and thus renews myth. All these terms are decisive if one understands the direction in which this type of novel produced by the writer takes us: he wrote it reconstructing the "reality" that the documents pretended to offer us as true. His instruments are the recreating imagination and the language, forger of images, with which myth is renewed. Let us examine this last point in *Santa Evita*.

It is very well known that since the origins of humankind, history and literature have been united by myth. The historian Mario Cancel explains this fact thus:

> lo que daba unidad a aquellos géneros era el fondo mítico que estructuraba la visión del mundo del ser humano. Detrás del deseo de "ordenar" la realidad circundante en un todo coherente estaba también la necesidad de saber cómo las cosas llegaron a ser ... Por eso la historia se compenetraba con el mito y tomaba ese cuerpo literario que le permitió convertirse en un instrumento de poder, en un mecanismo útil para justificar las estructuras políticas, aunque difícilmente hubiera podido convertirse en lo contrario.
>
> (Cancel, 45)
>
> [What gave unity to those genres was the mythical background that structured mankind's vision of the world. Behind the desire to "order" surrounding reality into a coherent total, there was also the necessity of knowing how things came to be.... Therefore, history and myth penetrated each other and took on this literary body that allowed it to convert itself into an instrument of power, into a useful mechanism for justifying political structures, although with difficulty would it have been able to convert itself into the opposite.]

The fact that a myth recounts history, that it is a significant part of it, has great transcendence when dealing with the history of a nation or a significant moment of it. Tomás Eloy Martínez found in full force the mythical value that Evita had among the Argentine people. What he did was harvest this myth, attending to its fundamental components, and contribute to its re-elaboration, to maintaining it alive. Whether he proposed to or not, he magnifies the concept that already existed, by means of which he succeeds in producing a complete identification between the figure of "Santa Evita" created by those who believe in her with veneration and of the other Evita seen by those who demonize her. He also manages to make the myth more current by relating it to the political fight that took place during the long period of active presence of Peronism in Argentina. Argentina lived (and probably still lives) two histories: one of full acceptance of the mythical dimension of the defender of the shirtless ones and another that impugns such acceptance in order to destroy this myth with the worst qualifiers. Both sides use the myth of Evita in their struggles for power.

The appropriation of myth in *Santa Evita* has a meaning that seems very clear to us: to make relative the official histories of so many essays— and fictions—that have been written about the real person and to propose a new version that will include, as we said, the modes of interpretation of this figure by social and political groups. The author re-elaborates tales with which a significant number of Argentines identify and which grant or confirm the meaning of their existence. All mythical tales, all narrations with this dimension, touch the receiver in some way. The receiver thus feels part of the past that is being narrated to him, because it gives him security about his own beliefs and conceptions, granting to him a sense of belonging to a community that shares the same assessments of the actions of their heroes or anti-heroes. Myth, in contrast to history, can either coldly or with scientific serenity distance itself from its characters. It allows for the action of the imaginary and produces a tale with which those sectors of the community will be able to identify. The pro-Peronist group looks at the story of Evita as *its* story, when her tale is told with all its mythic power. I am not affirming that Tomás Eloy Martínez has intended to cede to the demands of determined readers—we know that he maintained that a writer, in contrast to a journalist, should never take into account "para quién escribe" [for whom he writes]—but I do judge that, upon respecting the mythic dimension of Evita, he was able to create a literary character—the fictitious entity that is every novelistic character—that comes to his readers as such (whether or not they accept the validity of this concept). They also know that this person has lived historically and served as a referent for the fictitious character. In his essays on Eva Perón, Tomás Eloy Martínez touched upon this mythic component with critical distance, but in the novel it appears fully incarnated.

The myth of Eva Perón is complex, which is why one must see how Tomás Eloy Martínez renews it in the novel. I propose that he does so by disarticulating the elements that most markedly comprise that myth. Just as *La novela de Perón*, *Santa Evita* is composed of various discourses that overlap, crisscross, are juxtaposed, and fertilize one another. Along with the metaliterary reflections that recur throughout the novel, there are narrations of fictitious lives that have real referents (the most important of which is the part that refers to Colonel Carlos Moori Koenig, along with which there are many others), and the pithy fictionalization about the investigations that seek to inform themselves about the destiny of the embalmed body. The scrutiny and commentary of a large part of the writings on the theme are also added: "en *Santa Evita* intenté recuperar la esencia mítica de un personaje central de historia argentina reuniendo en un solo texto todo lo que los argentinos hemos imaginado y sentido sobre Eva Perón durante dos o tres generaciones" (Martínez, "Argentina entre la historia y la ficción," 23) [In *Santa Evita* I tried to recover the mythic essence of the central character of Argentine history collecting in a single text everything that the Argentines have imagined and felt about Eva Perón during two or three generations].

The literary visions of Perlongher and Ezequiel Martínez Estrada, among many others, are gathered in the novel. Tomás Eloy Martínez received, then, an ample variety of discourses and *re-wrote* (the author knew that his was one more re-writing, not the definitive one) the myth(s) of Evita, renewing them. The narrator recognizes that he is "arming a jigsaw puzzle," conscious of the fact that he is creating a *history* that is *literature*, fiction, but *true fiction*. What historiography was impotent to show, perhaps the novel can illustrate. The emptiness, the silence of history faced with the body of Evita, will be filled, spoken, with the word of the imaginary, until other renovations of the same myth appear.

The myth of Eva Perón has its generating elements in the tales about Eva Perón's dark origins, premature death (like Christ or Che Guevara), her "miracles," the profaned mummy. However, one must act with precaution faced with what happened with these myths after the death of Evita, if one wishes to understand both what Sebreli has called her "ossification" as well as what Tomás Eloy Martínez has done in his novel upon revivifying these myths. Sebreli, in his classic work *Eva Perón, ¿aventurera o militante?* [*Eva Perón, Adventurer or Militant?*] has allowed us to see that:

> El mito de Evita como expresión simbólica de los anhelos de justicia e igualdad de las mujeres y los trabajadores argentinos, sólo a medias realizados en la realidad, y a la vez como expresión del temor por la pérdida de sus privilegios por parte de las clases burguesas, fue como tal un mito de carácter dinámico, creador y progresivo, estaba dirigido hacia el futuro y no hacia el pasado, como los regresivos. Pero después de la muerte de Evita comenzó el proceso de cosificación del mito, la tendencia a convertir la imagen del mito en algo fijo e inamovible, esencia eterna de un pueblo ahistórico, estático y sin desarrollo.
>
> (Sebreli, 109)

> [The myth of Evita as a symbolic expression of the desires for justice and equality of Argentine women and workers, only partially achieved in reality, and at the same time as the expression of fear for the loss of their privileges on the part of the bourgeois classes, was as such a myth of dynamic character, creative and progressive, directed toward the future and not toward the past, like regressive myths. But after the death of Evita, the process of ossification of the myth began, the tendency to convert the image of the myth into something fixed and immobile, the eternal essence of a historic people, static and without development.]

Tomás Eloy Martínez does not allow the myth to become regressive: whether or not he proposes it to himself, he makes it recover its driving force of new processes of historical development. Its renovation reveals unresolved conflicts in Argentine society; it remits us "a un pasado cristalizado que la evolución incesante de los acontecimientos históricos va dejando atrás" (Sebreli, 109) [to a crystallized past that the incessant evolution of historical events has left behind] and, thus, allows us "enrique-cernos con nuevas experiencias de nuevas situaciones ahora más extremas" (Sebreli, 109) [to enrich ourselves with new experiences of new situations that are now more extreme].

The image that *Santa Evita* gives us of the death of the champion of the shirtless ones coincided with the end of the power that Sebreli him-self has designated as "el ala plebeya del peronismo" (Sebreli, 109) [the plebian wing of Peronism]. It also coincided with the weakening of the General Office of the Workers, the emergence of the General Office of Entrepreneurs, and Perón's capitulation (not without resistance, although his surrender of power in 1955 took place without any fight) to the bourgeoisie, the Armed Forces, and imperialism.

Faced with the populist sector of the bourgeoisie interested in develop-ment that tries to appropriate the figure of Evita, Tomás Eloy Martínez's novel rescues Evita's plebian image, among others. *Santa Evita* shows the struggle between classes—the same thing that Martínez did in his previ-ous novel. The image that he provides of the Peronist phenomenon and of Eva Perón is not one of neutralizing and depoliticized integration. The image is presented in vital relation to social and political reality. It is not a mere object of contemplation, admiration, and repudiation, as are the great, "exceptional" personalities, but rather presents the image of Evita within concrete ideological contents that are in permanent battle among themselves. That is, by trying to recover Evita's mythical essence, he suc-ceeds in denying its fossilization into a museum object, its neutralization and process of becoming de-politicized. As Sebreli indicates:

> Contra las necrofilias de ciertos peronistas que reclaman la momia de Evita para convertirla en un objeto mágico de adoración mística, prefiero que la tumba de Evita siga abierta y que su tumba siga perturbando las conciencias.
> (Sebreli, 112)

> [Against the necrophilia of certain Peronists who reclaim Evita's mummy in order to convert it into a magical object of mystical adoration, I prefer that Evita's tomb continue to be open and that her tomb continue to perturb consciences.]

What Tomás Eloy Martínez achieves in *Santa Evita* has been to de-mystify the myth (his audacity was to title his work as he did: the title induces the reader to think that the image of the historical figure is univocal, when, on the contrary, it is presented in all its multidimensionality). There is a de-mystification of both Evita's angelic version as well as her diabolical one. Thus, this is the way in which he has made the following appear to the consciousness of his readers (above all those who are most committed and cognizant of themselves):

> que una severa censura interna y externa nos impone ocultar, es una de las maneras—la que corresponde al escritor más que al político—de contribuir al esclarecimiento de la conciencia de la clase trabajadora y de las mujeres argentinas, o por lo menos de sus posibles dirigentes, de los cuadros, de quienes depende que la transformación social del país, el cambio histórico deje de ser un mito nostálgico en el que se proyectan las esperanzas y los sueños más ardientes de una gran parte del pueblo.
>
> (Sebreli, 112–113)

[That which a severe internal and external censure makes us hide. It is one of the ways—that which corresponds to the writer more than the politician—of contributing to the clarification of the consciousness of the Argentine working class and of Argentine women, or at least their possible leaders, of the pictures of those who depend upon the social transformation of the country, in which historical change stops being a nostalgic myth that projects the most fervent hopes and dreams of a great part of the people.]

Tomás Eloy Martínez is skeptical with respect to this supposed responsibility of the writer, or at least, the efficacy of his discourse:

> En verdad un libro, la literatura en general, por eficaz que sea, raramente contribuye a cambiar nada ni a que nadie tome conciencia de nada. Contribuye solamente a establecer un lento diálogo, a operar como un sedimento en la conciencia. Pero no a plazo inmediato, sino muy largo. Si uno piensa en la obra de Kafka, que tuvo que esperar más de treinta años para que se dieran las consecuencias de narraciones como *La colonia penitenciaria* en los campos de concentración . . . Ni la obra de Hemingway, ni la obra de Faulkner, ni la de Borges modifican nada en los imaginarios nacionales.
>
> (Coddou and Figueroa, 343)

[In truth, a book, literature in general, however effective it might be, rarely contributes to changing anything or makes anyone become conscious of anything. It only contributes to establishing a slow dialogue, to operate like sediment in the conscience. And not short term, but rather long term. If one thinks of the work of Kafka, who had to wait more than thirty years for narrations like *The Penal Colony* to have their predicated events realized in the concentration camps.... Neither Hemingway, Faulkner, or Borges's work modified anything in the national imaginaries.]

However, despite such reticence, there is no doubt that Tomás Eloy Martínez has succeeded through his works in changing the image of both Perón and Evita. In *La novela de Perón*, "fue apareciendo un Perón que

nadie había querido ver: no el de la historia sino el de la intimidad"
[a Perón was appearing that no one had wished to see: not the historical Perón but rather the private Perón].[10] Thus, just like we know that
the Evita who we today value is not the same as the one we knew before
the author's imaginary proposal, few now doubt that the events from the
"blind ditches" covered by fiction are not "true" or did not "really happen."
It is sufficient for whoever wishes to *know* what young Evita thought and
felt when her father died or what Evita said to Colonel Perón when she met
him or what the First Lady felt when faced with the demands of the people
that she accept the candidacy to the vice presidency in 1952, to read what
the novel indicates as irrefutable facts. It is in this manner that Tomás Eloy
Martínez recreates the myth—with certain facts about what happened,
documentable events, and above all, his powerful imagination, which is
not his "exclusive property" because it takes into account, with responsibility, as he himself recognizes, that the novelist recovers: "el imaginario
y las tradiciones culturales de la comunidad y que, luego de apropriárse-
las, les da vida de otro modo" (Martínez, "Argentina entre la historia y la
ficción," 23) [the cultural imaginary and traditions of the community and
after appropriating them, gives them new life in another way].

When he was asked to clarify what the myth of Evita consisted of
(and this inevitably leads to an extreme oversimplification), Tomás Eloy
Martínez responded, connecting his figure to that of Che Guevara and
Christ:

> Latin American myths are more resistant that they seem to be. Not even the
> mass exodus of the Cuban people or the rapid decomposition and isolation
> of Fidel Castro's regime had eroded the triumphal myth of Che Guevara,
> which remains alive in the dreams of thousands of young people in Latin
> America, Africa and Europe. *Che as well as Evita symbolize certain naive, but
> effective, beliefs: the hope for a better world; a life sacrificed on the altar of the
> disinherited, the humiliated poor of the earth. They are myths which somehow
> reproduce the image of Christ.*
>
> (Martínez, "Evita or Madonna," 32)

And later on, in the same answer that he gave to whoever challenged him
to reflect on the fact that if formerly imperialism appropriated resources
like copper and rubber, in the present Hollywood was appropriating much
more, "the myths themselves of national culture," the novelist responded:

> The myth of the real Eva Perón will begin after the fires of the film have died.
> Her image is already installed in history with such force and with as many
> lights and shadows as that of Henry the VIII, Marie Antoinette or JFK. The
> immortality of great personages begins when they become a metaphor with

which people can identify. Evita is already several metaphors: *she is the Robin Hood of the 20th century, she is the Cinderella of the tango and the Sleeping Beauty of Latin America.*

(Martínez, "Evita or Madonna," 32–33, my emphases)

As one can clearly see, Tomás Eloy Martínez had very distinct ideas about what the myth of Evita represents, in all its complexity. This is why he can proceed to reformulate it in a novel in which such a myth, as we have already said, is both affirmed and re-signified.

Myth and Symbol

Tomás Eloy Martínez installs himself and us in Argentine reality through the configuration of his narrative language, thus complying with what Michel Foucault describes as the manner in which human beings create and recognize their own reality:

> los códigos fundamentales de una cultura—los que rigen sus lenguajes, sus esquemas perceptivos, sus cambios, sus técnicas, sus valores, las jerarquías de sus prácticas—fijan de antemano para cada hombre, los órdenes empíricos con los cuales tendrá algo que ver y dentro de lo que se reconocerá.
>
> (Foucault, *Las palabras y las cosas*, 5)
>
> [the fundamental codes of a culture—those that govern its languages, its perceptive schemes, its changes, its techniques, its values, the hierarchy of its practices—set beforehand for each man, the empirical orders with which he will have something to do and within which he will recognize himself.]

And it is thus how the writer from Tucuman, in those propositions of "truth" about Perón, Evita, and Peronism that constitute his novels, should respond to a complete collection of conditions under which such propositions are going to be judged precisely as such, as *true*. In this group of conditions, the "presuppositions" matter greatly. According to Ducrot and Lyotard, the presuppositions should be true in order that the proposition can be considered true or false.[11] The "true" character of a proposition depends on both its verification (Russell, 83) and its credibility in the eyes of the listener or the reader.[12] It presupposes the intention of truth (or deception) in the emitter of the discourse, as a condition so that the act of communication can be accomplished. Tomás Eloy Martínez insisted that every novel is a *lie*. "Narrar significa licencia para mentir" [narrating means license to lie] is the phrase that he reiterates in essays and interviews. Nonetheless, the author expects that the reader accede to the truth of what is narrated to him or her, although the truth can be sheltered, disguised, in the *lie* through the protection of social convention. As Víctor Bravo points out, when Saint Agustín maintains that "mentir es decir lo contrario de lo que uno piensa, con la intención de engañar" [lying is saying the contrary of what one thinks, with the intention of deceiving], he is giving way to the possibility of conceiving of "permissible lies" along with lies "with the intention of deceiving" (Nietzsche spoke of damaging lies) (Bravo, 24). On the other hand, credibility, we said, makes us easily accept as true what are *certain lies.* Tomás Eloy Martínez had a long and recognized career as a journalist when he wrote *Santa Evita* and had always been faithful to his conviction that in journalism it is an ethical mandate to tell only the truth. That is, the credibility of his word—of any of his words—was guaranteed by his established prestige. And since in his novel he employed the techniques of journalism, he achieved what he did not expect: that *everything* that he told there would be judged to be true. However, the decisive thing is that the truth that he was interested in establishing remained disguised in the *lies* of his fiction. And this was so not only because of his confidence in the power of the imagination to accede to hidden zones of reality, but also because he held the conviction that invention is a dimension of language where liberty not only is possible but also *necessary*: "yo creo que la novela es el género de la libertad, y en esa medida cualquier confusión genérica es posible, cualquier elemento bastardo, marginal de la realidad es introducible en la novela .... La única fidelidad del novelista es a sí mismo, a su propia libertad" (Neyret, 19) [I believe that the novel is the genre of freedom, and in this measure any generic confusion is possible, any bastard element, any marginal element of reality, is introducible in the novel .... The only fidelity of the novelist is to himself, to his own freedom].

Maurice Blanchot points out that the novelist "es un hombre sometido por entero a la ley de verosimilitud" (Blanchot, 203) [is a man entirely subjected to the law of verisimilitude], and thus suggests that fiction has a secret aspiration to completely rid itself of the impositions of truth. Tomás Eloy Martínez's postulates and their achievement in his novels allow us to see that *true fictions* (*La novela de Perón* and *Santa Evita* are of this nature) possess the same power to answer the "regimens of truth" as they do to demystify (in the sense that they attack established myth) and to unmask the *established truths*: the author, as we know, subversively faces official historiography. Carlos Fuentes, citing Tomás Eloy Martínez, has said as much in the following words:

> "Mito e historia se bifurcan y en medio queda el reino desafiante de la ficción." [TEM] quiere darle a su heroína [Evita] una ficción porque la quiere, en cierto modo, salvar de la historia: "Si pudiéramos vernos dentro de la historia—dice TEM—, sentiríamos terror. No habría historia porque

nadie querría moverse." Para superar ese terror, el novelista nos ofrece, no vida, sólo relatos.

(Fuentes, http://www.literatura.org/TEMartinez/cricf.html)

["Myth and history fork and in the middle remains the challenging kingdom of fiction." [TEM] wants to give his heroine [Evita] a fictional existence because he wants to save her from history to a certain degree: "If we could live within history—says TEM—we would feel terror. There would be no history because nobody would want to move." To overcome this terror, the novelist offers us not life, only tales.]

We could give many examples of the great quantity of affirmations from the Argentine writer that allude precisely to what Carlos Fuentes considers with respect to *Santa Evita.* Thus, for example, in a pithy essay of his, suggestively titled "Mito, historia y ficción: idas y vueltas" ["Myth, History and Fiction: Comings and Goings"], Tomás Eloy Martínez cites "historical" works by Carlo Ginzburg, Robert Darnton, and Phillippe Aries and other "fictional" ones by D. M. Thomas and Julian Barnes. He concludes that in these works "la ilusión lo envuelve todo y el hielo de los datos va formando un solo nudo con el sol de la narración" (Martínez, "Mito, historia y ficción," 109) [illusion envelops everything and the ice of the facts forms a single knot with the sun of the narration]. He then rhetorically asks:

¿Con qué argumentos negar a la novela, que es una forma no encubierta de ficción, su derecho a proponer también una versión propia de la verdad histórica? ¿Cómo no pensar que, por el camino de la ficción, de la mentira que osa decir su nombre, la historia podría ser contada de un modo también verdadero o, al menos, tan verdadero de los documentos?

(Martínez, "Mito, historia, ficción," 119)

[With what arguments can we deny a novel, which is an undisguised form of fiction, its right to also propose its own version of historical truth? How can we not think that, through the path of fiction, of the lie that dares to say its own name, history could be told in a way that is also true, at least, as true as in the way it is narrated in documents?]

With these queries he seems to be giving convincing answers upon questioning his teacher Barthes (Tomás Eloy Martinez effectively was the disciple of the French theorist and thinker):

La narración de los acontecimientos del pasado, que en nuestra cultura, desde los griegos en adelante, ha estado sujeta a la sanción de la "ciencia" histórica ligada al estándar subyacente de lo "real," y justificada por los principios de la exposición "racional," ¿difiere, en realidad, esta forma de narración, en algún rasgo específico, con alguna característica

indudablemente distintiva, de la narración imaginaria, como la que encontramos en la épica, la novela o el drama?

(Barthes, *El grado cero de la escritura*, 22)

[The narration of past events, which in our culture, since the Greeks on
forward, has been subjected to the sanction of historical "science," [is] connected to the underlying standard of the "real" and justified by principles of
"rational" exposition. Does this form of narration differ, in any specific characteristic, with any undoubtedly distinctive characteristic, from imaginary
narration, as we find it in the epic, the novel, or the drama?]

Barthes himself elsewhere points out that writing is also "un acto de soli-
daridad histórica" [an act of historical solidarity] meaning that one must
integrate the practice of language as a dichotomy and interaction between
text and historical context. This affirmation appears to gloss, amplify, and
make more profound that which Tomás Eloy Martínez maintained in his
recently cited essay:

La ficción y la historia se escriben para corregir el porvenir, para labrar el
cauce de río por el que navegará el porvenir, para situar el porvenir en el
lugar de los deseos. Pero tanto la historia como la ficción se construyen con
las respiraciones del pasado, reescriben un mundo que hemos perdido y, en
esas fuentes comunes en las que abrevan, en esos espejos donde ambas se
reflejan mutuamente, ya no hay casi fronteras: las diferencias entre ficción e
historia se han ido tornando cada vez más lábiles, menos claras.

(Martínez, "Mito, historia y ficción," 109)

[Fiction and history are written in order to correct the future, to carve out
the riverbed across which the future will navigate, in order to situate the
future in the place of desires. But history, as well as fiction, is constructed
with the breaths of the past, they re-inscribe a world we have lost, and in
these common fountains from which they drink, in those mirrors where
each are mutually reflected, there are hardly any boundaries; the differences
between history and fiction have become more flexible, less clear.]

In his book, *El sueño argentino*, Tomás Eloy Martínez provides us with the
fundamental clues we need to see how he deconstructs the myth of Evita in
his novel in order to later reconstruct it in another manner. He recognizes
that in the process of rereading undertaken by him in his own work (a process that included the reading of others: of critics of the novel, of historians
that considered it in their investigations on the character and her circumstances), he found clarity, clarity that was not so obvious in the moment
of writing the plot. *Santa Evita*'s plot, based on the mythic body of Eva
Perón, sketched another myth "el del cadáver nómade que de algún modo
simboliza la errancia de la Argentina" (Martinez, *El sueño argentino*, 347)

[that of the nomadic cadaver that in some way symbolizes the wandering of Argentina]. In other words, the embalmed body of Evita, in permanent and difficult displacement, is a sign whose presence evokes another reality suggested or represented by it. The myth of Eva Perón's wandering mummy evokes an Argentina in search of itself. Tomás Eloy Martínez wrote:

> Si Evita logró ser ella misma sólo desde que murió es porque esa muerte revela tanto su historia como la historia de la Argentina en los últimos cuarenta años. Fuimos como esa muerta, un país nómade, sin lugar, sin rumbo fijo: alguien que fue desaparecido, vejado, enterrado en el anonimato, sometido, oprimido, negado.
>
> (Martínez, *El sueño argentino*, 320–323)

> [If Evita managed to be herself only since she died it is because this death revealed not only her history but also the history of Argentina in the last forty years. We were like this dead woman, a nomadic country, without a place, without a fixed destination: someone who was disappeared, humiliated, buried anonymously, subjected, oppressed and denied.]

Saussure posits that there exists a certain analogy between a symbol and reality or a symbolized idea. The symbolizer (in this case, the wandering and mistreated body of Evita) and the symbolized (the Argentina that lost itself) present not only a *motivated relationship* (the cadaver converted into an ambulatory mummy suggests the analogy with the idea of a country with a feminine name, la Argentina, that is frozen in a moment of history, living a delirium of greatness that it already lost a long time ago), but also an *unnecessary relationship*[13] (Argentina exists and has its own "function" on the margin of the idea of its wandering in the sense that we are seeing).

Santa Evita gives us both the desire for abomination and destruction about which Borges, Cortázar, Onetti, Silvina Ocampo, and Martínez Estrada wrote as well as the desire for Evita's canonization, veneration, and eternal preservation that is reflected in the conduct of the shirtless ones who adored her, those who said mass and made pilgrimages for her health, those who proclaimed the 18th of October as Santa Evita day, and those who made Parliament designate her "Spiritual Chief of the Nation."

Tomás Eloy Martínez once said that the novelist tries to make the dead "remain detained in some gesture of eternity," which returns the bodies from history to reality ("a la frágil realidad de las ficciones" [to the fragile reality of fictions] converted into icons of culture, into another avatar of tradition. He added, however: "y, al hacerlo, muestra que el ícono es apenas una construcción, que las tradiciones son un tejido, un pedazo de tela, cuyos hilos cambian incesantemente la forma y el sentido del dibujo, tornándolo cada vez más fragmentario, más pasajero" (Martínez, "Evita, la construcción de un mito," 361–362) [and, upon doing so, it shows that the icon is hardly a construction, that the traditions are a fabric, a piece of material whose threads incessantly change, form, and alter the sense of the drawing, turning into something each time more fragmentary, more fleeting.]

This affirmation doesn't do anything but respect the multidimensionality, the semantic multivalence of the myth of Evita and her possible symbolic meaning. To the question, What does Tomás Eloy Martínez bring to this myth? (because there is no doubt that this myth exists), the author's answer is absolutely meritorious:

> *Santa Evita* procura ser el *inventario* [subrayo yo] de un mito argentino pero a la vez, de manera involuntaria, es también una confirmación y una ampliación de ese mito . . . . Las manos que mueven el telar de los mitos son ahora muchas y vienen de infinitas orillas, que ya ni siquiera es fácil distinguir dónde está el centro ni qué pertenece a quién. Así son las imágenes con las que el pasado reescribe, en las novelas, la historia del porvenir.
>
> (Martínez, "La construcción del mito," 361–362)

> [*Santa Evita* tries to be the *inventory* [my emphasis] of an Argentine myth but at the same time, in an involuntary manner, it is also the confirmation and amplification of this myth . . . The hands that move the loom of the myths are now many and come from infinite shores, so that it is no longer easy to distinguish where the center is or what belongs to whom. Such are the images with which the past rewrites, in the novels, the history of the future.]

Notes

1. Note that this translation and all others, unless otherwise indicated, are mine.
2. It seems pertinent to me to recognize here the wise idea of John S. Brushwood, which has not always been taken into account when dealing with not only the description but also the valuation and organization of the so-called new Spanish American narrative. Six years after Vargas Llosa's affirmations, the critic stated: "Although the terms *new Latin American novel* and the *boom* sometimes appear synonymous, they really indicate two different aspects of a single phenomenon—the maturity of fiction in Latin America" (1975, 211). Then he proposes to date the moment in which the continental narrative begins to reaffirm itself at the end of the decade of the 1940s. He also finds a change in valuation in the years following *Pedro Páramo*, when there is an unprecedented international interest in the Spanish American novelists of the 1960s, a time that produced a spectacular increment in the number of high-quality novels that would come to be known by the much debated term, *boom*. All of the authors mentioned by Ángel Rama in his book *La novela*

latinoamericana. Panoramas 1920–1980 [*The Latin American Novel: Panoramas 1920–1980*] are legitimate continuers of the boom as are those who in Mexico, Argentina, Chile, and other countries continue to offer works of undisputable value, recognized not only by cultured readers, but also by the mass public.

3. This project and its realization makes us see that *Santa Evita* approximates what Luiz Costa Lima calls "una narrativa concebida y creada, siempre, a partir del otro lado" [a narrative conceived and created always, from another side]. The Brazilian critic defines: "lo que llamamos narrativa a partir del otro lado significa que el autor simula hablar de los *percepta*, para en verdad, construir una narrativa toda ella concebida por la focalización desde lo imaginario. Ahora bien, por supuesto, es innecesario insistir que esta tematización no excluye la realidad material e histórica. Recusa, eso sí, la documentalidad" (Costa Lima, 179) [What we call narrative from another side means that the author simulates speaking of the *percept*s, in order to construct a narrative entirely conceived of by its focalization from the imaginary viewpoint. Of course, it is unnecessary to insist that this way of creating themes does not exclude material and historical reality. However, it does challenge documentation.]

4. On this topic read the essays "Ficción e historia en *La novela de Perón*" (1998), "Historia y ficción, dos paralelos que se tocan" (1996), and "Mito, historia y ficción: idas y vueltas" (1996) by Tomás Eloy Martínez.

5. The entire text is available on the webpage www.literatura.org/TEMartinez/Santa_Evita.html.

6. Exactly the same thing happens in other systems of representation of reality: myth, historiography to which Tomás Eloy Martínez has referred in various of his essays.

7. Tomás Eloy Martínez's work should be understood as a symbolic act directly focused toward "el gran discurso colectivo y de clases en el cual un texto es poco más que una *parole* individual o una *utterance*" (Jameson, 76–77) [the great collective discourse of classes in which a text is little more than an individual *parole* or an *utterance*].

8. See Mikhail Bakhtin's chapter on "The Problem of Discursive Genres," in *Estética de la creación verbal* [*The Aesthetics of Verbal Creation*].

9. Note that this translation is taken from the English translation by Asa Zatz.

10. This is a paratext from the edition of the novel published by Legasa in Buenos Aires in 1985.

11. Oswald Ducrot, *Dire et ne pas dire* (1972), and J. F. Lyotard, *Le différend* (1983). Each has examined in depth the function of presupposition—an idea proposed by Gottlob Frege—regarding speech.

12. See Víctor Bravo's discussion of lies, truth, and presuppositions in "La verdad, la mentira, y el poder creador del lenguaje."

13. See Ferdinand de Saussure, *Course in General Linguistics,* for a discussion of this conception of symbolization.

Works Cited

Bajtín, Mijail. *Estética de la creación verbal*. México: Siglo XXI Editores, 1998. Print.

Barthes, Roland, et al. *Análisis estructural del relato*. Buenos Aires: Edición Tiempo Contemporáneo, 1970. Print.

———. *El grado cero de la escritura*. Buenos Aires: Siglo XXI, 1973. Print.

Bravo, Víctor. "La verdad, la mentira, y el poder creador del lenguaje." *Ateneo de la Laguna* 5 http://www.ateneodelalaguna.es/pdf/ATENEO5/pdf/verdad.pdf. Web.

Brushwood, John S. *The Spanish American Novel: A 20th Century Survey*. Austin: University of Texas Press, 1975. Print.

Cancel, Mario. "Sobre la historia y la literatura: Una visión de conjunto en Ana Lydia Vega, Fernando Picó y Juan Gelpi," in *Historia y literatura*, Ed. A. Gaztambide, San Juan: Historias-Posdata, 1995. 39–60. Print.

Coddou, Marcelo and Ana Figueroa. " *El vuelo de la reina* o el viaje al otro lado del espejo. Entrevista a Tomás Eloy Martínez." *Alpha* 19 (2003): 339–350. Print.

Costa Lima, Luiz. *Sociedade e discurso ficcional*. Río de Janeiro: Editorial Guanabara, 1986. Print.

Foucault, Michel. *Las palabras y las cosas*. Mexico: Siglo XXI Editores, 1968. Print.

———. *El orden del discurso*. Barcelona: Tusquets, 1974. Print.

———. *La verdad y las formas jurídicas*. Mexico: Gedisa, 1983. Print.

Fuentes, Carlos. "Santa Evita," http://www.literatura.org/TEMartinez/cricf. html. Web.

González Bermejo, Ernesto. *Cosas de escritores*. Montevideo: Marcha, 1971. Print.

Genette, Gérard. *Figures I*. Paris: Editions de Seuil, 1987. Print.

Jameson, Fredric. *The Political Unconscious: Narrative as Socially Symbolic Act*. New York: Cornell University Press, 1981. Print.

Martínez, Tomás Eloy. *The Peron Novel*. Trans. Asa Zatz. New York: Pantheon, 1988. Print.

———. *La novela de Perón*. Barcelona: RBA Editores, 1993. Print.

———. "Argentina entre la historia y la ficción." *Página 12*, 5 de mayo de 1996a, 18–23. Print.

———. "Historia y ficción: Dos paralelos que se tocan," in *Literaturas del Río de La Plata hoy: De las utopías al desencanto*. Ed. K. Kohut. Frankfurt: Vervuert Verlag, 1996b. 90–100. Print.

———. "Mito, historia y ficción: idas y vueltas," in *Visiones cortazarianas. Historia, política y literatura hacia el fin del milenio*. Ed. Alejandra Mora. México: Aguilar, 1996c. 109–133. Print.

———. *Santa Evita*. Novela. 12th ed. Buenos Aires: Editorial Planeta, 1996d. Print.

———. "Ficción e historia en *La novela de Perón*." *Hispamérica* 17 (1998): 41–49. Print.

———. *El sueño argentino*. Barcelona: Editorial Planeta, 1999. Print.

———. "Ficción, historia, periodismo: límites y márgenes." (2004) http:// americat.net/docs/biblioteca/catedra/3%20catedra%20america%20mart. pdf. Web.

Martínez, Tomás Eloy. "Mito, historia y ficción: idas y vueltas," in *Visiones cortazarianas. Historia, política y literatura hacia el fin del milenio.* Ed. Alejandra Mora. México: Aguilar, 1996, 109-133.

———. "Evita o Madonna, whom will history remember?" *New Perspectives Quarterly*, vol. 14 (Winter 2007): 32–33. Print.

Mora, Miguel. "Entrevista: Tomás Eloy Martínez-Escritura," in *El País*, 8 de noviembre de 2002. http://elpais.com/tag/argentina/a/. Web.

Neyret, Juan Pablo. "Novela significa licencia para mentir. Entrevista con Tomás Eloy Martínez." *Espéculo. Revista de Estudios Literarios* 22 (2002): 18–26. http://www.ucm.es/info/especulo/. Web.

Rama, Angel. *La novela latinoamericana. Panoramas 1920–1980.* Bogotá: Colcultura, 1982. Print.

Russell, Bertrand. *Significado y verdad.* Barcelona: Ariel, 1983. Print.

Saussure, Ferdinand de. *Course in General Linguistics.* New York: McGraw Hill, 1959. Print.

Sebreli, Juan José. *Eva Perón, ¿aventurera o militante?* 4th ed. Buenos Aires: Editorial Pléyade, 1971. Print.

Vargas Llosa, Mario. "Novela primitiva y novela de creación en América Latina." *Revista de la Universidad de México* 23.10 (1969): 29–36. Print.

White, Hayden. *The Content of the Form: Narrative Discourse and Historical Presentation.* Baltimore: The Johns Hopkins University Press, 1987. Print.

7

Chaos and Simulations
of History in *Mujer en traje*
de batalla

Fátima R. Nogueira
Translated from Spanish by Bruce K. Fox

The novel *Mujer en traje de batalla* (2001) [*Woman in Battle Dress*], by Antonio Benítez Rojo, constructs a biographical fiction of Henriette Faber, one of the first female Swiss doctors, situating her within a broad Western historical and cultural context that moves between 1791 and 1870. This time period deals with the great historical events affecting Europe and echoing through Latin America: the Haitian and French Revolutions, the Napoleonic Wars, the experience of colonial Cuba, and the Renovation of Paris carried out by Haussmann under the reign of Napoleon III. These historical events have no chronological order. On the contrary, by means of a history with an uneven development, the recovery of historical memory is achieved through the recollection of the octogenarian Henriette Faber, who, in a desperate struggle against time, tries to write about the abominable imposition that the supposed necessity of history exerts on the individual.

The title of the novel, *Woman in Battle Dress,* refers to the transvestism of its protagonist, who was forced to disguise herself as a man in order to attend medical school. This transvestism, which prefigures the idea of illusion or masquerade, is a metaphor for the struggle between the ahistoric subject and a history anchored in cultural "truths," such as history's ethical value, that eventually will be revealed as simulacra produced by human invention. The novel exposes the invention of a metanarrative in which history, driven toward progress, functions as an instrument of the emancipation of the human spirit. In the novel, Faber reflects on the fallacy that History serves as an ethical lesson: "La campaña rusa de 1812 fue un hecho irreversible y ningún *si* de político o historiador jamás lo podrá remediar. Tampoco servirá de lección para que algo semejante no se repita en el futuro" (394) [The Russian campaign of 1812 was an irreversible fact and no *if*, from any politician or historian, could ever fix or prevent it. Nor will it serve as a lesson to avoid something similar happening again in the future.[1]]

The temporal extension of the novel induces a reflection about modernity, by focusing on the great epistemological discontinuity of Western culture achieved, according to Foucault, on the threshold of the nineteenth century. This era implied radical change in historical analysis, resulting in the emphasis on temporal continuity, the loss of the representative power of language, economic studies directed toward production, and biological research that privileged the organism (body).[2] Benítez Rojo's novel focuses on these transformations, achieving a critical analysis of history and its textual production, as well as of the Cuban historical and social anachronisms with regard to methods of sugar production and the transformation of the medical sciences. However, it should be taken into account that Benítez Rojo's work, published at the beginning of the twenty-first century, produces another series of historical anachronisms. These anachronisms are corroborated through the novel's theoretical references, emphasizing what could be interpreted as another epistemological discontinuity that happened in the second half of the twentieth century—the development of the Theory of Chaos,[3] which ended up spreading from the exact sciences to fields that comprise the humanities, including diverse artistic manifestations.

Benítez Rojo has proposed the Theory of Chaos as a productive rereading of Caribbean culture in the essay *The Repeating Island* (1989), conceptualizing the Caribbean as a meta-archipelago "that 'repeats' itself, unfolding and bifurcating until it reaches all the seas and landing of the earth" (3). He also emphasizes that the repetition in the discourse of chaos "is a practice that necessarily entails a difference and a step toward nothingness" (Benítez Rojo, *The Repeating Island*, 3). However, by supposing that the Theory of Chaos was applied by the Cuban writer based on the geometric fractal model—which makes possible the description of "regularidades dinámicas" [dynamic regularities]—Camayd-Freixas postulates that both the theory and the model represent systems that reflect human existence, posing a dialectic between the application of this theory in *The Repeating Island* and *Mujer en traje de batalla*. The critic describes the relationship between the essay and the novel in the following terms:

La novela como toda (meta)máquina opera en su cronología discontinua conforme a una secuencia de flujos e interrupciones. Así el flujo de la vida de Enriqueta lo interrumpen otros flujos, los de sus amores y amistades, de modo que cada parte es la misma, pero distinta. En cada etapa de su vida tiene que volver a encontrarse, a reinventarse. En definitiva Enriqueta es: la mujer que se repite.

(Benítez Rojo, *The Repeating Island*, 22)

[The novel like any (meta)machine operates in its discontinuous chronology in keeping with a sequence of flows and interruptions. So the flow of Henriette's life is interrupted by other flows, those of love affairs and friendships, so each part is the same, but distinct. In each step of her life she has to return to find herself, to reinvent herself. In short, Enriqueta is: the woman who repeats herself.]

It should be noted that the novel is composed of six parts, each named for the character whose encounter with the protagonist produces an important modification in her life. It is also important to note that throughout the story, Henriette assumes a set of identities in which the character adopts varied positions, and even different names, identifying herself as Henriette (or Enriqueta) Faber Cavent, Enrique Fuenmayor, and finally, Enrique Faber.

The novel *Mujer en traje de batalla* repeats and adopts the chaotic image of the universe produced in the essay *The Repeating Island,* transferring it to the construction of a personal life whose inscription is subjected by time to her intervening memory:[4]

Mis recuerdos están tan desparramados como los astros en el firmamento. Estrellas brillan aquí y allá en la oscuridad de mi memoria; puntos de luz que debo enlazar con trazos imaginarios para que dibujen constelaciones y así hasta darle por obra y gracia de las palabras una apariencia figurativa a mi pasado, a mi cielo, a mi existencia, que de otra manera, lejos de formar este ordenado relato que construyo con mi pluma, sería un caótico reguero de materia estelar. (265–266)

[My memories are so scattered like the stars in the firmament. Stars that shine here and there in the darkness of my memory; points of light that I should connect with imaginary lines so that they could draw constellations and thus give, by work and grace of words, a figurative appearance to my past, my sky, my existence, that in another manner, far from forming this ordered account that I construct with my pen, would be a chaotic trail of stellar material.]

Based on this image in which the memories of the protagonist and chaos are mixed, this study centers on two dimensions of Benítez Rojo's novel.

The first, of which the previous quotation is emblematic, is the perceived relationship between life and chaos, the relationship between personal existence and history. The second dimension involves theoretical positions that explore the intersections of art and chaos. I do not refer, therefore, to the relative theories of quantum physics—explored in the essay by Camayd-Freixas—but rather to some propositions of a philosophical nature. The first dimension of the novel engenders a particular conception of history related to life in which chance plays a preponderant role and which will be illustrated in terms of the application of the Theory of Chaos. The second dimension takes into account the ideas that Deleuze and Guattari developed in *What Is Philosophy?* and deals with the importance that transvestism acquires in the composition of the novel, relating equally to historical formations and the personal life of its protagonist. By applying these authors' theory of the rhizome, which implies a chaotic structure, I will show how the artistic composition of the novel is also "chaotic" in the sense of positing a multiplicity of identities, beginnings, and endings that branch out from the initial concept of transvestism.

The convergence of these two dimensions in the narrative development constructs a vision of life in which chance and the human condition are joined. A veiled fascism constitutes an outstanding feature both in individual lives and in historical formation. Another emphasized point in *Mujer en traje de batalla* is the tendency toward masquerading that commands not only social relationships but also the subject herself. This propensity for disguise provokes a reflection about the usefulness of mimicry, sometimes considering it as a means to guarantee biological or ideological survival, and other times as a principle that acts in the world of live beings, to which Caillois refers as the principle "of pure disguise," whose impulse is identified with "a leaning towards the act of passing oneself off as something or someone else" (75). The notorious side of this principle is to a certain extent made explicit in the work's title whose referent is a painting found by doctor Henriette of the Napoleonic army, which she carried with her until her expulsion from Cuba for the crimes for which she was convicted.

The painting represents a beautiful woman of the same age as the protagonist in combat uniform and functions as an allusion to two important themes in the novel. The first theme is the presence of a certain personification that links the painting to the young Faber, connoting her constant fight to affirm herself as a woman and a doctor. From there, it is perceived that the battle dress not only refers to the military gear but also to the transvestism assumed by the character until her withdrawal from the island. The second theme, equally related to transvestism, draws a correspondence between disguise and sexual drives because the painting functions as a point of convergence between Faber and other women with whom she maintains homosexual relationships. Nadezhda, the nurse who took care of the protagonist in the hospital when she was injured in the Russian campaign, physically looks like the woman portrayed in the painting. The novel also presents Fauriel, who acts like a double of the protagonist in several instances. One example of the mirage that unites the two characters refers to a game of a sexual nature that happened during a carnivalesque dance: "Al verme reflejada en su rostro enmascarado sentí llegar el temblor del orgasmo. Ella me miró. Por un instante fuimos una" (373) [Upon seeing myself reflected in her masked face, I felt the tremor of orgasm arrive. She looked at me. For an instant we were one.]. Although the painting in question only appears in the story beginning with the Russian campaign, it is spread throughout the entire novel since, to a certain extent, all of the female characters are obligated to wear a "battle dress" in some manner, transforming "la mujer del cuadro, [en] la Mujer, la suma de todas las mujeres" (462) [the woman in the painting (into) the Woman, the sum of all women].

It is worth noting that the mirage disseminated from the painting contributes to the transformation of Henriette (the woman who recurs, according to the interpretation of Camayd-Freixas) into the point of convergence for the representation of various fictitious female characters (such as Maryse, Fauriel, and Nadezhda, among others) as well as emblematic historical figures with whom the protagonist identifies, notably Sor Juana and Madame de Staël. The experiences of these two figures inspire Henriette's life. In the case of Sor Juana, the parallel is produced in a shared transvestism and integrated into the respective biographies of the Mexican writer and of the doctor. The reiterated allusions to the nun make it impossible not to perceive the connection between them when reading the protagonist's sensations as she disguises herself as a man in order to study medicine: "Fue algo así como meterme a monja" (290) [It was something like becoming a nun.]. To a certain extent, these sensations evoke Octavio Paz's interpretation of Sor Juana, centered on a supposed exchange between the disguises of man and nun. In the case of Sor Juana, her simultaneous rejection of marriage and desire for knowledge and education gave rise to a process of masculinization.[5] In turn, Benítez Rojo brings the lives of these two historical figures (Henriette Faber and Sor Juana) together because in distinct epochs, they were both obligated to resort to disguise in order to educate themselves. This need for disguise associates both women with the repressive social forces that tried to destroy them.

A more subtle point of the principle of disguise deals with its transposition to historical formation, on the one hand, and its adoption as a means of individual survival, on the other. In the first case, the characteristic tendency of history to appropriate situations of the past in order to validate ideologies of the present is denounced. The second case exposes Faber's individual struggle when sociocultural structures oblige her to disguise herself in order to attain a position that is traditionally denied to women. The evocation of an imaginary ludic impulse is situated between these two axes (historical formation and individual survival) and contributes to the transformation of the individual, according to the suit that she adopts: the role of Napoleon's hussars in the composition of the war machines; the transvestism of the central character, which many times goes beyond necessity; and, in the artistic sense, the metamorphosis of the actors of Maryse's nomadic variety theater.

This emphasis on disguise and repetition of historical situations leads to another chaotic conception of history with which truth value cannot be associated. In this conception, history develops erratically, following the footsteps of chance in order to begin again indefinitely, without apparent purpose. History follows a cosmological model that, by approximating chaos, permits the repetitions to multiply with infinitesimal differences mimicking the same process as generation of life. Clearly, we are faced with a supposition that would annul the idea of history as a succession of events linked together by an organizing principle, obeying the mechanism of intelligibility. This vision of history suggests a poetics of chaos that Benítez Rojo employs in his novel. This poetics endeavors to accomplish the impossible task of transforming the "stellar material" into an organized story, refuting both a chronological linearity and the transformation of history into metaphysics.[6]

The network of connections among history, art, and chaos operates on several fronts. The first is the constant questioning of the relationship between historiographic and literary discourse. The second is the existence of a plane of consistency oriented toward chaos and based on fortuitous encounters, which Deleuze conceptualizes as ethology, the study of relations of velocity among different bodies and their capacity for communication. In *A Thousand Plateaus*, Deleuze and Guattari refer to the plane of consistency as the disposition of forces among individuals in a chaotic universe. These forces are perceived according to the circumstances and the manner in which they are fulfilled in order to form power relations among different individuals.[7] The third front is the presence of a plane of composition that, upon being connected to the plane of consistency, proposes a rhizomatic text structured on the convergence of various lines into one point. The plane of composition indicates a union among diverse artistic forms.

The German philosopher Nietzsche had already noted a certain correspondence between history and chaos, spreading it throughout his work. In the essay *On the Use and Abuse of History for Life,* he exposes it clearly by questioning the status that history and science acquired in the time in which he lived, admonishing his contemporaries:

> Arrogant European of the nineteenth century, you are raving! Your knowledge does not complete nature, but only kills your own. For once just measure your height as a knower against your depth as a person who can do something. Of course, you clamber on the solar rays of knowledge upward towards heaven, but you also climb downward to chaos. Your way of going, that is, clambering about as a knower is your fate. The ground and floor move back away from you into the unknown; for your life there are no supports any more, but only spider's threads, which every new idea of your knowledge rips apart. (52)

Nietzsche concludes his essay by offering the ahistoric and the suprahistoric as antidotes to historical sickness. One antidote is based on the capacity of forgetting and the other on the ability to look toward that which confers upon existence an eternal and immutable character, as religion and art do (64–65). In other words, Nietzsche, by recognizing the suprahistoric as a form of organization of chaos, questions any study of history that separates itself from life, as well as from a superior vision or an artistic revelation.

Considering Nietzsche's philosophy makes sense in this study because, his association of history and art, as well as his demonstration of the relationship of both of these subjects with chaos, helps the reader to appreciate Benítez Rojo's poetics, an amalgam of the ahistoric and supra-historic, in which art becomes a privileged place from which to contemplate chaos.[8] Moreover, a complex relationship between historiography and literature insinuates itself at the convergence point between chaos, history, and art. Many times the roles of history and fiction are exchanged, given that, by virtue of its chronological axis, historiography assumes a fictitious character, hiding the phantom of its origin. The complexity of this relationship is due in great part to the ambiguity of historiographic discourse. Although this discourse is constructed upon the basis of a rational and logical content—the truth—it adopts the form of narration. Michel de Certeau notes the split that occurs between historical fact and event, since the latter is not related to signification, but rather to intelligibility, constituting a form of transformation of disorder into order or an imaginary support through chronological organization. However, the French thinker specifies that sometimes the event "is no more than a localization of disorder: in that instance [it] names what cannot be understood" (96).

This fissure, by revealing the instability of historiography, explains to a certain extent the philosophical attitude of postmodernity, which refuses, as Lyotard postulated, the metafictions of legitimization and the fable of origin that gave direction to modernity.[9] In this sense, by questioning the metaphysical category of the hidden truth in a primordial origin, postmodernity recognizes the coexistence of several possible and provisional truths, attributing to them equally the rule of constructed realities. These observations permit the revelation of one of the exponents of postmodernity found in *Mujer en traje de batalla,* since the reflections that Henriette Faber makes about the truth are not typical of the modern epoch in which the character lived, but rather the reflections acquire postmodern tones, thus creating a kind of anachronism, as seen in the following quotation: "en este mundo no hay verdades completas" (567) [in this world there are no complete truths]. The constant confrontation between historiographic text and fictitious creation is brought about by means of the reiterated interruptions of Henriette Faber's personal story in which Henriette, as the writer of her memories, reflects about writing and historiography. This again raises the question of the relationship between history, reality, and language. The character equally assumes a postmodern orientation by carrying out a questioning of the historical truth at the same time as she reflects on the methods and discursive forms shared by historiography and literary creation.

The digressions of the character about history and literature reveal their affinities with the theoretical post-structuralist framework, as well as with a late-nineteenth-century philosophical current that denounces the great imposture of history. I am referring specifically to some ideas developed by Nietzsche and Marx with respect to the French Revolution. The novel's affinities with post-structuralist theory can be illustrated following Foucault's tendency to relate the subject to history, emphasizing the position of the historical subject vis-á-vis the practices that historically constituted Western subjectivity. In this sense, it could be argued that the reflections about these discursive practices are aided by a game of changing identities described as the possibility of putting the same woman in a lot of situations. Clearly, the binding to post-structuralist thought is not limited to the philosophy of Foucault, even if one could easily track veiled references to the French philosopher concerning history, the history of medicine and of sexuality, the practices of vigilance and punishment in the segment about the protagonist's trial in Cuba, and the connection between the war and the plague in Haiti.

In addition to the post-structuralist aspect of Benítez Rojo's textual construction, the resonance of the ideas developed by Deleuze and Guattari can be seen in what they refer to as a rhizomatic structure of the literary text. The nexus where history, literature, and theory converge leads once again to the connection between *Mujer en traje de batalla* and postmodern literature, since it permits the verification of the link between the novel and a certain type of writing that Hutcheon identifies as historiographic metafiction, attributing to it a preponderant role in the formation of the postmodern novel.[10]

The plane of composition (union of diverse artistic forms) in the case of *Mujer en traje de batalla* is established in relation to a plane of consistency (disposition of forces among individuals in the chaotic universe). The plane of composition fictively represents the confluence of lives that come together and separate at random, but also annex the diverse arts, principally, painting, music, theater, and literature. In the aforementioned citation that brings the cosmos and personal life together, the association of the two planes can be observed, which confers upon them the possibility of ordering, to a certain extent, the chaos and entropy that rule all material composed of time: the universe, historical formation, and human life. In this way, writing history would presume to retake in a certain sense the ahistoric, resuscitating deceptive memories, by removing them from oblivion. Likewise, writing history would arrange a way to defeat death, recovering, therefore, the supra-historic, by making a life that is being extinguished persist, and communicating it with the future: "escribo para que todo eso perdure más allá de mis días, vuele como una luciérnaga sobre un mundo cuyos rasgos no puedo ni siguiera imaginar" (267) [I write so that all of this will last beyond my days, fly like a firefly above the world whose traits I cannot even imagine].

Benítez Rojo's novel is presented as a network in which reflections about discourse (historical and literary) and writing are superimposed upon the universe and its plane of consistency, which in turn is juxtaposed on to the production of the work. All of these aspects get mixed up in the development of the narration, thus making possible an opening toward the chaos that ties them together. It is unnecessary to reiterate that chaos should not be understood as a disorder, but rather as a random order that favors the happening of one possibility among so many other things that do not come to be or take place. Thus, a combination of the forces of the individual and those of nature is privileged in order to compose the intense and vast "world symphony."

Mujer en traje de batalla is a narration about accidental encounters with a rhizomatic structure reflected in its organization (the fictionalization of a historical character with a random selection of dramatized events, as well as the protagonist's encounters with characters that effectively change the direction of her personal history). Also, this rhizomatic structure is perceived in the unmasking of the irrationality that controls historical formation, which is equally subjected to random combinations. Such combinations might potentially generate either the composition of more elevated forces or the decomposition and destruction of an individual or a social body. Some historical episodes, such as the propagation of the plague and the genocide that took place in Haiti under the dictatorship of Rochambeau, exemplify this last perspective. Moreover, the association between history and chaos as the only viable explanation of the disastrous Russian campaign of 1812 also illustrates this idea. In the segment related to the Russian campaign, a series of fortuitous encounters is combined with different impulses such as hunger and nature. This composition of forces, tied to the necessity of moving in order to survive, summarizes the great lesson that Henriette Faber learns from the war: "Para sobrevivir era necesario caminar" (443–444) [In order to survive it was necessary to walk]. This is also the experience that will lead to the last lines of her writing: "esa pérdida incesante que cada día me deja al medio de las cosas, pero con la determinación de seguir" (692) [this incessant loss that each day leaves me in the middle of things, but with the determination to continue]. From these citations one thus concludes that assimilating, understanding, and accepting the chaos, from an existential perspective, leads to an essential valuation of life, even when death is recognized as the inevitable destiny.

The acceptance of loss as an intrinsic part of the generation of life is poetically incorporated into the text in the fragment that portrays an unusual dance on the occasion of the withdrawal of Napoleonic troops from Russia. This occurs during the military march, also known as "La coja," which accompanied the steps of the defeated and crippled soldiers. Two points stand out in the description of this march. The first is related to art's capacity to capture life contemplating death: "Fue marcha de vida y de muerte" (471) [It was a march of life and death.]. The second evokes the breakdown of the formidable Napoleonic war machine, setting itself against the description of the disciplined figure of Robert and the French emperor's hussars as an effective war machine. In such disintegration, what stands out is the de-romanticizing of death, faced plainly and therefore deprived of the fascination of heroic death longed for by Napoleon's hussars, who "vivían para la muerte, y era el encanto de la muerte lo que los definía" (102) [lived for death, and it was the spell of death that defined them]. In other words, the segment that closes the Russian campaign simultaneously portrays the contemplation and ordering of chaos, since the function of music and also of writing seems to be that of providing to the dead left along the road a burial grave and a tribute at the same time as survival is celebrated. In other words, a history ruled by life is created.

The counterpoint to this image is found in the description of the plague and the genocide that took place in Haiti under the tyranny of Rochambeau, which was enclosed in silence and concluded with Maryse's refusal to continue her narration. In the narration of the episode, the propagation of the plague and the sexual orgy are brought together, confirming, therefore, a cultural conjoining (promulgated in the nineteenth century) of madness, physical decomposition, and degeneracy:

> Pronto ya no hubo médicos que se ocuparon de los enfermos. La gente moría en la calle. Incluso en los banquetes y en los bailes. Centenares y centenares de cadáveres insepultos. Los echaban al mar, y volvían. Y, encima de todo eso, la putería . . . . Todos en cuero, bailando sobre las tripas y la mierda. Bailando la música de la muerte, cada uno intentando cubrir el miedo con la máscara de su propia y más secreta perversión. (248–249)

> [Soon there were no doctors to take care of the sick. The people were dying in the street. Even in the banquets and in the dances. Hundreds and hundreds of unburied cadavers. They threw them into the sea, and they returned. And, on top of it all, the whoring around . . . . Everyone naked, dancing on top of the bowels and shit. Dancing to the music of death, each one trying to cover the fear with the mask of his own and secret perversion.]

In *Discipline and Punish,* Foucault compares the model of the exclusion of leprosy victims with the disciplinary scheme of the plague. Foucault notes that each deals with different political ideals: "the first is that of a pure community, the second that of a disciplinary society" (198). In the case of the novel, both abstractions (incorruptibility and absolute discipline), whose potentiality depends on closed and meticulously ordered spaces, fall apart due to the incidence of the plague presented in the preceding quotation as a model of chaos, which, consequently, deteriorated regulatory forces in both political and medical fields. The political aspect deals, in this case, with the complete liberation from the evil illustrated by the tyranny of Rochambeau.

From the point of view of medical regulation, the eruption of chaos dissipates the protection that medical regulation offers against confusion, thus leading to the exhibition of unburied bodies whose return mixes life with death. Bodies and anonymous individuals appear and disappear or live and die in the most complete disorder. The vision of the plague as a real and imaginary figure of anarchy goes in two opposite directions in the episode of the incidence of the plague in Haiti. On the one hand, the image of the plague as a literary fiction is recovered, described by Foucault as the suspension of laws and prohibitions, the frenzy of time that passes, the lewd mixture of bodies, and the unmasking of individuals who reject an identity under which they were recognized, revealing a diverse truth.[11] On the other hand, the return of the repressed (supposing the rescue of dark forces that populated the human imagination through the times) erases the borders between corruption and decay of the flesh, liberating sexual fantasies in order to compose an unusual association of pleasure and pain.

In such a combination, the figures of madness, licentiousness, crime, and sickness mix and multiply. In other words, the return of the repressed (represented by monstrosity and scatology) reveals the complicity between desire and crime, tying together licentiousness and perversions with delinquency and madness. The closeness between the sexual and pathological camps reveals that the beast resides in the deepest point in human nature.[12] In this sense, the terror of the plague was not only restricted to contagion and physical putrefaction, but also reached the dissemination of an aberrant sexuality, conferring upon sex a frightful power, due to the ignorance of the forces behind its functioning.

The novel's mixture of the Foucauldian models of leprosy and the plague, with their political correlates of purity and discipline, expands the former to their maximum level by means of an excess that concludes with an explosion that annuls the aforementioned ideals of purity and discipline. In other words, the desire for order, brought to its limits, culminates, on the one hand, in the apocalyptic vision in which the union between war and plague prefigures the end of time. On the other hand, this desire degenerates into genocide due to the necessity to purify the species and to separate the races, thus exercising control over the phenomena that reach the population. It is worth noting that the experiences with race, as well as the means to exterminate the blacks, occupy a great part of the second section of *Mujer en traje de batalla,* beginning with the experiences of Despaigne in *La Gloire* (an immense sugar plantation in Haiti) in order to "purify" the race and concluding with the tyranny of Rochambeau.

In reality, the episodes of the Russian campaign and of Rochambeau's tyranny deal with the proximity of the historical events to chaos, obtaining diametrically opposed results. In the episode of the Russian campaign, death is tamed, offering to the corpses a burial that allows historiography, together with art, to fulfill its role of organizing the chaos. In the second episode about Rochambeau's tyranny, chaos dominates, making it impossible for the narration to unite the figures of madness and death, presented in their macabre dance in which their horrible specter incessantly returns. The suspension of discourse, in this sense, does not simply represent the nothingness of death, but rather is a reminder that death contaminates life, making it lack any meaning, and connecting, therefore, death, life, and madness. The final result of this macabre dance, foreseen by Foucault in *History of Madness,* culminates in the revelation of life as a mask that hides the skeleton of death beneath the flesh: "The carnival mask and the cadaver share the same fixed smile. But the laugh of madness is an anticipation of the rictus grin of death, and the fool, that harbinger of the macabre, draws death's sting" (15).

Returning to the plane of consistency and the existence of encounters that liberate creative energies, it should be noted that one of the most significant examples in *Mujer en traje de batalla* is found in the association between Henriette and Maryse that overcomes the divisions of visible gender. Gender is seen from a critical perspective, as a sociocultural operation, historically constructed, in which the roles corresponding to each sex are arbitrarily distributed. As Henriette and Maryse become conscious of this absurd division, they imagine a utopian country where women and men are treated alike. This game is what, to a certain extent, motivates the protagonist to disguise herself as a man in order to study medicine, inspired by Leonore de Fidelio. This episode shows that although, on the one hand, social forces weaken women, on the other, this fact does not impede bodies and minds from uniting to compose greater forces. In this case, the encounter between Henriette and Maryse is revealed as a productive alliance, making possible the admission of the protagonist to the university, since it will be Maryse who, from Cuba, sends Henriette the false identification of Enrique Fuenmayor. These fruitful meetings are those that bring happiness, which, in the case of Henriette, is summarized in the joy of "romper con ese falso sentido de seguridad que nos da el orden cotidiano" (291) [breaking with this false sense of security that daily order gives us] and launches her in the direction of the unknown.

Another important point for this study is that the indetermination of the beginning and end of the novel, as well as the crossed flow of the diverse lives of its characters, approaches Deleuze and Guattari's rhizomatic model. Their model is opposed to the arborescent paradigm of Western thought, given that it rests on concepts of cartography, unusual connections, a-signifying ruptures, heterogeneity, multiplicity, lines of territorialization, deterritorialization, and reterritorialization. This model's plane of consistency connects to the Deleuzian concept of ethology, which permits a circulation of intensities, velocities, and states in which beginning and end are unimportant, and only chaotic evolution matters. In this manner, the model of a monumentalized history is rejected, since such a concept, at heart, is lacking in humanistic principles. The middle point is essential to the rhizomatic model because it is at this point that its lines acquire speed and can continually connect among themselves. It is important to note that the middle point should not be confused with a central axis, given that this system does not have a center or signification, and is equally associated with the natural and the artificial.[13] This last connection permits a correspondence between rhizome and book, since in Deleuze and Guattari's model, the book and the world compose a rhizome with the latter's characteristic capacity for reterritorializing and deterritorializing.

The rhizomatic model is important for this study, not only because it refers to the flows of lives that cross in *Mujer en traje de batalla* or the narrative's tendency to be disconnected from a beginning or an end, but also because in another of the novel's anachronisms, Henriette associates her writing with a rhizomatic text, relating book and life: "[El poder generativo de la vida] construye los relatos verdaderos, los relatos rizomas, donde el que escribe un silencio o una acción siempre está en el medio de las cosas" (625–626) [(The generative power of life) constructs the true stories, the rhizomatic stories, where he who writes a silence or an action is always in the middle of things].

The poetic incorporation of the rhizomatic model to the text concedes importance to the middle, to movement, to a creative plane of composition in which a story joins with others intertextually, connecting itself equally to a plane of consistency that captures the movement of life; confirms the composition of the rhizome book-world; as well as deterritorializes the story in the universe. Inevitably, this direction leads the writing to an encounter with chaos that is extricated from the cosmos, to an (ex)centric order, to a non-genealogy and non-signification associated with the rhizomatic process. It is both a reflection about the inevitable nature of existence and a critique of the supposed constructions of the order(ing) of history that deep down obey chaos.

The association between writing and chaos likewise explains another ambition of the novel, related to Deleuze and Guattari's assertion about books: "the ideal for a book would be to lay everything out in a plane of exteriority, on a single page, the same sheet: lived events, historical determination, concepts, individuals, groups, social formations" (*A Thousand Plateaus,* 9). This ideal is fulfilled only in a composition plotted on this plane of exteriority with its relationships of forces, flows, and intensities. It is a plane in which chance carries out a preponderant role, capable of changing both personal lives and historical and social formations according to the cosmological model. It is a matter of chain reactions outside of or beyond reason or a cause-and-effect relationship. With its web of unusual connections, open cartographies, and constant ruptures crossed by lines of flight, Benítez Rojo's story explains its process of gestation in its metaliterary reflections, even alluding to the idea that a rhizome, by possessing neither beginning nor end, can connect its lines at any point. Such a tendency is observed when Henriette comments on the notes written in the *Collector* as the only spontaneous lines of her memories because of her insistence upon following the novel's protagonist in her nomadism. Henriette confesses that the point of her connection to the novel will be decided subsequently. These transformed lines in the prologue of the novel are not important so much for their location in the text, but rather for their germinating capacity or their rhizomatic tendency of being incorporated into a text in constant metamorphosis, initially taking on the form of a letter, later that of an autobiography, and, finally, that of a novel. This structure consequently refutes the illusion of a history that guides a civilizing occurrence.

The metamorphic aspect of the text deepens the perspective of the transvestism of the writing, which goes beyond any generic character that writing might acquire, given that its task of fixing memory in words displays its own traps. Writing centers on the fact that its potentiality for catching a glimpse of chaos confronts it with its own limits. This transvestism principally acts in three directions related to the potential dissimulation of writing. The first direction concerns the potentiality for diluting concepts, like that of identity and subjectivity, given that writing transforms the "I" into the "other": "¿Seré yo la Henriette que va emergiendo del tintero?" (265) [Will it be me, Henriette, who gradually emerges from the inkwell?]. The second is related to writing's capacity to situate itself among memory and forgetting, as well as among words and silence, organizing, suppressing, removing, and selecting certain events and characters to the detriment of others; in short, writing masquerades in order to please: "todo es lograr la justa inclinación, aunque en el fondo da lo mismo, saltimbanquis de papel, o mejor, complacientes prostitutas a diez francos la leída" (211) [everything is to achieve the precise inclination, although at heart it's all the same, paper acrobats or better yet, prostitutes who aim to please for 10 francs per go]. The third direction, still connected to disguise, refers to the destructive dimension of a writing that conceals death under the appearance of life. Clearly, this third face of writing relates it to time: "¡cuánto por decir y se me acaban los días! mi relato no son estas páginas que lees sino aquello que en mi carne ha escrito el tiempo, escritura que ni siquiera yo misma puedo sacar a flote" (625) [so much more to say and my days are running out! My story is not these pages that you read, but rather that which time has written in my flesh, writing that even I can't keep afloat].

Another aspect of transvestism that is raised in the text concerns the dissimulating capacity of history mentioned by Marx in his essay "The Eighteenth Brumaire of Louis Bonaparte," which was indirectly alluded to in Maryse's observations upon being informed of Napoleon's coup d'état and of his later self-proclamation to first consul of the French government. Marx reflects in his essay about history, reaffirming that historical events and characters are repeated twice, the first as a tragedy, and the second as a farce: "the Revolution of 1789 to 1814 draped itself alternately as the

Roman republic and the Roman empire, and the Revolution of 1848 knew nothing better to do than to parody, now 1789, now the revolutionary tradition of 1793 to 1795" (329).

Nietzsche, in turn, confers upon the French Revolution the same farcical character, diverting it toward a special type of parody in which the bourgeoisie imitates the nobles. For the aforementioned philosopher, the recovery of Roman antiquity fails because it was guided by resentment:

> The French Revolution: the last political nobility in Europe, collapsed under the instincts of popular *ressentiment*. Admittedly, the most monstrous and unexpected thing happened in the middle of all this: the ideal of the ancients itself emerged in *flesh and blood* and with unheard-of splendour before the eyes and conscience of mankind.
>
> (*On the Genealogy of Morals*, 36)

The Nietzschean idea of resentment, tied to the slave's morale, functions as a motor force for some collective actions in several parts of the novel related to the trial of Henriette in Cuba. In these parts, the character is subjected to ridicule and violence in the town, serving as a kind of scapegoat responsible for individual frustrations in a society tied to false moralism.

The constant reference to art, principally to theater and literature, complements the different meaning that transvestism acquires in the text, by opposing it to the traditional sense of history as superfluous buffoonery, involving a repetition that is based on the return to the similar, presented as a backward movement. Clearly, historical agents, by identifying with figures from the past in order to create something new, are presented as actors in a scene. However, according to Deleuze in *Difference and Repetition* (90–93), it is not events, but rather historical conditions, that are repeated and permit the new to be created. In this way, repetition is only realized as comic transvestism when the past crystallizes, impeding the possibility of transformation of the present, which is ultimately inspired by a tragic and creative repetition. The French philosopher, referring to Marx, comments that the temporal order of "Décimo-octavo brumario" [Eighteenth Brumaire] (first tragedy, then farce) is justified only when the abstract independence of these two moments is based on the separation of the genres. Thus, the comic follows the tragic due to a creative failure, impeding a metamorphosis. What interests me about this point is Deleuze's perspective in which these two moments do not separate, coexisting in order to give the appearance of a third temporal instance. This third instance, the eternal return, promotes that which is completely new, incorporates a dramatic repetition, sketches future scenarios, and does not depend on historical subjects.[14]

In this line of Deleuzian thought, the present can be metamorphosed only through the aid of a future repetition, brought about by a temporal synthesis in which past and present are nothing more than future dimensions. This temporal synthesis, based to a certain extent on a drama without heroes, would be possible only if history, imbued with an artistic sensibility, could achieve the capability of conjuring the dead to create a space of life. It is possible that the greatest ambition of the writing of *Mujer en traje de batalla* is to achieve this temporal synthesis, imbuing it with an artistic sensibility. With this purpose, the idea of origin is played with, displacing the beginning of the story and dispersing the time of the writing. Such displacement consists of a transfer of the origin, and consequently of a temporal opening, in which in place of a point of origin of the narrated story, various beginnings are offered. In this way, the novel can begin in the prologue with Henriette's boarding the schooner that brings her to New Orleans. This beginning therefore coincides with the end of the story. The novel also can start in the year 1805, chosen by the protagonist to begin her memoirs, or with a hypothetical present identified with the time of the writing that unfolds, referring sometimes to New York at the end of the nineteenth century, and at other times to a contemporary present of the production of *Mujer en traje de batalla,* that is, to the beginning of the twenty-first century. Neither the individual nor history concurs in this vision as subjects of an order, a statute, a principle, or a foundation, but rather as utopias.

In this way, the displacement of a supposed present of the narration toward the future (that replaces it) is achieved, by, on the one hand, Henriette's reference to possible readers, exemplified by the following quote: "Tú que me lees, si puedes viajar a través del tiempo no dejes de visitar el Prater de mi juventud" (95) [You who read me, if you can travel through time be sure to visit the Prater of my youth]. On the other hand, by giving complexity to this temporal displacement, Henriette bifurcates it, creating another insinuating textual present in which the time of the writing of *Mujer en traje de batalla* is presented as a re-writing of Henriette Faber's memoirs: "[quizá] un novelista que aun está por nacer descubra tus memorias y te reconstruya como heroína" (290) [(perhaps) a novelist yet to be born will discover your memoirs and reconstruct you as a heroine]. As can be seen, a distant past and a remote future meet in the text, mediated by an uncertain present. This present functions like the temporality of a constantly interrupted writing that advances and recedes in time. Moreover, the novel does not end: "sé que no tengo fuerzas para continuar, aún cuando me fuera posible alumbrar con la pluma mucho de lo que he vivido, habría que concluir que mi relato también acabaría en un final tentativo, necesariamente abierto" (691–692) [I know that I do not have the strength to continue, even if it were possible for me to shed light on more of what I have lived with my pen, I would have to conclude that my story would also finish off in a tentative, necessarily open ending.].

Another possibility for masking history with an artistic sensibility relates to the manipulation of the novel's varied aesthetic expressions. In this sense, a creative transvestism is revealed and celebrated, not only in the reference to diverse plays and operas whose plots likewise center on disguise, but also in the novel's title. The novel thus breaks with chronology and juxtaposes spaces, tying together the personal and universal histories under a common denominator. This common denominator is a writing whose fundamental role consists of demonstrating the failure of an attempt at organizing chaos, which would suppose, certainly, the acceptance of a linear, ordered, and productive history. In the novel, one of the most successful examples of the dilution of time and space can be observed in the description of Café Procope, located on the street with the *Comédie Ancienne*. There, several periods from 1550 until 1806 are mixed together, composing the history of France (with an emphasis on the French Revolution) starting with some houses on the street and different cafés replacing one another. Thus, actors, playwrights, painters, sculptors, art critics, journalists, philosophers, writers, revolutionaries, and the upwardly mobile bourgeoisie successively file by this street. Fictitious and historical characters and spaces in Europe and America are mixed together by means of the association of Despaigne—the fictitious character who has positivist experiences related to "scientific racism" in Haiti—with Marat. Similarly, the historic and the ahistoric fuse, since anonymous characters also circulate in the café, as well as in the houses on the street that lacks official history. The description concludes with an eloquent image that associates history, violence, and chaos, letting us know that Dr. Guillotine lived in one of the houses.

In *Mujer en traje de batalla,* the two lines that I am following on their plane of composition—the plane of consistency dominated by an ethology and the preeminence of transvestism on the personal and historical level—converge in an implicit feminism in the novel's concluding narration of the protagonist's trial in Cuba. This implicit feminism is spread throughout the novel, as demonstrated by some scenes that are discussed in this study. Benítez Rojo's novel opens a privileged space for some women who stood out throughout history, like Sor Juana and Staël. He also creates memorable female characters, such as Henriette Faber, a fictionalized historical character, and Maryse, a fictitious character who acquires a leading role in the novel, acting like a kind of mother, older sister, and counselor to Henriette. It would be impossible to not give due consideration to the emphasis that the author bestows on the female characters.

As for the two dimensions examined in this work and their relationship with feminism, it should be emphasized that the first of these—transvestism—is justified as a way to confront the social injustices committed against women throughout history. Likewise, cross-dressing, in all of the instances in which the term is attached to women's condition, signifies wearing the "battle dress" in order to fight against these injustices. This is why the painting for which the novel is named is presented as the sum of all women. Moreover, with regard to the Deleuzian concept of ethology that is sustained on the plane of consistency, elaborated by the French philosopher with strong connections to the philosophy of Spinoza, it is worth stressing the utility of this concept for considering problems posed by feminist theory. Now and in recent times, Spinoza's philosophy of immanence has been studied by some theoreticians of feminism who recognize in it a way to more productively approach the dichotomy established between biological sex and the sociocultural construction of gender. In other words, thinking of the difference between the genders in consonance with a plane of bodies in movement that are mutually affected allows us to understand the division of genders not as a preexisting and immutable biological condition, but rather as a social construction, based on a power relationship. In this sense, in *Part of Nature* (160–168), Lloyd points out that focusing on a relationship between the development of the individual power of the bodies and social corporations to which these bodies belong permits a reconsideration of gender differences and helps us see that they depend on a social distribution of power. They are therefore able to transform themselves according to the socio-historical times and contexts that maximize or diminish them. In this way, there always exists the possibility to transcend these differences. One thus understands the emphasis that the author of *Mujer en traje de batalla* confers upon certain female characters who were able to excel, fighting against unfavorable conditions.

The critical vision of history observed throughout Benítez Rojo's novel is transposed to current times, since, by fabricating a life for Henriette Faber, the reader is led to reflect on reality, to consider problems that seem to endure through time, such as the condition of women and the historical tendency toward fascist formations. By projecting life, history, and writing onto the image of the universe, a poetics of chaos is implied within the narration. This poetics, removed from any sentimental inclination, seeks to achieve the ideal of the rhizomatic text, composing a nexus in which the sensations provoked by lived events come together and meet, as do the repercussions of certain historical and cultural determinations. In this sense, Benítez Rojo's story does not specifically deal with France's history, nor with that of the Caribbean, although it has them as its background, since transposing the poetics of chaos to history does not consist of relating events that are supposedly linked together, but rather of contemplating, like the angel in the story of Benjamin: "one single catastrophe which keeps piling wreckage upon wreckage and hurls it in front of his feet" (257).

In this way, the reader observes that the experience related by the characters in *Mujer en traje de batalla* consists of visualizing the chaos inserted in history, as can be verified in the episodes of the withdrawal from Russia or the tyranny of Rochambeau, narrated by Henriette and Maryse, respectively, and by reiterating the idea that history does not progress. The importance that these episodes obtain in the making of the novel is not related to the act of enumerating a legion of deaths, but rather to putting a special emphasis on the capacity that these women had to contemplate chaos and return to life. Perhaps this return was made possible only insofar as these characters have a strong connection to art, possessing, therefore, a talent for keen perception. It should be equally noted that Benítez Rojo explores the ambiguity inherent in the proximity of historiography and literature, profoundly investigating certain historical formations of the nineteenth century in order to fictionalize them and thus create a special relationship between literary and historiographic discourses. Literature operates as an element that generates discontinuities and interruptions in history, destabilizing and corroding it, since both are on the same level as producers of reality. The critical vision of history coincides with a poetics of chaos that deals with the celebration of life, of nomadism, and of metamorphosis in the description of systems of open chains that are permanently moving and proliferating in diverse spaces.

Notes

1. Unless otherwise noted, all translations were done by Bruce Fox.
2. Regarding this discontinuity, consult the introduction to *The Order of Things* (xxiii).
3. According to Stephen Kellert, Theory of Chaos originated in mathematics as a way of studying dynamic systems whose sensitivity to small differences caused very different outcomes, thus destroying the idea of predictability (32).
4. The visual image of the Caribbean as meta-archipelago is transcribed in *The Repeating Island* thus: "the spiral chaos of the Milky Way, the unpredictable flux of transformative plasma that spins calmly in our globe's firmament, that sketches in another shape that keeps changing, with some objects born to light while others disappear into the womb of darkness, change, transit, return, fluxes of sidereal matter"(4).
5. For Octavio Paz, the rejection of matrimony and love, in favor of knowledge, are determining causes of Sor Juana's decision to embrace monastic life and triggers her process of masculinization: "para saber hay que ser hombre o parecerlo. La idea de disfrazarse de hombre, cortarse el pelo y, en fin, neutralizar su sexualidad bajo el hábito monjil son traducciones de su deseo"

(159) [to know, one has to be a man or seem like one. The idea of disguising herself as a man, cutting her hair and, in the end, neutralizing her sexuality under the nun's habit are translations of her desire].

6. The concept of history as metaphysical is connected, according to Derrida, not only to linearity, but to a more broad schema in which an entire system of varying implications meet, among them teleology, scatology, accumulation of sense, tradition, truth, and so on. For more information about this topic, consult *Positions* (48–60).

7. Regarding the Deleuzian concept of ethology, consult *Spinoza Practical Philosophy* (124–126).

8. In *What Is Philosophy?* Deleuze and Guattari see philosophy, science, and art as a means to organize and confront chaos, specifying that "chaos has three daughters, depending on the plane that cuts through it: these are Chaoids as form of thought or creation" (208).

9. In *The Postmodern Condition,* Lyotard refers to two narratives of legitimization of knowledge: one is a politics that emphasizes humanity as hero of liberty, while another refers to the philosophical ideas of German idealism. We all know the importance that history acquired in this philosophical current. The thesis of the French researcher is that postmodern society distrusts these narratives: "In contemporary society and culture the grand narrative has lost its credibility, regardless of what mode of unification it uses, regardless of whether it is a speculative narrative or a narrative of emancipation" (37).

10. In *A Poetics of Postmodernism,* Hutcheon considers the problematizing of history as a primordial element of the postmodern novel, generating the concept of historiographical metafiction. The researcher develops this concept in Chapter 7, pages 105–123.

11. For more about this topic, consult *Discipline and Punish,* pages 196–198.

12. For more information about this theme, consult *History of Sexuality I,* pages 36–49.

13. Clearly, all of the concepts related to Deleuze and Guattari's rhizomatic model cannot be explained in this work, which is the reason I limit myself to citing them. For a complete understanding of these concepts, consult the introduction to *A Thousand Plateaus* (3–25).

14. These ideas explain my interpretation of Deleuze's theory, and are therefore subject to errors and oversimplifications.

Works Cited

Benítez Rojo, Antonio. *The Repeating Island: The Caribbean and the Postmodern Perspective.* Trans. James. E. Maranise. Durham, London: Duke University Press, 1996. Print.

———. *Mujer en traje de batalla.* Madrid: Santillana Ediciones Generales, 2005. Print.

Benjamin, Walter. *Illuminations.* Trans. Harry Zohn. New York: Schocken Books, 1968.

Caillois, Roger. *The Mask of Medusa.* Trans. George Ordish. New York: Clarkson N. Potter, Inc., 1964. Print.

Camayd-Freixas, Eric. "El fractal de Mandelbrot. Del travestismo al caos: Fuentes del nuevo realismo aleatorio de Antonio Benítez Rojo." *Caribe: revista de cultura y literatura* 10.1 (2007): 7–48. Print.

Certeau, Michel de. *The Writing of History.* Trans. Tom Conley. New York: Columbia University Press, 1988. Print.

Deleuze, Gilles. *Spinoza: Practical Philosophy.* Trans. Robert Hurley. San Francisco: City Lights Books, 1988. Print.

———. *Difference and Repetition.* New York: Columbia University Press, 1994. Print.

Deleuze, Gilles and Félix Guattari. *What Is Philosophy?* Trans. Hugh Tomlinson and Graham Burchell. New York: Columbia University Press, 1994. Print.

———. *A Thousand Plateaus: Capitalism and Schizophrenia.* Trans. Brian Massumi. Minneapolis: University of Minnesota Press, 1987. Print.

Derrida, Jacques. *Positions.* Trans. Alan Bass. Chicago, London: The University of Chicago Press, 1981. Print.

Foucault, Michel. *The Order of Things: An Archaeology of the Human Sciences.* New York: Pantheon Books, 1971. Print.

———. *Discipline and Punish: The Birth of the Prison.* New York: Pantheon Books, 1977. Print.

———. *The History of Sexuality.* Trans. Robert Hurley. New York: Vintage Books, 1988. Print.

———. *History of Madness.* Trans. Jean Khalfa. London: Routledge, 2006. Print.

Hutcheon, Linda. *A Poetics of Postmodern: History, Theory, Fiction.* London, New York: Routledge, 1988. Print.

Kellert, Stephen H. *In the Wake of Chaos: Unpredictable Order in Dynamical Systems.* Chicago: University of Chicago Press, 1993. Print.

Lloyd, Genevieve. *Part of Nature. Self-Knowledge in Spinoza's Ethics.* Ithaca: Cornell University Press, 1994. Print.

Lyotard, Jean-François. *The Postmodern Condition: A Report of Knowledge.* Trans. Geoff Bennington and Brian Massumi. Minneapolis: University of Minnesota Press, 1984. Print.

Marx, Karl. *Karl Marx: Selected Writings.* Ed. David McLellan. Oxford, New York: Oxford University Press, 2000. Print.

Nietszche, Friedrich W. *On the Use and Abuse of History for Life.* Trans. Ian Johnston. Arlington, Virginia: Richer Resources Publications, 2010. Print.

———. *On the Genealogy of Morals.* Trans. Walter A. Kaufmann. New York: Vintage Books, 1967. Print.

Paz, Octavio. *Sor Juana Inés de la Cruz o Las trampas de la fe.* México: Fondo de Cultura Económica, 1995. Print.

8

The Plural History of Memory: A Polyphonic Novel by Ángela Hernández

Ester Gimbernat González
Translated from Spanish by Javier F. González

Fibras (181) [Fibers][1]

The possibilities offered by the historical novel as a means of highlighting complex and multiple identities, situations, inquests, and injustice have been used to great effect by women writers in recent times. As de Groot explains, the virtue of the historical novel is that it enforces on the reader a sense of historicized "difference," and it is a mode that has an effect on the normative experience of the everyday and the contemporary world (4). There are numerous recent studies that analyze the evolution of historical novels written by women. These studies have shown the gradual shift of how this sub-genre[2] is assessed critically and why these novels have been such a success for the publishers. These writers of historical novels have been offered a context so that their historical settings are focused directly or indirectly on

> a female consciousness and explore female fears and desires. Perhaps even more important for women writers has been the way that the historical novel has allowed them to invent or "re-imagine" (to borrow Linda Anderson's term [1990, 129], the unrecorded lives of marginalised and subordinated people, especially women, but also the working classes, [...] the lives of the conquered, the victimised and the marginalised, those left out of traditional histories written by the (male) victors.
>
> (Wallace, 2)

It is common to note that in all official historical discourse, there has been a tendency (1) to not fully represent the active role and participation of women; (2) to diminish the degree of importance of their past actions; and (3) at times simply, to leave them out altogether by selecting a set of facts that favor certain points of view or ideologies that do not take them into consideration. Linda Anderson has noted: "women cannot simply be added on to history—expanding the boundaries of historical knowledge empirically—without putting under pressure the conceptual limits that excluded them in the first place" (130). However, the historical novel as a genre offers a varied set of possibilities for an unexpected model of female agency, because writing such novels also allows the female writers to imagine and reconstruct a history that retrieves a matrilineal genealogy, which has been erased from history.

"Franquicias en lo abierto" (290) ["Franchise in the Open"]

Ángela Hernández's 2003 novel *Charamicos* [*Fine Kindling Wood*][3] has been studied and referred to as a historical novel, *bildungsroman,* a testimonial novel, and a novel of "uprising," among other genres.[4] The complexity of the historical plot, in addition to the narrative composition focused through the lens of gender, allows for multiple readings and interpretations. For a reader unfamiliar with the peculiar circumstances of Dominican history, reading *Charamicos* is a different experience than that of the reader with the knowledge of historical facts and the subtleties conveyed by national myths.[5] The knowledgeable reader is able, in turn, to discern which historical figures are represented by the fictional names. For the outsider, because there are no historical guidelines to latch onto, the reading of the novel turns into an exploration of hazy, unknown territory. Such a challenge opens the possibility of studying it like a cultural memory, which in a certain sense draws upon the history on which it is constructed, but widens its scope by suggesting new perspectives and historical consequences.

When a novel focuses on memory, as Huyssen makes clear, it can also mean "the strengthening and expansion of the public spheres of civil society" (36). In its recounting, a cultural memory functions as a counter-narrative to the officially sanctioned accounts. This occurs because these texts can be circulated in a public sphere, expressing collective suffering and achievement, as well as allowing for the public to take stock of lesser-known events. As Victoria Hesford has observed, as counter-narrative, cultural memory is a turn toward the past that acts as a disruption rather than as a repetition, and the present becomes something that has to be articulated in relation to the past and not just assumed as its (inevitable) outcome. Deploying cultural memories as counter-narratives, then, can also be about enacting the future, a practice that is dependent upon reaching out to others (the dead, the not-yet-born, the forgotten, the suffering), and acknowledging our interdependence with them. To be affected by others, to remember them, and to reach out to them is to open up conditions of possibility in the present for a different future (7).

In presenting the cultural memory in a fictionalized manner, there is an intention of representing a present that is linked to a past whose latency is still relevant, as opposed to an assumed past that has led to inevitable results. The cultural memory can function as diverse replicas of the past. However, like with all echoes from the past, these replicas are filled with indeterminacies that leave gaps through which facts and meaning are lost. Whatever clarity is gleaned from the events enters the realm of conjecture. Thanks to these gaps, which are by no means empty, the path between different points in time, as well as past and present meanings referring to such events, is enriched.

Recent comments made by Ángela Hernández in an unpublished interview have convinced and motivated me to focus my analysis on this type of cultural memory. She said that she relishes the uncertain atmosphere of the time: chimerical, hard, framed by illusion, naive, cruel, mean-spirited, and fleeting are all terms that define those years. Pragmatism, orthodoxy, ambiguity, polarity, being spellbound, global knowledge, peculiar misinformation, secret trends, and clandestine work characterized the era. All of these elements were mixed together to create something elusive to historians, which literature eventually succeeds in translating to some degree.

This comment, like many other declarations made by the author in referring to this novel, stresses the importance of an era and the effect of having multiple voices in its textual reconstruction. In this sense, the multiple voices imply a fragmentation that blurs the singular vision of history, composed of exact and congruent facts and occurrences. The novel's text has a primary basic goal, as Quiroz said, to recognize the youth who fought the twelve years of Balaguer; it does not matter if they were wrong or not. There was a vibrant, participating youth, a generation that was stranded along the way, and perhaps that explains the title of the novel, *Charamicos*,[6] fine kindling wood that is good to start a fire, but not to keep it burning. Nonetheless, the novel's plot questions and challenges the gradual fading away of the deep feeling and complexity lived in that era. Beyond the historical facts, which in some ways are still elusive because of their being complex and controversial as well as relatively recent, there are other versions that express the close proximity of that time on a daily basis.[7]

The construction of *Charamicos* turns into "a complex engagement with the ways in which representations of history change over time and their relation to structures power, not least of all those of gender" (Wallace, 204).

Hernández undoubtedly makes the most of the advantage that writers of cultural memory have over historians. From the fragments of history that emerge through *Charamicos,* the novel creates a frame containing the overall scene within the university environment and recounts events from the tumultuous times during the 12 years of Joaquín Balaguer's regime (1966–1978).[8] As Lämmert points out, in cultural memory there is

> [a] definite advantage over professional historiography: here, the ordinary folks, the actual people about whom the historian, especially one who relies on the sources, is unable to write even one authentic word because practically they do not exist as individuals, fill the scene, as they did in reality, with their deeds and suffering, thus affirming the fate of their own. Only a "fantasy of facts" makes the story appear "as it was" and grants a continuing existence to those denied individual treatment by the historian, who is bound by the written documents before him. (233)

Patricio Manns, in his study about the clash between history and historical novel, presents a similar point when he writes that for history, the people are anonymous, subdued masses. These faceless masses function like a choir in the background, which emphasizes the univocal silhouette of the heroic deeds inscribed in marble. It is natural that one day, a certain type of writing and a certain band of novelists will invest themselves in the particular parcel of history that motivates them to offer a corrected version by means of fiction. These books develop a fictional discourse, which is simultaneously factual. None of them intends to shatter an adulterated reality and reorganize it afterward, but instead attempts to recover certain materials confiscated directly or indirectly from history with the end goal of reworking them (231–232).

Also, María del Carmen Aldeguer proposes that the author of the historical novel is not so interested in the faithful transmission of information about a particular historical epoch, but the re-creation of it from the perspective from which she writes (119). In an interview, Ángela Hernández elaborated on this topic by saying that history in this novel is the backdrop of the times, something in the air, a motion of starts and stops that simultaneously elevates and crushes those who were most exposed. This particular historic time contains the passage of the "cold wind" (of the postwar, of Balaguer, of the military and paramilitary), evil, confinement, and also heroism and honesty. It was the background and the hot spell that lingered over the fates of individuals (www.elcaribedigital.com.do).

In the case of *Charamicos,* the cultural memory expands its scope and widens the focus of what was previously stated. Beyond its recovery of the murmurs forgotten in history, it propounds a new concept: " . . . to engender and stimulate [. . .] new modes of conceptualization, new theories and models adequate to the complexity and hitherto unrepresented qualities and characteristics of women, the feminine and sexual difference" (Grosz, 41). From a feminine narrative, *the self opens itself* to a plurality of voices that convey stories of women and other marginalized citizens who were previously ignored or poorly represented, especially dealing with verifiable occurrences forgotten in official Dominican history.[9] In an oblique way, the novel defends a woman's right to better herself, use her mind, and bring about a political, intellectual, and personal emancipation.

In *Charamicos* the action revolves around two protagonists, Trinidad and Ercira. Both are fictional characters[10] who share the profile of many students who arrived at the Universidad de Santo Domingo from the countryside with the aid of the Movimiento Renovador Universitario.[11] Trinidad is the first-person narrator in the 61 chapters that are only numbered, but do not have titles. Her initially naive perspective regarding what is occurring around her slowly becomes more complex. Her perspective eventually evolves into a metaphorically multifaceted, plural voice in the first person. This occurs, as Wallace explains, because "women writers increasingly turned to the historical novel, or rather to new versions of the genre which they shaped to reflect their sense of history as subjective, multiple, contingent and fragmented" (Wallace, 203).

Ercira appears in the majority of the other 27 chapters, which are differentiated from the chapters narrated by Trinidad because they have titles. In these chapters, the first-person witness narrating the facts becomes obscured. Nonetheless, there appear to be one or two details (suggested by the verb tenses used) that refer back to Trinidad, the first-person narrator. These titled chapters, dedicated to Ercira's story, or to individuals in her circle, or to historically verifiable events, maintain a certain testimonial character mixed with a private, intimate tone. The latter is achieved by means of a poetic prose that suggests, in many cases, more than what is said relative to the historical facts and the imagined emotions.

At the beginning, the numbered chapters focus on Trinidad's experiences, which she narrates herself. In contrast, the titled chapters emerge from an intrusive look into the occurrences in Ercira's life. Some of these are seen from a pseudo-omniscient point of view expressed in the writing of Trinidad, or in a diffused flow of consciousness. However, as the chapters advance, the narrating "self," as can be gleaned from the novel's first sentence, becomes more complex: "Los hechos que voy a referir son responsables de trastocar mi mirada y mi manera de ser" (7) [The facts

I refer to are responsible for disrupting my view and my way of being]. The first person becomes blurred and the chapters, regardless of whether they are numbered or titled, may or may not refer to what has been witnessed by the first person. As a result, the first-person narrator loses the authority and thoroughness attributable to a first-hand witness, which upon becoming undefined enriches the polyphonic environment that it aspires to cover.

The two main characters are rural, dark-skinned women who are extremely intelligent and young, dedicated to the sciences, and unconcerned with small love affairs. In choosing these women as main characters, one can note the intention of dismantling the prejudices against everything that these characters could potentially symbolize. In this way, it also relates them directly to the benefits brought about by the development and the effects of the Movimiento Renovador Universitario, which aided so many of the "cero-once."[12] The movement itself is mentioned only in passing in the novel. Through these circumstances, the rural mentality comes face to face with the urban mentality, the cultural struggle between center and periphery becomes more obvious, as is the constant preoccupation about reworking language, a concern carried from childhood,[13] which is in the process of being further reworked and refined in the university environment. Beyond that, there is also the intent to create a matrilineal genealogy within history.

By means of Trinidad and Ercira's learning process, a variety of routes are posited in the novel, routes that ramify their implications upon bringing together loose ends from the immediate and distant past. The two fictional feminine characters, represented within every specific space and time frame that are largely ignored by Dominican history,[14] outline a comprehensive area of the collective memory of an era in order to widen its scope and project its significance onto the present. Hernández said that interpretations of the characteristics of that time are nebulous. Rapprochement by means of a free imagination can perhaps shed a bit of light, not the light of a historical document, but that which originates from the human desire to understand humankind's own condition, its limits, its constant challenges. It is said that the Dominican people forget easily: *Charamicos* refutes this prejudice ("Entrevista").

Through the two women protagonists who represent a complex *collage* of "anonymous" women for history, the novel inscribes and integrates the Dominican woman within a legible historical plane. In that way, an almost endless number of stories about unknown and ignored women are told alongside mentions of women like Mamá Tingó (52),[15] the Mirabal sisters (283),[16] and Manuela Aristy[17]—figures who are readily recognized by both the Dominican people and the official historical discourse. This heterogeneous group, which was active in different levels of society, represents and bears witness to the most common injustices and forced obscurity perpetrated by the patriarchal model against them as women and society's needy. As Diana Wallace points out, "The re-imagining and re-evaluation of women's lost histories . . . is still an important part of this contestatory dialogue with traditional history" (205).

"Planos adyacentes" (121) ["Adjacent Planes"]

In a recent study, "¿Cómo narrar el (neo)trujillato?" [How to narrate the (neo)trujillato?], Rita De Maeseneer points out that much recent Dominican narrative continues exploiting the character of the dictator as the guiding principle of the stories, turning to the genre of the so-called dictator novels (2011, 21). This is not the case in *Charamicos*, although the persecutory practices do imply Balaguer's silent presence. In De Maeseneer's estimation, an alternative for docile imitation of the great models focused on the dictator perhaps would consist of focusing on the rebels (28). She also refers to the oppressed, those who search for ways to survive under dictatorial regimes (31) and keeps them as the central focus of the novels that wish to represent an era well on its way to being forgotten. She points out that two techniques allow for the continued presence of authoritarianism: narrating public/historic events from the private realm and dealing with the historical topic in a tangential manner, through contiguity (42). Although De Maeseneer does not mention *Charamicos* in her study, this novel responds to what critics point out is a necessity of displacing the authoritarian systems from the public realm and researching them from the private realm (49). It is within the gaps between the private and public realms where the best versions can originate. As de Groot observes, "It is here, in the gaps of history, in the spaces between knowledges, in the lacking texts, within the misunderstood codes, that historical novelists work, and it is the very insubstantiality of the past that allows them to introduce their version of events" (182).

The plot intertwines and juxtaposes two themes: (1) the public and personal history reconstructed from the women protagonists' lives of dissidence at the university and (2) the trajectory of the two large, antagonistic groups that permeated the history of the *Doce Años* [Twelve Years]. One of the factions consists of President Balaguer, with a group of generals and a sinister paramilitary group, named "La Banda Colorá."[18] Opposing them, the reader discerns the constant, invisible presence of a traveler named "Hombre-brújula" [Compass-Man] who will come to liberate the nation with the help of some of his faithful and indefatigable followers.

By putting details of the vicissitudes and anxieties that are typical of the urban war experience in perspective and at a distance, a dynamic background emerges that emphasizes not only the action but also the evolution taking place with the women at a local level. The effort, support, and invisible presence of the "non-spellbound" groups, the "non-historic" groups,[19] and especially the women refer the reader to the everyday life and minutiae experienced in a specific time and space. This space is demarcated by the strict boundaries between the university and the rural villages from which the protagonists originate.

The degree of importance of several of the male characters, easily recognizable by those who remember or know the history of the 12-year Balaguer regime, is not obvious to the reader who is unfamiliar with details about Dominican history. Probably this is because they do not appear with their historical names. For example, the "Hombre-Brújula" character refers to the leader of the constitutionalist government, Colonel Francisco Caamaño;[20] Aridio Hormelo, head of "Los Ciguayos," is, without a doubt, historically speaking, Amaury Germán Aristy,[21] the leader of "Los Palmeros";[22] General Vizcaíno may refer to General Pérez y Pérez;[23] "La Gamba" is undoubtedly the Frente Joven Democrático Anticomunista y Antiterrorista (The Democratic Anticommunist Antiterrorist Youth Front), commonly referred to as "La Banda Colorá," among many others.

If the novel's main purpose were to extol the heroic acts as much as the sinister ones that occurred during those years, the names of all of these historic protagonists would appear with the weight given by official documents. The importance of historical facts is disturbed by the use of pseudonyms. As a result, more emphasis is put on the two fictional characters whose personal stories organize the chapters. The relationship of both protagonists with their rural past and their present at the university puts them in the proximity of one historical character in particular: Aridio Hormelo. This historical figure was the leader of the resistance and the lynchpin of one of the heroic events during the persecutory years of the Balaguer regime. Hormelo's engaged, active nature contrasts with the general passiveness associated with the majority of the subversive student groups.[24]

Those student organizations become known to the reader through Trinidad and Ercira's participation within them. Outside of secret meetings and organizing several tumultuous street protests, they were apparently not armed or violent. The most metaphoric and representative of their actions is the preparation of a "pedo químico" (97) [chemical fart], which they intended to use to ruin a governmental festivity. The applicable chemical knowledge that exists within the university allows subversive students the opportunity to prepare this discomforting stink bomb. Nonetheless, once it is ready, they do not use it at the planned event. The length of time these groups remained subversive can be equated to some extent to the ephemeral quality of the fetid gas, never reaching its target. Had it reached its target, it only would have scattered its pestilence, eventually fading to nothingness, like "charamicos." Retelling the deeds of the subversive students allows the author "freedom to examine *masculinity* as a social and cultural construction. The acts of reading and writing *across* gender have been central to the woman's historical novel right through the twentieth century" (Wallace, 8).

Aridio Hormelo, as one of the few active opposing parties that existed among these student organizations, is undoubtedly the historic figure who dominates the action within the novel. He participates with "Los Ciguayos," defending the sovereignty of the national territory before the arrival of the revolutionary invasion of "Hombre-brújula." These actions lead them to their heroic demise. To this day, Dominican history does not offer much information about this event. The epic eight-hour standoff that the novel narrates in detail (see Chapter 55) is the apex of an invisible struggle with all its forces concentrated on a fleeting, burning moment that remains in the historical memory for only a brief time, despite its intensity. Hormelo and the subversive group believed in the revolution that "Hombre-brújula" was to bring, and they gave their lives so that moment of triumph could come to be.

The novel makes them characters whose presence is far stronger than how they appear in Dominican history—a history that diminishes them and blurs their very existence with their passing mention. The novel gives Amaury Germán Aristy and "Los Palmeros," hidden under the guise of pseudonyms, a presence that makes them part of the present. The cultural memory that is constructed from the diverse voices reaches a dimension that historical fact in itself cannot: Amaury Germán Arisy, converted into Aridio Hormelo, reaches a mythical depth within his human dimensions. The creation of occurrences within his life, for example, the circumstances of his marriage, the stories that are repeated and "colored" by popular hearsay, plus the historical marks left by his participation in subversive groups, augment his being within the historical present of the Dominican Republic. As Jerome de Groot explains:

> History is other, and the present familiar. The historian's job is often to explain the transition between these states. The historical novelist similarly explores the dissonance and displacement between then and now, making the past recognisable but simultaneously authentically unfamiliar. (3)

Aristy's historical dimension is reinforced by the recurring names of two unmistakable historical characters, Father Bartolomé de las Casas (and his writings)[25] as well as Oliborio o Liborio[26] and his Palma Sola followers.

They also function as another foundational reference point regarding what being Dominican means to Amaury Germán Aristy, Hormelo in the novel. The constant presence of historical characters of such importance, and their mention for different reasons by different characters within the plot, conveys a significant polyvalence. As Fernández Prieto explains, incorporating the names of historical characters into a fictional world generates expectations in the reader different from those that can be generated by an imaginary character. The proper name causes a reaction in the memory enabling connotative networks that integrate the cultural competence of the readers and raises certain restrictions for the novelist. However, the character functions as historical only while it is recognized as such by the readers, that is, provided that there is a common code shared by the writer and audience.

If one is to ask what to do with the resources provided by the great texts that precede the novel, or what to do with the already canonic "message," we can say that Enriquillo, Liborio, and Aristy/Hormelo are riddles to be answered. This is particularly the case from a feminine perspective, because they are still alive in the sense that they can alert us to generic behaviors and change attitudes from the political to the aesthetic realm.

Aristy was born in the town named after Father Bartolomé de las Casas. He also read Las Casas's writings from a young age. The most significant relationship is the one that exists between the writings by the Father from the Dominican order and the most praised Dominican historical novel: Manuel Galván's *Enriquillo*. Within this character, chosen by Father Las Casas as an example *par excellence* of what bravery, justice, and heroism are within the Dominican context, there is a convergence of the conditions experienced by the besieged native who is pushed into an armed conflict with the domineering and disdainful colonizer. In *Charamicos*, Father Las Casas is remembered as the defender of the indigenous people who wrote that the uprising of the Indians was not a war, but instead legitimate "autodefensa natural" (220) [natural self-defense].

The novel makes reference to the historical figure Enriquillo (137), but Galván's novel of the same name is not mentioned. In referring to a history for the "Ciguayos," Hormelo explains why he preferred that name over that of Enriquillo saying that when the time came to choose a name, he hesitated between Enriquillo and Ciguayo. He chose the latter because it is an Indian word and it does not name an individual, but a lineage (220). Both Las Casas's writings and Galván's novel have been recognized in the official and literary history, where they maintain their privileged status.

That is not the case with Oliborio o Liborio and the persecutions suffered by his followers in the Cordillera Central in 1922 and in Palma Sola in 1962. Liborio and his followers are linked to Palma Sola, the site of their persecution, and the 1962 "Palma Sola Massacre." The name responds to a fact registered by the official history, but the place itself slowly seems to be forgotten within the culture, even more so were the government to have any say in the matter. What is intriguing about this past occurrence is that it continues to grow in the present. The versions of what occurred, and the facts surrounding it, continue to multiply in literary, journalistic, and artistic interpretations—projecting the event in a multifaceted fashion toward the future. It is a phenomenon with a life of its own. Its complex past and its expansion toward the present allow for the exploration of the converging elements in the repressive elimination of the messianic phenomenon that killed the followers of Olivorio Mateo, or Liborio. There are a variety of explanations and possible truths behind the reason for the existence of this messianic movement. One scholar on the subject, Lusitania Martínez, sustains that it was a social protest movement, led religiously, due to a present and immediate cause: the oppression of the peasant group as a result of the penetration of capitalism in the countryside (Ikemendez).

The existence of multiple, circulating versions regarding both historical occurrences referring to Liborio has prevented the event from fading to obscurity with the passage of time. Instead, it has grown into something else, allowing writers the opportunity to retell what little is known of the actual historical occurrence in more depth, utilizing fictional modes to recreate it. In confronting the event from a literary perspective, from fiction, there is no direct conflict with what is verifiable from the official history. Instead, the fictional approach is more concerned with finding the appropriate voice to refer this past with hidden, present repercussions.

"El elemento agridulce" (42) ["The Bittersweet Element"]

In their constant questioning, both Trinidad and Ercira confront situations that mirror a reality rendered as a temporal and spatial diorama within which they search for responses to the most paradigmatic patriarchal structures. Both, even without knowing, ask themselves about their relationship with the patriarch and patriarchy, with authority of all types, the university, the student groups, the nation, and their very relationship with history.

Trinidad relates the case of Oliborio Mateo, his miracles, persecutions of him, his sanctuaries, and the massacre at Palma Sola to the negligent, almost inexplicable, absence of the father figure in a literal and figurative sense. Two stories told by the groups in conflict coincide at Palma Sola—both of which concern the protagonist. First, on a personal level, is the story of the father who is a follower of the new prophets of Liborism, the Twins. Somebody told her that the "mangrino" of her dad, that "démontrer" bird, was in Palma Sola. He abandoned her to go with the warlocks, the famous twins of Palma Sola. Her daddy was among those who were there from the start, but there he was called Avelino (329). Recounted in second- and third-hand accounts, Trinidad hears a version of what occurred in Palma Sola from the prejudiced, rural point of view of her mother's friend. The fact that the friend did not believe in Liborio explains the negative attitude she puts forth when she said that he would go everywhere with the twin Plinio. She mentioned that night and day, at Plinio's behest, he followed his steps. He kept his knife for him. Supposedly, this Plinio had only three more days before completing his mission. But the soldier jumped them and bam! Plinio fell in his arms. At first, Avelino thought it was a vision. That vision had taken away her father's voice and Avelino, just like in his visions, hit the machine-gun captain with a club (330).

Seriously hurt in the incident, Trinidad's father, Avelino, spends a long period convalescing far away from home, remaining in the neighboring areas by Palma Sola, eventually starting another family. As she is told: "ese sin vergüenza vive en El Teterito de Padre Las Casas.... Tu papá, ese sinajuste, tiene tres hijos" (329) ["that scoundrel lives in the Teterito of Padre Las Casas. Your incorrigible father has three children" (331)]. This unexpected story regarding the father's role and location produces "extrañamiento, casi escándalo" (331) [estrangement, almost a scandalous feeling], which indefinitely postpones the reconciliatory meeting between father and daughter. At the end of the novel she says she will think about it.

On a national–historic level, we have "Hombre-brújula," who, according to the official archives and popular retellings, was responsible for the attack on the group of believers in 1962 and was the only seriously injured individual in the uneven fight during the Palma Sola massacre. It is precisely Avelino, overwhelmed by the visions and the knife of the Messiah that triggered the storm. Hombre-brújula attempted to take the weapon away from the mute Avelino. He resisted and Plinio joined the struggle. A bullet pierced his heart. Avelino hit "Hombre-brújula" (281–282).

This version of events involving "Hombre-brújula" differs from the previous version as it exempts the military from its direct culpability in the massacre. That very character is the one that many of the students and idealistic youth are waiting for to aid the poor and re-establish the constitutional order of the nation in the early 1970s. As the narrator reflects, " 'El Hombre-brújula', su participación en la matanza de Palma Sola . . . , bueno, a su favor, hay que pensar que pudo ser sorprendido, o haber caído en una trampa"(281) ["Hombre-brújula," his involvement in the Palma Sola massacre . . . well, in his favor, one could think that he was surprised, or could have fallen in a trap]. In these versions of the Palma Sola massacre, the father figures are implicated directly. First, there is the father whose family is awaiting his return someday. Also, there is the figurative father of the social movement who has been far away and whose return is so unquestionably certain that his followers are willing to give their lives for the cause championed by the absent father.

What the narrator refers to as the "penumbras e interrogaciones de mi pensamiento" (169) [shadows and questions in my mind] complicates the clarity necessary to face events so profusely narrated through the years. In the versions found in the novel, the two "fathers" confront each other in a confusing and ambiguous way: in one, "Hombre-brújula" supposedly initiates the firefight, while in the other, Avelino, affected by his visions, attacks the "Hombre-brújula." She even asks herself if her father's assault of the military leader, the future leader of the revolutionary group, would awaken a new commitment to the people: "El Hombre-brújula fue de los pocos militares malheridos. Comportiría algún significado especial que Avelino, un campesino fervoroso le abriera de un palo la cabeza? Sería a partir de allí que la mentalidad del Hombre-brújula empezó a transformarse a favor del pueblo?" (282) ["Hombre-brújula" was one of the few military personnel who were hurt. Is there a special significance that Avelino, an ardent farmer, would break his head open with a club? Would it be from that point on that the consciousness of "Hombre-brújula" began to shift toward favoring the people?]. One affirmative answer to these questions would endow Trinidad's father, who was then earning a living renting mules, an epic patriotic dimension. The "mute" man, with nothing beyond his faith and his club, manages to change the fate of many. "Hombre-brújula" is an enemy to everything that Avelino represents. Avelino, in literally breaking his head open with a club, also figuratively liberates his mind and changes his future course.

When thinking of "Hombre-brújula," who fails to arrive on time and disembarks only to die quickly from having been betrayed, Trinidad asks herself: "¿cómo lo vería la posteridad? ¿Qué ejemplo sería el suyo? ¿Quién iba a detener 'el viento frío' que soplaba sobre esta tierra?" (346) [How will posterity see him? What kind of example will he set? Who was going to stop the "cold wind" blowing over this land?].

Both of Trinidad's "fathers" are an enigma because of their absence, failures within their respective legacies of loneliness, and neglect. Both represent an opportunity for her to question the patriarchal historical archive, which presents these oft-repeated events without an endpoint that sheds light upon them in the present.

"Mínimo razonable" (207) ["Reasonable Minimum"]

Ercira, whose name is likely drawn from Sagrario Ercira Díaz,[27] is the focus of observation of a narrator in the majority of the poetically titled chapters.

In these chapters, their narrator chooses a vantage point, the focused eye of the camera capable of showing the heart of the most intimate fictional and historical events. Ercira is also profoundly marked by a complex relationship with a father figure whose Spanish name, Agramonte, implies that he is hard-working but also alcoholic. She said his head was like a gloomy gourd full of shrews (33). When he would get drunk, he had nightmares about his interactions with opportunistic landowners, forces of the American occupation, and corrupt Dominican police when working as a watchman. In the rural family, the father's domestic altercations with the mother, Ercira, and Santos, the handicapped and mentally disabled brother, drove Ercira to feign weakness. She worked but did not speak and also decided to not show the physical pain caused by the punishments she received—even horrifying ones such as forcibly burning her hand in a fire. On that occasion, in front of the thorny javilla bush, she promised herself to never weep a single tear, even if someone were to cut her flesh strip by strip (58). The father's unjustified violent episodes motivate Ercira to define herself and opt for a different future outside her home: "tu furia crecía como una nube, hasta volverse completamente oscura, de plomo Fenecio Sánchez Agramonte sacaba lo peor de ti y en esto peor te habías revolcado" (59) [Your anger grew like a cloud until it became completely dark, heavy like lead. Fenecio Sánchez Agramonte brought out the worst in you and you were immersed in it.].

Violence from a father figure, in one degree or another, is a constant in each institution with which Ercira involves herself. The worst case occurs in a prison when she is systematically tortured under the control of "Los Intelectuales,"[28] who cannot explain her capacity for suffering without uttering a word. There are more than five chapters in which oblique references have been made to Ercira's torture.[29] From the vantage point that brings us closest to what is most intimate within her; there is a vacillation between her torment and how the mind of the tortured escapes to other situations. At another point, she also becomes indignant with herself for becoming a prisoner: "llena de ira consigo misma por haber caído tontamente entre estas garras, es un NO al vampire que la está escrutando con pretendida inteligencia, convencido de que un revolucionario es una alimaña pozoñosa" (232) [full of ire with herself for having fallen foolishly in the grasp of those claws, it is a NO to the vampire who is scrutinizing her with alleged intelligence, convinced that a revolutionary is a poisonous vermin].

The figure of Father Las Casas as a defender of the oppressed is obliquely embodied in the form of a Dutch priest, Father Erasmo Amir. It is he who teaches Ercira to untiringly aid the defenseless and to fight for change and ending social injustice. The chapter titled "El elemento agridulce" (42–43)

[The Bittersweet Element] appears to be narrated by Father Amir, who addresses a "tú" [you] who is a nearby observer. More accurately, murmuring to the observer without knowing if Ercira hears what he says, he states: "Inteligencia y rabia impregnaban tu arisco carácter" (42) [Intelligence and anger permeated your contentious character]; "No era tuya una típica crisis de pubertad, sino una pugna entre la reciedumbre de lo posible, solo intuido y y la hostilidad de lo inmediato; y en medio el torrente de tu naturaleza" (43) ["Yours was not a typical crisis of puberty, but a struggle between the moral strength possible, just guessed, and the hostility of the immediate, and amid the torrent of your nature" (43)].

Undoubtedly, the paternal figures of Agramonte and Balaguer, the father of the family and the father of the government, respectively, are joined by the cruelty and unpunished violence they put forth. Regarding male supremacy within the patriarchal society, we can add the leaders of the dissident groups at the university, though their actions are less outrageous. Ercira, the prototypical independent woman, faces up to all of them, emancipated from within, with grand ideals of fairness and rectitude. This made her uninterested in young love and convinced that marriage would not be part of her future at the young age of 12: "Viviría sola. Tendría numerosos amigos, le agradaba entablar amistad con los hombres. Ser parte de sus conversaciones" (290) [She would live alone. She would have many male friends as she enjoyed befriending them, being part of their conversations]. She does not count on discovering a different type of man in the secret group meetings with Hormelo—the type of man who, from his position of distance, accepts women's equality in the struggle with which she is committed. Upon being captured and tortured, the goal that saves her from madness during the torment is to ask Hormelo to marry her. Through the efforts of Father Amir, they are able to marry in absentia. When her husband dies in battle without having seen her again, Ercira, protected by a human rights delegation, receives recognition from the "father" of the government, Balaguer. As such, she achieves a mythic stature within the novel. Of course, Balaguer's discourse is a political maneuver to absorb her into the magnanimities of power, after having been the victim of its torturers and precisely when she becomes untouchable due to the protection imparted by international human rights. This was one of Balaguer's practices during his dictatorship. In the novel, it is a polyvalent way of denouncing governmental rhetoric and simultaneously aggrandizes Ercira's character (347).

By integrating the historical leader's speech from a specific date into the story of a fictional character, the borders between history and fiction are blurred. It also ennobles the many invisible women embodied by the character, women who have tolerated the same indignities and violence perpetrated by the Agramontes, Balaguer, and the "Intelectuales," an "engendro de astucia represiva" (196) [an engenderment of repressive ploys].

Contrasting with Trinidad's story, which flows in a certain chronological order, Ercira's is presented in a plot that intertwines past and present. The interweaving of the students' stories disarticulates both the act of writing and the act of reading. A fabric of diverse threads drawn from historical references and poetic flourishes constructs the complex puzzle of Ercira's character, who complements Trinidad. Everything that Trinidad does not encompass in her rural life comes to life in the daily violence, the personality engrossed in questioning, and the fierceness dramatized by Ercira. She is the other, the exemplary face and the supplementary equal of Trinidad's transformation: "Ercira me arrastró por una mano, le quitó una bandera a un estudiante y me la entregó a mí" (7) [Ercira dragged me by the hand, took a flag from a student, and handed it to me]. Interspersing fragments of Ercira's life in the pseudo-biographical memory is a way of intervening in, interfering with, and enriching the official history, because it is well worth dreaming of young people with a disposition to make history do justice (13).

The narrator's self needs to create its other facet. The "tú" [you] will allow for this self to be a multiple historical presence. The protagonists, as characters, reach a dimension that surpasses the fate of a single life: "Esta es la vida? Sólo esto es la vida? (...) Esto es todo cuanto es la vida? En esa interrogación tu espíritu prosperaba a la manera del guayacán y de la flor del maguey" (154) [This is life? This is all that life is? This is everything regarding life? On that question your spirit flourished in the manner of the guayacán and the maguey flower.].

The "tú" [you] of the titled chapters, which undoubtedly refers to Ercira, is a powerful tool in the construction of a narrator who is a *voyeur*, who asserts herself like a witness, with an authority that reconstructs her and permits seeing her in all her complexity and growth: "Dentro de ti, fluían ríos disidentes" (181) [Within you, dissenting rivers were flowing]. Seen from an outside, yet interested, vantage point, a protagonist on a par with history is constructed: a wife of the same noble caliber as the husband, the heroic figure Hormelo. Her loyalty is established as the counterpart to the treasonous infiltrator represented by the Minda Silveira character who makes everyone around her uneasy. As they said, that woman made all the comrades, young and old, restless. She cannot explain where this concern arose from, perhaps it was because she brought with her the disruptive threat of women's liberation (158); they knew from a reliable source that Minda Silveira was a CIA agent (343).[30] One of the titled chapters, "Dejarse encantar" ["Allowing Oneself to Be Enchanted," 158], is dedicated to Ercira's and Minda's display of physical strength and dexterity in a scene of combat on a rubble-ridden mountainside, which emphasizes both women's agility and astuteness in battle (160).

By devising a character that is simultaneously unique and an embodiment of the experiences of an era, the author employs few characters to represent an entire generation of university youth, beyond their role as a force for social change that is reflected in the generic: "A su tiempo Ercira, lo supe. En ti el baile no era fiesta, sino contracción del vacío, pronunciamiento de naturaleza. Mil espectros andaban port tus huesos" (153) [In time, Ercira, I knew it. For you, the dance was not a celebration, but a conquest of the void, the proclamation of nature. A thousand ghosts walked through your bones.]. Ercira is herself, her past and present ghosts, a victim who does not want that fate, who refuses to be victimized. From the gradual growth engendered by her actions, the "voyeur" tells her: "Sabes que no estás sola. Hay nexus silenciosos, entibiándose como larvas de abeja en el panal soleado. Acciones y procesos sin suficiente coordinación pero movidos por el mismo espíritu que busca respirar a sus anchas" (177) [You know you're not alone. There are silent liaisons, warming up like bee larvae in a sun-soaked honeycomb. Actions and processes without sufficient coordination, but moved by the same spirit seeking to breathe at ease.].

The historical links in the novel are put forth, obviously, in the speech in which Balaguer (supposedly) names her and because of her relationship with Hormelo, who pushed her toward history, to cast her lot with him. These two poles, so disparate in reality, Joaquín Balaguer and Amaury Germán Aristy, ponder their place in history through Ercira's character. By means of both historical characters, Ercira represents so many others forgotten by history.

Imprevisiones (132) [Foresight]

The intense and painful historical facts of the Doce Años de Balaguer [Twelve Years of Balaguer][31] may be broadened and their ideological meaning reconsidered by means of the rhetorical strategies in *Charamicos*. By recovering material for the cultural memory, the feminine voice questions and confronts a historical plot of dissonance and difference through a discourse characterized by the integration and amalgamation of voices. The writing allows for a juxtaposition of intellectual discourse with discourse drawn from popular tradition, as well as the domestic and intimate realm. Fragments from oral histories, the use of false historical figures, along with the use of historically verifiable facts, and press clippings, among other techniques, are employed in the construction of the happenings of the era. The patriarchal hierarchies appear in the novel for the specific purpose of being questioned. There are numerous examples of confrontation: (1) in the family, Ercira and Agramonte; (2) in the student organization, Peñaló and Trinidad; (3) the Balaguer regime and the students with La Gamba and student groups, respectively; high and low/popular culture (baseball players, rural folk wisdom, semi-magical cures, the rondalla music groups from the university, and the traditional perico ripiao, etc.); (4) the urban and the rural; and (5) the feminine and the masculine. These opposites are presented in the writing of the novel, and both poles are questioned in order to redefine the cultural identity of an era and a nation. The literary discourse turns surreptitiously subversive when the hierarchies that maintain and guarantee a national way of being are confronted and find themselves threatened. The subversion emerges from the refusal to recognize the discourse (the already accepted, deep-rooted stability of such dichotomies) in the novel. From the feminine perspective, and from the margins of Hernández's writing, emerges a disquieting historical, political, literary facet, marked by gender.

Through the fresh foresight (making the most of the polyvalent sense suggested by "imprevisión" in Spanish) provided by the feminine textual voice, new approaches make accessible obscure historical moments on the verge of oblivion. By narrating the occurrences in the life of two women protagonists, the novel does not make the political realm its main topic, but instead it inscribes it within its very writing. By changing certain historical names and situations, which would be appropriate in referential or allegoric literature written under dictatorial regimes, this novel articulates a history as-yet untold, narrating it from the point of view of a marginalized self—marginalized both from being a woman and from not being part of the official history. As a result, the discourse regarding even the most commonplace events and that of the hidden history are equated. This makes the enigma present throughout the text function in two directions: either it leaves the underlying codes untouched and uninterpreted, or asks it the questions that may provoke as many answers as each reader can or will dare to accept.

From the feminine perspective, the novel does not cede to hegemonic discourses that invoke reconciliation or advocate having an inconvenient past fade away. The writing instead favors having an effect on the cultural memory, which returns to the past in order to speak of the present and to make a different future possible, not only on a governmental level, but also regarding the situation faced by women within the society. *Charamicos* can be considered the recuperation of an era, of a group of young people for whom, life, with its thirst for knowledge about life itself, with its righteous genes, makes them rise up, and what matters least are the words and ideological creeds. What moves them is an ancient air of freedom.

As a cultural memory *Charamicos* conveys the hope for the present and the future of courageous, intelligent, rural women, who, thanks to their education and active participation in the subversive movements, learned to think and question for themselves. The future is in Arelis, the orphan girl who Trinidad adopts and brings to live with her in the big city at the end of the novel. Arelis expresses what she desires in negative terms: "¡Tú no me vas a comprar una tambora. Yo no quiero una tambora!" (350) [You're not going to buy me a drum. I do not want a drum.]. The hopeful future for women from anywhere in the country is found in the music that both Arelis and Trinidad will play together—a future without negative assertions.

The cultural memory confronts the reader with a historical peculiarity that demands an active response on their part upon awakening a sense of *otherness* and, even, difference. This occurs because, although the chosen information that is integrated into the plot negotiates with the reader's encyclopedic knowledge, with what they supposedly know about the topic and what they supposedly ignore and want to know (Fernández Prieto), this same information can open up dissonant gaps that invite more questioning.

Considering the subjectivity of the feminine subject outlined by means of the two protagonists, the political aspect within the public and private realm, and the marginalization or obscurity forced upon the weakest, *Charamicos*, as a cultural memory, creates a dissident space in which diverse issues related to authority and the emancipated, thinking woman are at play. This memory reveals a rebellious disposition against historiographic discourse: "giving femininity, which usually has a walk-on part in the official history of our times, the lead role in the national drama" (de Groot, 68).

Notes

1. Every subtitle originates from a title of a chapter in *Charamicos*. Note that all translations are by Javier F. González.
2. See specifically *The Woman's Historical Novel* (2005) by Diana Wallace and *The Historical Novel* (2010) by Jerome de Groot.
3. Ángela Hernández Núñez, who was born in Jarabacoa, Dominican Republic, stands out as one of the most prominent women authors of her country today. She has published several collections of poetry including *Tizne y cristal* (1985), *Desafío* (1985), *Edades de asombro* (1985), *Telar de rebeldía* (1998), *Onirias* (2012). Her short stories have been collected in the following books: *Alótropos* (1989), *Masticar una rosa* (1993), and *Piedra de sacrificio* (1999). Many of

them have been included in Spanish-American anthologies. Her novels are *Mudanza de los sentidos* (2001) and *Charamicos* (2003). "Hernández's work offers a great challenge.... Her effective and coherent provocation is all the more powerful when one considers the impact of colonization, governmental repression in dictatorial regimes and the patriarchal literary forces that have shaped and continue to shape the Dominican Republic" (González, 135, 137).

4. See Sara Rosell, *La novela de escritoras dominicanas de 1990 a 2007*(46–48); Lucía Montas, "*Charamicos*: bildungsroman femenino o aprendizaje político a través de la memoria histórica"; Néstor Rodríguez, "*Charamicos* de Ángela Hernández"; Isabel Teresa Zakrzewski Brown, "Through the Looking Glass: Reflections of the Trujillo and Balaguer Regimes in Ángela Hernández' *Mudanza de los sentido*s and *Charamicos.*"

5. The historical novel is constructed with a recipient who is endowed with certain knowledge about the historical issue at hand. The discourse is forged from this competence or allegedly shared knowledge. On the one hand, it confirms, corroborates, and respects historical events at least sufficiently enough to make historical knowledge active within the text—the reader recognizes what he already knows, as you would expect. On the other hand, it also increases that knowledge, qualifying and completing it, incorporating information that is unlikely to be known by the general reader, and yet is necessary for the formation of the diegesis or for understanding the actions and the behavior of the characters (which depend, to a greater or lesser extent, upon which historiographical extratextual source the text is drawing from). Finally, it is reworked using the procedures of fiction and generic rules, and may even question it, disassemble it, or subvert it. But always, the use made of that realm feeds the need to operate as such in a historical novel (Fernández Prieto).

6. About using "Charamicos" as the title for the novel, the author says: "I like the word itself, 'charamicos', a dominicanism, that names thin and dry branches ideal for lighting the fire, but not to maintain it. The 70s generation burned and consumed itself quickly" ("Entrevista"). *Diccionario de Americanismos* defines the word as "Leña menuda, conjunto de ramas secas para hacer fuego" (494) [Twigs, dry branches to make fire].

7. One of the requirements for a historical novel is (according to Wallace, Fernandez Prieto, de Groot, and others) that the events occurred before the author's life.

8. The mandate of Joaquín Balaguer, in accordance with their US sponsors, had as its first goal the dismantling and destruction of popular groups who had participated in the Revolution of April 65. He used both the army and a paramilitary group of professional killers called "La Banda," who qualified in his speeches of "uncontrollable forces." It is estimated that more than 3,000 Dominicans were killed between 1966 and 1974 only. By the time he turned over the presidency in 1978, Balaguer had exterminated most promising youth and the most advanced ideas that the nation had, http://www.dominicanaonline.org/portal/espanol/cpo_balaguer.asp.

9. Undoubtedly, Hernández's novel fits into the fourth category of historical novels as put forth by Umberto Eco, who defines it as "the historical novel which uses made-up events and characters yet tells us things about a period which history books do not" (75).

10. Although they are fictional characters, many facts relating to Trinidad are linked to the life of the author as can be seen in "Los senderos elásticos," which recounts her life in a *sui generis* way. The author mentioned in an interview: "Sin duda hay detalles autobiográficos en la novela, pero también una voluntad de que ese 'yo' funcione como personaje de ficción: Estudié en la UASD en los setenta. Participé y conocí en lo posible uno de los mundos que allí sucedían (había otro mundo subterráneo, impalpable)" ("Entrevista") [There are undoubtedly autobiographical details in the novel, but also a desire that 'I' work as a character of fiction: I studied at the UASD in the seventies. Participated in what I could with what was happening (there was another underworld, impalpable)].

11. "Movimiento Renovador Universitario (University Renovation Movement) emerged from the national crisis of 1965 that the Dominicans have called 'the April War'. This new phase of the UASD [Universidad Autónoma de Santo Domingo] had a highly political and patriotic origin" (Hermann). "Only after the failed revolution of April 1965 was there a movement of renewal at the public university. Among other measures, they attempted to take away the Trujillista teachers and open the door to poor youth. The Renovation Movement, as it was called, was led by intellectuals and teachers linked to the left and the April Revolution" (comments on phone by Ángela Hernández).

12. "Cero-once era lo mismo que decir, le sale el verde por encima de la ropa . . . le sale el campo por los ojos, huele a mierda de vaca . . . . es una burra" (*Charamicos*, 10) [cero-once was the same as saying, you get the green over the clothes . . . the field comes out through your eyes, you smell like cow shit . . . you are a donkey].

13. There are many clichés, some of which are of a political-ideological nature. At the same time, Trinidad is constantly checking the dictionary to clarify many terms that urban and university life bring to her.

14. I have not found many facts in history books that refer to the 12 years of Balaguer and the repression against the UASD university. The most informative account is offered by *Balaguer and the Dominican Military. Presidential Control of the Factional Officer Corps in the 1969s and 1970s* by Brian J. Bosch. The following two history books, *The Dominican Republic. A National History* (392) by Frank Moya Pons, and *Dominican History* (303) by Jaime de Jesús Domínguez, pay more attention to the country's economic success and the political parties of the time than to the repression against the students. On July 2, 2011, Loyda Peña published an article "Hechos imborrables. La estela de dolor de los 12 años de Joaquín Balaguer" (Unforgettable Acts. The Trail of Pain of 12 years of Joaquín Balaguer) in *Hoy*, a digital Dominican newspaper. This shows the constant need for more information and remembrance of those fateful years.

15. Mamá Tingó is a symbol of the struggle for land and an example of rural women in the defense of the rights of the peasants in Latin America and the Caribbean.

16. The Mirabal sisters, marked by the persecution and injustice that led to their deaths, are part of the group of heroines who fought against the Trujillo dictatorship.

17. Manuela Aristy, mother of Amaury Germán Aristy, is still trying to have a monument built honoring "Los Palmeros," who died fighting against many troops of the Dominican government and US occupation troops (see interviews with Vianco Martínez). Also see YouTube: "Amaury Germán Aristy—Un héroe perdido en el tiempo" and "Homenaje a Los Palmeros_Amaury German Aristy.wmv."

18. The "Frente Democrático Anticomunista y Antiterrorista" was known as *La Banda*, a vigilante group in the service of Joaquín Balaguer, who operated in Santo Domingo with national and international fame in the 1970s. It was created to break strikes, and also made its contribution in training the staff of the "security services" responsible for the repression, torture, and disappearance of revolutionary youth (http://www.quisqueyavirtual.edu.do/wiki/La_Banda).

    To determine the magnitude of the violations and abuses committed by these gangs of thugs, we can cite the admissions by Brian J. Bosch: "His first goal was to terrorize those suspected leftists in the public schools and state university. During their raids, the classrooms were destroyed, teachers and students beaten [and] intimidated. . . . After the first month of mutilation caused by Banda, it was obvious that the scope of counterterrorism operations had gone beyond the original plans [. . .] Complaints against the excesses of Banda were expressed not only by the bishops and the entire society, but also the U.S. Embassy itself in the country, according to notes by former military attaché Brian J. Bosch in his book" (see Núñez).

19. "Ercira se confundirá con la historia. Mi frente no está *hechizada*. Yo no soy histórica. Lo que, en sí, no es una dicha, tampoco una fatalidad" (*Charamicos*, 350) [Ercira will merge with history. My face is not *spellbound*. I'm not historic. Which in itself is not a joy, not a fatality. (my emphasis)].

20. Col. Francisco Alberto Caamaño Deñó (1932–1973) was a Dominican soldier and politician, the 44th Constitutionalist President of the Dominican Republic. His entry into history books came during the Dominican Republic Civil War that began on April 24, 1965. He was one of the leaders in the movement to restore the democratically elected President Dr. Juan Bosch, who had been overthrown in a CIA sponsored military coup d'état in September 1963. This faction of loyalists came to be known as the *Constitucionalistas*, for their desire to return to a rightful and constitutional form of government, as opposed to the military junta that was in place. During the Winter of 1973, after several years staying low profile, Caamaño led the landing of a small group of rebels at Playa Caracoles, near Azua, and then into the mountains of the Cordillera Central, with the purpose of starting a peasant revolution to overthrow Dominican President Joaquín Balaguer. Balaguer's government was repressive and highly

centralized during this period, reminding many of the Rafael Trujillo regime in which Balaguer had been one of the dictator's puppet presidents and close advisers. After a few weeks of guerrilla warfare against Balaguer's regular army and not having received the much-hoped-for peasant support, he was wounded and captured by Dominican government forces, and then summarily executed. www.historiadominicana.com.do/historia/contemporanea.

21. Amaury Germán Aristy (1947–1972) turned at a very young age to the political ideas that emerged following the death of Rafael Leonidas Trujillo. In 1964 he formed part of the Directorate of the Revolutionary Students Union (EBU) and the Youth Section of the School belonging to the 14th of June, becoming one of its most notorious leaders. He struggled in RD waiting for Colonel Caamaño who was in Cuba training to lead the guerrilla outbreak that was finally aborted. Amaury, Virgil, Ulysses, and Bienvenido (Chute) fell heroically on January 12, 1972.

22. This revolutionary structure (Los Palmeros) born in 1968, boldly and courageously led by Amaury was hardly touched by the state security agency. It seemed that it was being left alone, but it was not until late 1971 when they were actually detected, located, and finally surrounded in January, 1972. We know that in the battles that were staged on January 12, 1972 Los Palmeros fought heroically against the troops who wanted to crush them. These brave men fought until the last minute, struggled until they fired their last bullet (GUASABARAeditor, Enero 11, 2011).

23. In 1968, General Enrique Pérez y Pérez, with the approval of President Balaguer, created from the San Isidro base a team of counterinsurgent assassins. Its specific mission was to eliminate individuals whom they considered terrorist leaders. The public only superficially understood the character of General Pérez y Pérez when he became the head of the country's security forces. His commitment to duty, self-discipline and emotional control were discussed as among the best that they knew. However, his absolute cruelty was not known to all. With Pérez y Pérez at the head of the National Police, preparations began to mount a terrorist project. About 400 young people from the lowest social strata were recruited to form the "Democratic Youth Front and Anti-Terrorism" that from the beginning of its activities, was known as "La Banda") (www.wikidominicana.edu.do/wiki/La_Banda).

24. University activist groups included in *Charamicos*: Frauer (7); Fedel, Student Liberation Front (14), PARCO, Communist Party of the Revolution (23), "the white hand" (24), LEC, Students Representative of PARCO (24), PBL, Flag of People's Liberation (27), "Red Star" (45), FED, Dominican Students Federation (45), PUNO, Party Worker Unity (46); a detailed list of every group and its acronyms working at the university (46).

25. Bartolomé de las Casas O. P. (1484–1566) was a sixteenth-century Spanish historian, social reformer, and Dominican friar. His extensive writings, the most famous being *A Short Account of the Destruction of the Indies* and *Historia de Las Indias*, chronicle the first decades of colonization of the West Indies, focusing particularly on the atrocities committed by the colonizers against

the indigenous peoples. In 1531 he began preaching in Puerto Plata against the Spanish colonists, whose superiors had moved to Santo Domingo. In this capital, in 1533, Chief Enriquillo, who had been rebelling since 1519, surrendered. In addition, Father Las Casas is associated with *Enriquillo*, which is the most recognized name in the historical novel of the Dominican Republic, and in which Manuel de Jesús Galván recreates the events that constitute the indigenous uprising against the injustices of the Spanish (www.jmarcano.com/mipais/historia/discovery).

26. On June 27, 1922, the occupation troops hunted Oliborio, the "rough and ordinary peasants." John Bartlow Martin, former ambassador to the Dominican Republic, who first came to the country in 1937, stated: "During the occupation of the American Marines, a man named Liborio had founded a religious cult, apparently opposing the occupation, and they said he had been killed by Americans" (ikemendez). For E. O. Garrido Puello the confrontation that led to the liquidation of Oliborio responded simply to the negative answer to the request of the military government emerged from the occupation by US troops to hand over weapons and "acquiesce to develop their activities under the order and the law" (Ikemendez).

27. Sagrario Ercira Díaz was murdered by the army in Santo Domingo on April 14, 1972, at 25 years of age in a strafing of students at the Universidad Autónoma de Santo Domingo campus (UASD). Over 50,000 people were at her funeral. She is considered a martyr of the government of 12 years of Balaguer.

28. I am not sure if the name "Los intelectuales" is historical, or is the name for this repressive historical group in the novel. See chapter "Los intelectuales" (195–199), which provides a historical account of this "brain M-1 (Department of the Air Force counterintelligence) and G-2 (Department of Army counterintelligence)" (*Charamicos*, 196).

29. The names of the chapters are "Los ciguayos" (220), "Duerme sintiendo" (225), "Corrida" (231), "Piedra de Rayo" (236), "El umbral del dolor" (241), and "Arrastre" (283).

30. The number and names of undercover agents of the CIA in the political movements of the era are a matter of interest, concern, and study, as shown in a recent article "La CIA y el MPD." Freddy Aguasvivas. http://www.hoy.com.do/investigacion/2011/2/13/362177 13 Febrero 2011.

31. "como historia sólo pueden interpretarla los que vivieron o investigaron ese agitado y doloroso periodo del acontecer reciente porque la distinguida escritora cambió casi todos los nombres de víctimas, héroes, dirigentes, militantes, asesinos, agentes, informantes, infiltrados, espías, sacerdotes de base, oficiales y agentes policiales. Lo que relata con claridad pormenorizada, reveladora, son los hechos" (Peña) [those who lived and researched that troubled and painful period of recent events are the only ones who can interpret the events as history because the distinguished writer changed almost all the names of victims, heroes, leaders, militants, murderers, agents, informants, infiltrators, spies, priests, and police officers. What she clearly describes in detail are the revealing facts.].

Works Cited

Aldeguer Beltrá, María del Carmen. "Técnicas de reconocimiento en una novela histórica de memorias," in *La novela histórica a finales del siglo XX*. Eds. Romera Castillo et al. Madrid: Visor Libros, 1996. 119–125. Print.

Anderson, Linda, Ed. "The Re-Imagining of History in Contemporary Women's Fiction," in *Plotting Change: Contemporary Women's Fiction*. London: Edward Arnold, 1990. 129–141. Print.

Bal, Mieke, Jonathan Crewe, and Leo Spitzer, Eds. *Acts of Memory: Cultural Recall in the Present*. Hanover (New Hampshire): Dartmouth College, University Press of New England, 1999. Print.

Bosch, Bryan. *Balaguer and the Dominican Military. Presidential Control of the Factional Officer Corps in the 1969s and 1970s*. London: McFarland and Company, 2007. Print.

Connerton, Paul. *How Modernity Forget*. Cambridge (UK): Cambridge University Press, 2009. Print.

Cookson, Catherine. *My Land of the North: Memories of a Northern Childhood*. London: Methuen, 1999. Print.

www.dominicanonline.org/portal/espanol/cp_balaguer.asp. Web.

De Groot, Jerome. *The Historical Novel*. London: Routledge, 2010. Print.

De Maeseneer, Rita. *Seis ensayos sobre narrativa dominicana contemporánea*. Santo Domingo: Banco central de la República Dominicana, 2011. Print.

Domínguez, Jaime de Jesús. *Historia dominicana*. Santo Domingo, República Dominicana: ABC Editorial, 2001. Print.

Eco, Umberto. *Postscript to the Name of the Rose*, Trans. William Weaver. London: Harcourt Brace Jovanovich, 1984. Print.

Fernández Prieto, Celia. "Poética de la novela histórica como género literario," http://bib.cervantesvirtual.com/servlet/SirveObras/. *Signa* [Publicaciones periódicas]: Revista de la Asociación Española de Semiótica 5 (1996). Web.

González, Ester Gimbernat. "Ángela Hernández Núñez," in *Notable Twentieth Century Latin American Women: A Bibliographical Dictionary*. Ed. Cynthia Tompkins and David W. Foster. Westport: Greenwood Press, 2001. 135–138. Print.

Grosz, Elizabeth. "The Time of Thought," in *Feminist Time against Nation Time: Gender, Politics, and the Nation State in an Age of Permanent War*. Ed. Victoria Hesford and Lisa Diedrich. London: Lexington Books, 2008. 41–56. Print.

GUASABARAeditor.blogspot.com. Web.

Hermann, Hamlet. "La historia de la UASD," 17 de mayo 2009. www.elcaribe.com.do Web. February 12, 2011.

Hernández, Ángela. *Alótropos*. Santo Domingo: Editora Búho, 1998. Print.

———. *La escritura como opción ética*. Santo Domingo: Editorial Cole, 2002. 101–115. Print.

———. *Charamicos*. Santo Domingo: Editorial Cole, 2003. Print.

———. "Entrevista" Periódico *El Caribe*, www.elcaribe.com.do. Web. January 25, 2011.

Hesford, Victoria and Lisa Diedrich, Eds. "Thinking Feminism in a Time of War," in *Feminist Time against Nation Time: Gender, Politics, and the Nation State in an Age of Permanent War*. London: Lexington Books, 2008. Print.

www.hoy.cm.do/investigacion/2011/213/362177. 13 de febrero de 2011. Web.

Huyssen, Andreas. "Present Pasts: Media, Politics, Amnesia," *Public Culture* 12.1 (2000). Print.

Ikemendez. "De San Juan Bautista a Oliborio y Palmasola—Tramado Cultural e Histórico Oliborio Mateo, Palmasola," http://ikemendez.multiply.com/journal/item/33/. Web. January 22, 2011.

www.jmarcano.com/mipais/historia/discovery. Web.

Kristeva, Julia. " 'Women's Time' in 'Thinking Feminism in a Time of War,' " in *Feminist Time against Nation Time: Gender, Politics, and the Nation State in an Age of Permanent War*. Ed. Victoria Hesford and Lisa Diedrich, 23–39. Print.

Lämmert, Eberhard. "Three Versions of Wallenstein. Differences of Meaning Production between Historiography, Biography, and Novel," in *Meaning and Representation in History*. Ed. Jörn Rüsen. New York: Berghahn Books, 2006. 224–238. Print.

———. *Encuentro con la narrativa dominicana contemporánea*. Madrid: Iberoamericana, 2006. Print.

Manns, Patricio. "Impugnación de la Historia por la Nueva Novela Histórica. La Nueva Novela Histórica: una experiencia personal," in *La invencion del pasado: La novela histórica en el marco de la posmodernidad*. Ed. Karl Kohut. Frankfurt: U Católica de Eichstätt, 1997. 230–236. Print.

Martínez, Vianco. "Manuela Aristy: 'A Amaury me lo dejaron solo,' " in *Dos entrevistas de Vianco Martínez*. Santo Domingo: Producción Globo, 2006. 5–13. Print.

Montas, Lucía María. "*Charamicos*: bildungsroman femenino o aprendizaje político a través de la memoria histórica," http://utc.academia.edu/LucíaMontásRíos/Papers/314108. Web

Moya Pons, Frank. *The Dominican Republic: A National History*. Princeton (New Jersey): Markus Wiener Publishers, 1998. Print.

Nuñez, Rafael. "La Banda 'Colorá.'" www.almomento.net. Web. Lunes 06 de septiembre de 2010. Web. 10 February 2011.

Peña, Ángela. "Los vaivenes de la izquierda en una novela de Ángela Hernández," *Periódico Hoy*. Web. Sábado, 20 de diciembre de 2003.

Peña, Loyda. "Hechos imborrables. La estela de dolor de los 12 años de Joaquín Balaguer." Hoy. www.hoy.com.do/el-pais/2011/7/2 web. Julio 2, 2011.

Popper, Karl. *The Poverty of Historicism*. London: Routledge, 1957. Print.

Quiroz, Fernando. "*Charamicos*, novela ambientada en el período de los 12 años," *Hoy*. www.hoy.com.do/el-pais/2004/3/13. Web. February 23, 2011.

www.quispqueyavirtual.edu.do/wiki/La_Banda. Web.

Ricouer, Paul. *History and Truth*. Trans. Charles A. Kelbley. Evanston: Northwestern University Press, 1965. Print.

Rodríguez, Néstor. "*Charamicos* de Ángela Hernández," http://www.schnuckelchen.blogspot.com. Web. February 12, 2011.

Rosell, Sara. *La novela de escritoras dominicanas de 1990 a 2007.* New York: Mellen Press, 2007. Print.

Rüsen, Jörn, Ed. *Meaning and Representation in History.* New York: Berghahn Books, 2006. Print.

Wallace, Diana. *The Woman's Historical Novel.* New York: Palgrave Macmillan, 2005. Print

www.wikidominicana.edu.do/wiki/La_Banda. Web.

Zakrzewski Brown, Isabel Teresa. *Culture and Customs of the Dominican Republic.* Westport: Greenwood Press, 1999. Print.

9

(In)submissive Imaginaries in the Contemporary Brazilian Historical Novel: A Reading of *Um defeito de cor* by Ana Maria Gonçalves

Maria Josele Bucco Coelho

Introduction

By considering the contemporary literary production of historical extraction[1] as a privileged reading space of the signs marginalized by hegemonic history, this chapter, in concordance with Esteves's study (2012), accentuates and defends the importance assumed by such narratives in the constitution of an American imaginary re-signified by means of the discursive strategies that (re)invent forgotten temporalities.

Following this perspective, by taking into account the fight of the Latin American woman "cifrada en una doble negatividad: porque es mujer y porque es mestiza" (Castro-Klaren, 430) [ciphered in a double negativity: because she is a woman and of mixed race], this chapter seeks to reclaim the role of the feminine, engendered in the processes of transculturation, within Brazilian literary and historical culture. I will present a succinct panorama of the historical literary production by Brazilian female writers that adheres to the paradigm of the simultaneity of oppressions as a fundamental aspect of the social and political marginality suffered by women.

Talpade-Mohanty underscores "la lucha por la supervivencia y el significado de la memoria y de la propia escritura en la creación de una agencia de oposición" (Talpade-Mohanty, 10) [the fight for survival and the significance of memory and of literature itself in the creation of an agency of opposition]. This idea characterizes the works that de(re)construct the history of Brazilian literature by recognizing the "impurity" of its origins, breaking the pact of silence and oblivion in order to rescue the fragments of the collective memory, which, because of the colonizing process, were not retained by official documents.

According to Bernd (2011), this rejection or incapacity to recall "shameful memories" led to the creation of mythologies of substitution. Thus, this investigative perspective, applied, above all, to the literatures of the Americas, allows us to unveil the simulacrum of the "absent presences"; that is, it allows us to begin to see how the narratives of historical extraction by women writers are constructed in a political space where the subaltern practices are re-signified through the reinterpretation of the signs of culture. They create new possibilities of signification and make possible the reconstruction of the feminine imaginary itself in the Americas.

Finally, by analyzing the representation of the feminine in the work *Um defeito de cor* (2006) [*A Defect in Color*], by Ana Maria Gonçalves, this study delineates the changes wrought by contemporary narratives by women in the history of the continent, redesigning the role that the feminine has occupied in official discourse.

Brazilian Historical Fiction by Women Writers

> Una novela, al igual que la historia, sirve para explicar la realidad, también sirve para manipularla o para integrar una idea del pasado al presente, pero también nunca será la realidad
>
> *Antonia Viu*

> [A novel, just like history, serves to explain reality; it also serves to manipulate it or to integrate an idea of the past into the present, but also will never be reality. (my translation)][2]

Hayden White conceives of the historical work as a verbal structure in the form of narrative prose discourse that is said to be a model, or image of past structures with the goal of explaining what they were, by representing them (White, 14). Such a definition allows for the legitimizing of literary discourse in its intent to explain past images in its own way, since the proximity between literary and historical discourses resides precisely in the fact that the two are constructed from the same material—language—and revolve around the same referent—the past. What distances one from the other are the rhetorical strategies, because, according to Barthes, since they are discourses with different motivations, their rhetorical strategies will vary. Thus, the objectivity, the veracity, and the referentiality that constitute official historiographical discourse are rhetorical strategies, and it is possible to affirm that the two types of narrative—historical and literary—are, equally, forms of representation.

According to Gaddis, "representar no es otra cosa que la reordenación de la realidad según nuestros fines" (Gaddis, 2) [representation is nothing other than the reordering of reality according to our goals]. For this reason, the role played by narratives of historical extraction in contemporary society relates to the presence of groups, societies, or segments that have not encountered a space within the hegemonic historical register. In this way, one perceives a greater emphasis on marginal and peripheral beings, as well as those who have been distanced from official discourse by a conscious distortion of history through exaggerations, anachronisms, the demystifying of the historical register, and a carnivalesque vision of history. Such narratives allow the problematizing of official historical discourse, of culture, and of what has been socially accepted.

With regard to the production of narratives of historical extraction by women writers in Brazil, Esteves points out that "aunque la novela histórica sea un género asociado a la autoría masculina desde sus orígenes, se puede encontrar una progresiva participación femenina y un interesante panorama de esa trayectoria en Brasil" (Esteves, 61) [although the historical novel is a genre associated with masculine authorship from its origins, one can find a progressive feminine participation and an interesting panorama of that trajectory in Brazil]. This production can be divided into three distinct phases.

The first phase is constituted by works that deal with the foundation of "nationality" in the nineteenth century and that follow the model of Sir Walter Scott. Of these, it is worth mentioning that the first historical novel of feminine authorship was published by Ana Luísa de Azevedo Castro (1823–1869) in 1859. This text recreates the first moments of Brazilian colonization with its cultural clash and process of cultural hybridization. The novel presents a feminine perspective on these phenomena through the romance between a young Portuguese woman and the son of an indigenous man.

The second phase is characterized by the presence of novels that still follow a traditional structure, but in which the fictional plot gains more

Table 9.1   Historical novels by women writers: phase 2, the 1930s and 1940s

Author	Date of publication	Title	Theme
Cacilda de Rezende Pulino	1938	*Florinda, a Mulher que Definiu uma raça (Florinda, a Woman Who Defined a Race)*	Criticism of slavery
Cecília Bandeira de Mello	1937	*A infanta Carlota Joaquina (The Princess Carlota Joaquina)*	The life of Carlota Joaquina—kingdom of João VI
Josefa de Farias	1933	*Diamantes Pernambucanos (Pernambuco Diamonds)*	A re-reading of the *Inconfidencia Mineira (Minas Gerais Conspiracy)*
Maria José Monteiro Dupré	1944	*Luz e Sombra (Light and Shadow)*	Slave society
Ofélia Fontes	1932	*Um Reino sem Mulheres (A Kingdom without Women)*	sixteenth-century Brazilian colonial period and the influence of Protestantism

meaning and importance. From this period, the works published from 1930 on are the ones in which, according to Tejada, "lo histórico irá cobrando protagonismo a juzgar por las descripciones del acontecimiento histórico y por la progresiva incorporación de abundantes datos verídicos" (Tejada, 72) [the historical will gradually claim protagonism judging by the descriptions of the historical occurrence and the progressive incorporation of abundant true historical facts]. During this period, the novel *Um reino sem mulheres* (1932) [*A Kingdom without Women*] by Ofelia Fontes stands out, which, influenced by Rousseau's ideas on the "good savage," presents the harmonious relationship between Indians and the fight against the French and their expulsion from Brazil. In addition to this novel, there are other important works, as summarized by Table 9.1.[3] The third phase is constituted by works that recover feminine characters that were marginalized in official history, constructing a space for re-signification of the past by means of parody, carnivalization, and innovation in narrative technique (e.g., the superposition of narrative times, etc.). They are novels that are thus organized according to

La necesidad de llenar los vacíos de las historia, de articular la visión del pasado desde la perspectiva de los sectores marginados, de deconstruir la historia para denunciar las condiciones de producción que han determinado la escritura, o de repensar el pasado a la luz de lo que encontramos en el presente.

(Viu, 22)

[The necessity to fill in the empty spaces of history, to articulate a vision of the past from the perspective of the marginalized sectors, of deconstructing history in order to denounce the conditions of production that have determined writing, to rethink the past in light of what we find in the present.]

From this perspective, one can affirm that such contemporary historical narratives share the same ideas and preoccupations that the philosophy of history developed throughout the twentieth century, in other words, the perception of history as a narrative discourse that represents reality and seeks to explain it, but that does not demand the status of truth. The contemporary novels of historical extraction, as well as history, can explain reality, at the same time that they also equally manipulate it, integrating an idea from the past into the present. Thus, they can be considered as representations, but never as the truth.

Of the women writers who belong to this phase that takes us to the contemporary period, Ana Miranda is the one who has most extensively fictionalized the Brazilian colonial period, re(de)constructing the political authority and Portuguese absolutism. According to Tejada, the skeptical vision of official history that permeates the writer's narrative characterizes other novels that belong to this phase (Table 9.2).

The progressively increasing space occupied by women in the conquest of a political consciousness contributes to the constitution of a semantically re-signified imaginary, which until then, from one (dominant) perspective, was subaltern and marginal. The recuperation, study, and analysis of such works permit not only the development of an (ex)centric vision, but also the materializing of a discursive in-between space where the mechanisms of coercion, extinguishment, and exclusion are questioned through a reflective praxis.

The novels that stand out in this phase are those that revisit literary history itself, un(re)doing the knots left by the hegemonic version. The canonical characters are, then, re-inscribed in that demystifying tradition that breaks with phallologocentrism and allows the reader to accede to other perspectives, in a game that is defined by memory and oblivion.

Table 9.2 Historical novels by women writers: phase 3, from the 1950s to the present

Author	Date of publication	Title	Theme
Ana Elisa Gregorio	1978	Os Barões de Candeia (The Barons of Candeia)	Period of slavery
Anajá Caetano	1966	Negra Efigênia. Paixão do Senhor Branco (Black Efigeina. Lord White's Passion)	The agricultural expansionism in Minas Gerais from the pro-African perspective
Ana Maria Gonçalves	2006	Um defeito de cor (A Defect in Color)	The story of Kehinde, the black and slave mother of the first black Brazilian romantic poet—Luis Gama
	1989	Boca do Inferno (The Mouth from Hell)	Ostracism—life of the baroque poet Gregorio de Matos
	1991	O Retrato do Rei (The Portrait of a King)	Cycle of gold in Brazil—colonial period
Ana Miranda	1995	A Última Quimera (The Last Chimera)	Life and work of the symbolist poet Augusto dos Anjos
	1996	Desmundo (Unworld)	Brazilian colonial period from the perspective of Oribela—an orphan sent by the Portuguese queen to Brazil
	1997	Amrik	The Lebanese colonization of Brazil
Dinah Silveira de Queiroz	1954	A muralha (The Wall)	The process of formation of São Paulo
	1960	A Princesa dos Escravos (The Princess of the Slaves)	The life of Princess Isabel, who signed the declaration of freedom for slaves
	1965	Os Invasores (The Invaders)	The invasion of Rio de Janeiro by the French
Helena Moura	1997	O ouro da Liberdade. A História de Chico Rey (The Gold of Liberty. The Story of Chico Rey)	Slavery

Isolina Bresolin Vianna	1997	*Masmorras da Inquisição (Dungeons of the Inquisition)*	Power and domination of the Catholic Church during the period of the Inquisition in Brazil
	1997	*Rosa María Egpicíaca de Vera Cruz. A incrível história de uma Escrava, Prostituta e Santa (Rosa Maria, Egyptian from Vera Cruz. The Incredible Story of a Slave, Prostitute, and Saint)*	The story of a mystical slave persecuted by the Inquisition
Luzilá Gonçalves Ferreira	1993	*Os ríos Turvos (The Turbid Rivers)*	Life of the poet Bento Teixeira and his wife, Filipa Raposa, during the Inquisition
Margarida de Aguiar Patriota	1991	*Mafalda Amazona: Novela a-Histórica (Amazonian Mafalda: A Historical Novel*	Brazilian national history narrated from the matriarchal perspective
Maria Helena Whately	1995	*Os seios de Eva (Eva's Breasts)*	Re-signification of the role of Eva in Western civilization
Maria Jose de Queiroz	1987	*Joaquina, Filha de Tiradentes (Joaquina, Daughter of Tiradentes)*	The history of Minas Gerais in the seventeenth century
Nélida Piñon	1984	*A República dos Sonhos (The Republic of Dreams)*	Period of national formation of Brazil
	1967	*Fundador (Founder)*	Formation of Brazilian society
Rachel de Queiroz	1992	*Memorial de Maria Moura (Memorial of Maria Moura)*	Recuperation of the character from official history—Maria Moura—guerrilla fighter and chief of an armed band during the nineteenth century
Rosalina Coelho Lisboa	1952	*A Seara de Caim (The Harvest of Cain)*	Slave society in the nineteenth century and the formation of the first Republic
Tânia Jamardo Faillace	1965	*Adão e Eva (Adam and Eve)*	Critical and parodic approach to patriarchal society and gender relations
Urda Klueger	1972	*Verde Vale (Green Valley)*	German colonization in Santa Catarina
Virginia Tamanini	1964	*Karina*	Italian immigration in Brazil

Source: Tejada (2004), Esteves (2010), Figueiredo (1994), Lobo (2008), and Weinhardt (2006).

The History of Brazilian Literature Revisited
by Contemporary Fiction

Uno tenía la sensación de estar escribiendo alrededor de un agujero negro,
que no se podía tocar, y que era lo único sobre lo que tenía sentido escribir.
Y todo lo demás era banal, era trivial, y era inmoral. Era inmoral estar
usando la palabra para algo que no fuera contar lo que nos estaba pasando.
(Ana María Shua)

[One had the sensation of writing around a black hole, that could not be
touched, and which was the only thing about which it made sense to write.
And everything else was banal, trivial, and immoral It was immoral to use
words for something that was other than telling what was happening to us.]

In Brazilian literature, as in the rest of the Western countries, phallologocentrism has predominated for a long time. Toward the end of the
nineteenth century, one begins to see small changes and the insertion of
female participation in literature. Nonetheless, such changes, which can be
concretely seen in the tables that were previously presented on narratives of
historical extraction,[4] have intensified in the twentieth century and female
authorship, until then marginalized in official literary history, comes to
occupy an outstanding space.

   Considering the self-reflective role that the novels of historical extraction contemporaneously play and their transgressive and parodic character, one perceives that the works by women writers engender a vision that
deconstructs the double (or multiple) colonizations to which women have
been subjected in Latin America, chipping away at the universality of the
traditional hegemonic critical discourse. In this sense, one can signal the
importance of the works that, by means of the (re)visitation of the history of official literature, present to the readers the possibility of re-reading
the role of women in the constitution of that imaginary, revealing the
simulacra, the absent presences, "forgotten" or "marginalized" by official
discourse.

   Ana Miranda's literary production stands out in this regard. Miranda
fictionalizes characters from Brazilian literature in many of her works.
In *Boca de inferno* [*The Mouth from Hell*], a novel published in 1989, she
narrates the story of the baroque poet Gregorio de Matos, known by the
nickname "mouth from hell" because of his criticism and satire about
Bahia, a Brazilian state, during the colonial period. In addition to Gregorio
de Matos, in this work Miranda also fictionalizes the writer/priest Antonio
Vieira, icon of colonial literature in Brazil. In the novel, both the political and the literary activism of the poet is rescued, making him into a
representative figure of "Brazilianness." It is important to point out in

this context that Gregorio de Matos has been excluded from the work *Formação de la literaria brasileira* [*The Formation of Brazilian Literature*], published by Antonio Candido in 1957, and that he became one of the classics of national literary history.[5] Thus, this novel re-inscribes Gregorio de Matos in history not only as a poet representative of a literary period, but also as an individual who had a fundamental role in the era in which he lived.

In *A ultima quimera* (1995) [*The Last Chimera*], a work similar to *Boca de Inferno*, one can see the ample historical investigation that allows the reader to comprehend the metaphysical preoccupations that consumed the symbolist, Parnassian, pre-modernist poet, Augusto dos Anjos and that was concretized in his poetic expression. The great historical events of the period—the formation of the Republic, the political disputes, the Chibata Revolt, and the famous duel between the poet Olavo Bilac and Raul Pompeia—are fictionalized by the author who de(re)constructs the tragic death and indifference of Anjos's contemporaries through the labyrinthine memories of the poet's childhood friend.[6]

In *Clarice Lispector—o tesouro da mina cidade* (1996) [*Clarice Lispector—the Treasure of Mine Town*], Ana Miranda appropriates Lispector's style in order to give voice to one of the great icons of Latin American literature by women writers. The reception of the work by critics was, perhaps, a little harsh, considering that the novel was written as a financed project for the Fundação Rio Arte and published, in 1999, by the Companhia das Letras, with a cut in the title, so that it became known as simply *Clarice.*

The last work by Ana Miranda, *Dias e Dias* (2002) [*Days and Days*],[7] narrates the life of the renowned Brazilian poet Gonçalves Dias through the voice and romantic, passionate viewpoint of Feliciana, a woman who has access to the poet's correspondence. This work, like the ones presented before, share what Hutcheon calls a "profunda y aguda consciencia del proceso de construcción" (Hutcheon, 150) [a profound and sharp consciousness of the constructive process]. By appropriating the simple style that predominated in Romanticism, Feliciana's memories are presented as a mnemonic device through which the fictionalized poet himself becomes an ethereal and untouchable being.

In addition to Ana Miranda's production, the work *Os ríos Turvos* [*The Turbid Rivers*] (1993) by Luzilá Ferreira Gonçalves deserves to be singled out. This work, in contrast with the others that were previously mentioned, presents the fictionalization of a character from Brazilian literary history, Bento Teixeira, author of *Prosopopeia [Prosopopeia]*, in a less direct manner. The narrative is centered on the story of his wife, Filipa Raposa, who was assassinated by the poet after having denounced him to the Inquisition as a Jew and bad Christian. The story allows the reader to comprehend Bento Teixeira's process of literary production, characterized by arduous, rational work and counterpoise it to the natural and instinctive poetry written by his wife. This work de(re)constructs part of the colonial feminine imaginary considered as perverse and malignant, since Filipa's voice presents the feminine vision of events that official history crystalized.

Finally, Ana María Gonçalves's work, *Um defeito de cor,* published in 2006,[8] revisits 80 years of history between Brazil-black-Atlantic-Africa through the voice of Kehinde, possibly Luiza Mahin, the mother of the black poet Luiz Gama. The novel consists of 1,000 pages, and is considered by Millor Fernandes (in his prologue to the first edition) to be one of "los mejores libros leídos en nuestra lengua" ([one of] the best books in our language) and by Miguel Wisnik as one of the great Brazilian novels written in the past 50 years,[9] following the production by Guimarães Rosa. The novel rescues the black heritage forgotten by Brazilian letters, signaling the influence of the black Atlantic culture in the formation of Brazilian literature, by operating like a tool for re-signification of a marginalized and denied past. The institution of a feminine black ancestry proposed in the narrative is the theme for reflection that makes possible the configuration of the (insubmissive) contemporary imaginary that (re)invents the temporalities forgotten by official discourse.

Um defeito de cor: The Black Atlantic in Contemporary Brazilian Literature

The term *Black Atlantic*, utilized by Paul Gilroy, is imbued with the defense of the importance of black culture from "both sides" of the Atlantic and connotes the consideration of blacks "como agentes, como pessoas com capacidades cognitivas e mesmo com uma história intellectual—atributos negados pelo racismo moderno" (Gilroy, 40) [as agents, as people with cognitive capacity and also with an intellectual history—attributes that have been denied by modern racism]. Thus, the hybridization and transculturation become, for him, the mechanisms through which modern life is founded and cannot be left unconsidered in current studies.

Ana Maria Gonçalves's novel, seen in this light, can be considered as one of the legitimate expressions of the Black Atlantic in the south,[10] since it relates the mechanisms of oppression engendered by the slave regime in Brazil and in Africa from the perspective of a poor enslaved black woman. It deconstructs the romantic, nationalist discourse that defends purity of African origin by revealing the internal division—of gender and class—that allowed the implantation and retention of three centuries of slave trade.

The protagonist of the novel, Kehinde, is presented to the reader from the perspective of extreme violence. Her mother and her brother are assassinated by men that defend King Adandazor, an African dictator who incites violence between the tribes as a way to maintain the arms commerce, the traffic of slaves, and his own power. The mother is raped in front of her siblings, because of the accusations that her grandmother is a sorceress. Kehinde and her twin sister, who are still little girls, both suffer sexual violence and flee with the grandmother seeking a new life in Uidá, where they are captured and made into slaves. This description reveals the mechanisms of oppression that made Africa into a space fragmented by internal battles, where the search for survival led to the sale of even family members.

In this process, the work denounces the fact that the first oppressors of the Africans are the Africans themselves. Kehinde—or Luiza Gama, her Brazilian name—after facing all kinds of violence as a slave in Brazil, upon returning to Africa, becomes an arms and slave dealer:

> Anos depois, quando paramos de fazer comercio com eles, soube que tinham me enganado, que não eram pessoas tão corretas quanto eu imaginava. [. . .] Soube que, além das mercadorias locais, eles também faziam um pequeno tráfico de escravos, encomendas especiais.
>
> (UDC, 793)

> [Years later, when we stopped dealing with them, I found out that they had deceived me, that they were not such honest people as I had imagined . . . I found out they also had a small slave traffic, special orders].

It is important to point out that Kehinde was conscious of the fact that the activity she realized financed the violence of her continent but she justified herself by affirming that someone would have to do it, and if it were not her, then another person would. In this way, the narrative suggests a model that rejects current essentialism, centering upon human action and escaping from racial categorization in order to justify, comprehend, and reflect on human actions.

Another constituent factor of the Black Atlantic is, according to Gilroy, the mobility to which different cultures are subjected and the importance gained by transculturation that is achieved by means of transit. Various types of mobility are forged in the narrative—spatial, temporal, linguistic, and discursive—but the spatial displacements lived by Kehinde predominate.[11] She leaves Savalu, the city where she was born, and moves to Uidá, the coastal city where she is captured and taken to Brazil with her twin sister, Taiwo, and her grandmother.

In Brazil, she passes through diverse places: Isla de los Frades, where she remains until her purchasers are certain that the recently arrived slaves are not infected, and then later San la isla de Itaparica, where she is made a slave by José Gama, her first owner, by whom she will become pregnant through rape. The changes in her life occur after the death of her master and the family's transfer to San Salvador, where she manages to buy her freedom by working as a Gano slave.[12] Shortly thereafter, she meets a Portuguese merchant with whom she has a child, and then goes to live on a ranch in a village that she later abandons for Maranhão, where she becomes initiated in Vodun, the religious practice of her ancestors.

During this period, because of her involvement in various rebellions, she must remain far away from her child who is sold into slavery by his father, in order to pay off various debts. Once again, the narrative organizes itself on the basis of Kehinde's different displacements in search of her son: Rio de Janeiro, São Paulo, Campinas, and once again San Salvador until she returns to Africa, to Uidá, and then finally, old and blind, to Brazil.

Spatial mobility is clearly one of the constituent elements of the narrative structure and forces Kehinde into a constant process of adaptation and replacement of cultural and identifying values. By means of her displacements, the reader is inserted into the existing differences among members of the Brazilian black population, perceiving how the cultural differences brought from Africa are maintained in Brazilian territory and are the motive for conflicts and prejudices:

> Ao andar pelas ruas e mesmo pelos mercados [de escravos] eu tinha a mania de ficar olhando para esses pretos e tentando adivinhar de onde eran [...] O piripiri me instruí a não dizer que era do Daomé, mas sim uma crioula nascida na Bahia, pois os eves e os fons, ou preto-minas, como nos chamávamos, eram minoria em São Sebastião e não se davam bem com outros africanos.
>
> (UDC, 648–665)

> [While walking through the streets and (slave) markets I looked at the blacks and tried to guess where they were from .... Piripiri instructed me not to say that I was from Dahomé but rather a creole born in Bahia, because the *eves* and the *fons,* the black-mines as they were called, were a minority in San Sebastião and did not relate well to other Africans.]

Moreover, upon returning to Africa and establishing herself as a merchant, Kehinde, in a controversial process, comes to value her Brazilian identity, perceiving that this might be useful to her, once she considered her own people to be savages. This surprising change suffered since one of her last transits illustrates, once more, the power relationships established by one class of blacks who, having fled to Brazil because of the terrible conditions imposed on slaves, feel superior to those who remained behind. The knowledge of the world, the observation of the functioning of commerce, allows them to act in an effective manner in Africa, rapidly turning into a group that no longer feels a part of that culture. It is for this reason that Kehinde feels ashamed when she sees African women with their breasts revealed: "era estranho ver mulheres com o peito de fora, a sentí um pouco de vergonha por estar olhando elas, que também olhavam para mim quase com o mesmo espanto" (UDC, 745) [it was strange to see women with their breasts out, I felt a little ashamed for looking at them, who also looked at me with almost the same astonishment].

Thus, the novel demonstrates the transcultural process to which Kehinde/Luiza is subjected without converting her into a heroine exempt from faults and who was always susceptible to the pragmatism of life. In Africa she becomes rich, adopts a new Western name—repudiated while she was in Brazil—and becomes Doña Luiza, or Sinhá Luiza—the one who introduces customs, foods, and Brazilian architecture to the Gulf of Benin.

Moreover, this pondering of the similarities and differences between black cultures that the novel throws into relief underscores the asymmetrical relations that have constituted and continue to constitute the black Atlantic, establishing a discussion about the ties created by the postcolonial relationships still perpetuated within the twentieth century and that directly relate to the reflection on contemporary cultural identities.

Therefore, for Gilroy, one cannot refrain from considering that the intense trade that occurred in the nineteenth century because of slave traffic and the commercial relations established along the route—America, Europe, and Africa—was one of the factors that stimulated modernity and the processes of fragmentation of identity lived by contemporary society. Indeed, the defense of this idea finds support in Ana Maria Gonçalves's work through the first-person narration that describes the lack of identification into which the African diaspora was thrown and that remits to the constitution of a rhizomatic identity.[13] For Kehinde, those who return to Africa are no longer Africans, nor do they recall the customs and celebrations that are part of Brazilian culture, which forces them, in a transcultural process, to reinvent such customs and religious celebrations, converting themselves into something that, while they were living in Brazil, they had rejected. This process results in a religious syncretism and in the construction of hybrid and fragmentary identities.

Another important point regarding these processes of identification is that the transit lived by Kehinde throughout her life allows for the development of a consciousness regarding the devices that should be, in a given moment, emphasized to guarantee life. This process of cultural identification that the postmodern individual utilizes, as Hall (2002) defines it, is lived by Kehinde even at the beginning of the nineteenth century, when she offers to her friends the rings of *muçurumins*—blacks of Muslim origin who, because of their religiosity, refuse to subjugate themselves to domination by another who is not Allah. If their revolt were successful, the black Muslims intended to kill the whites and enslave the other blacks who were not converted to Islam. In this manner, the ring would function as a mechanism for identification, a piece of attire that could mean the continuation of one's own life. In addition, upon returning to Africa, she decides that her children born in Uidá—twins—should receive Brazilian names because this would give them a greater possibility to triumph in life. They are therefore named Maria Clara and João.

As far as the constitution of blacks as agents of history is concerned, the novel relates the experience of frustrated insubordination that became known as the Revuelta de los Malês [Revolt of the Malians]. In the narrative, Kehinde associates herself with the *muçumirins*, described as intelligent and haughty sorcerers, and for these reasons, they are despised by the other Africans who judge them as superior. The religious practices occur in hidden places where the presence of non-converts is not tolerated. The treatment given to women is also different. The men do not look them in the eye and are not authorized to speak to them without the permission of a husband, son, or responsible man.

Therefore, when Kehinde decides to rent her former bakery to a group of Muslims, despite the fact that she is black like them, also speaks various languages, bought her freedom and that of her son, and was a successful merchant, she is despised by the black man who refuses to speak directly to her and wants to negotiate with her son who is still a child.

The disparagement of the feminine condition and lack of consideration to which Kehinde was subjected amused Kehinde, because for her, the fact that that man would ask for approval from her son, a child, to deal with her, was, at the very least, ridiculous. Thus, by means of satire, we approach the mechanisms of power that demonstrate the processes of marginalization that occur between subjects that are considered subaltern.

This description illustrates how the black woman suffers a double exclusion: by white, slave society, and black men, equally patriarchal and sexist. She is thus subjected to multiple colonizations and her fight is, for that reason, different than that of men. She is simultaneously subjected to the power structure of family, religion, and the state. This position represents the ideas expressed by Talpade-Mohanty (1991), for whom Latin American women should fight in parallel against society's sexist, racist, and imperialist structures, constructing thus an agency of opposition against the experience of political and social marginality.

From this perspective, the differences and internal conflicts such as those faced by Kehinde are converted into tools through which a rupture in the organization of communities is established. Memory and writing are constituted as tools of subversion against the hegemonic state and contribute to the creation of this agency of opposition. Perhaps this is the reason why the novel *Um defeito de cor* invokes the ascendancy of the first black Brazilian poet through the story of his mother, Luisa Mahin/Kehinde, recovering the role of the (black) feminine in the constitution of the Brazilian nation and in literary history.

Toward a (Black) Feminine Genealogy in Brazilian Literary History: (In)submissive Imaginaries

According to Ironides Rodrigues (2007), black literature is that which is developed by an author who considers himself black or mulatto and who writes about race seeking to explain the meaning of being black and the black color in a deliberate form, discussing the problems in relation to society, religion, and racism.[14] Bernd, in consonance with this concept, emphasizes that such texts signal the presence of an "enunciating I" that proclaims itself the descendant of Africans. In this sense, one can affirm that the novel *Um defeito de cor* inserts itself within this tradition.[15] However, it is important to underscore that, considering the constitution of Brazilian society and, therefore, of its literature, the term *Afro-Brazilian* perhaps is the best one to indicate semantically the process of cultural mixture and hybridity that installed itself in the Americas and that is reflected in the novels by Ana Maria Gonçalves.

This Afro-Brazilian vein in Brazilian literature is born beginning with the publication of the work *Trovas burlescas* [*Burlesque Ballads*] by Luíz Gama, and the novel *Ursula* by Maria Firmina dos Reis, in the 1850s. Luíz Gama, Bahian abolitionist poet, was born free and then sold as a slave by his father—a Portuguese man who had debts because of his gambling addiction. In a letter sent to a friend, the poet declares:

> Sou filho natural de uma negra, africana livre, da Costa da Mina (Nagô de Nação) de nome Luíza Mahin, pagã, que sempre recusou o batismo e a doutrina cristã. Minha mãe era de baixa estatura, magra, bonita, a cor era de um preto retinto e sem lustro, tinha os dentes alvíssimos como a neve, era muito altiva, geniosa, insofrida e vingativa. Dava-se ao comércio—era quitandeira, muito laboriosa, e mais de uma vez, na Bahia, foi presa como suspeita de envolver-se em planos de insurreições de escravos, que não tiveram efeito.
>
> (Gama)

> [I am the illegitimate son of a free, black, African woman from the Coast of Mina (Nagó de Nación) by the name of Luiza Mahín, a pagan, who always refused baptism and the Christian doctrine. My mamma was short, thin,

pretty, her color was dark brown and without shine, she had very white teeth that were like snow, she was witty, haughty and vengeful. She worked in commerce—she was a trader, very hard-working and more than once, in Bahia, she was jailed on the suspicion of being involved in slave plans for insurrection that had no effect.]

The analysis of this document permits the reader to perceive the similarities between the life of Luiza Mahin and her corresponding literary character, Luiza Gama/Kehinde. The fictionalized character exactly repeats the characteristics of the poet's mother and her life. Just like Kehinde, Luiza Mahin also disappeared from her son's life without leaving any trail.

The interesting thing is that the literary narrative seeks to fill in the "gaps" through the first-person tale narrated by Kehinde. The reader of the text discovers that the search for the lost child, fruit of the (symbolic and emblematic) encounter between a Portuguese man and the African woman, is a constant in the life of the character. However, it is necessary to perceive that the figure of the mother, dedicated and absorbed in the care of her children, is subverted in the text, because Kehinde flees from the traditional sexual roles. Despite her preoccupation with her son, she does not fail to live passions—with Piripiri in San Sebastião (Rio de Janeiro) and with John, when she returns to Africa. Moreover, she manages to realize her road to self-discovery, upon entering in the terrain where Vodun religion and orgies were being practiced and in which she underwent the rites of initiation.

One can also point out her intense work as a trader, since from a young age, she learned that an individual's freedom depends first and foremost on financial independence. It was this perception that led her, for example, to leave the Portuguese father of her son, affirming that she was happy to be able to support herself alone, without depending on a man for survival. This determination to stay financially independent resembles the ideas expressed by Virginia Woolf, icon of the contemporary feminist movement, who defends this idea in her work A Room of One's Own (1929).

Thus, one can affirm that the work breaks with bourgeois morals and the Latin American religious tradition characterized by the double position Eve-Mary, explained by Lucía Guerra, by re-inscribing the feminine without repression of women's passions or libido. In this process, the representation of the resistance of the black woman occupies a privileged space, in contrast to that of the white woman, where the free exercise of her sexuality is not reprehended for they maintained themselves de-colonized from the current Christian moral code.[16]

This opposition between the sexuality of women characterized by the binarism white/submissive and black/free is reinforced in the novel when the narrator explains that, many times, the white women were infertile because of herbs that the black women put in their food. Moreover, the consciousness that these black women had regarding the desire that their strong bodies inspired is also emphasized. These acts reveal the "oppression" exerted by black women and show the need to break with the idea that all whites are exploitive and all blacks are victims.

It is clear that these situations suggest the avoidance of dichotomies and traditional Manichaeism without failing to denounce the violence of slavery and the privileges of the whites. The text represents the American imaginaries in their first instance of rebellion, emphasizing the role of the black as agent of history, reclaiming the importance of women within a black subaltern literary system.

This perception is only established at the narrative's end, when the reader discovers the great discursive node constructed in the work, and that the thousand pages read are in fact the letter that Luiza/Kehinde writes to her son. The identification of the text's narratee, the poet Luiz Gama, precursor of Afro-Brazilian literature, is the key point for the configuration of the criticism planted in the text, since it vindicates the female presence in history and denounces the presence/absence of women in the constitution of literary history.

Final Considerations

The reflective character of historical meta-fictions constitutes one of the most potent mechanisms for subversion and re-signification of the past. The criticism of multiple and intertwined oppressions reveals the complex relations of power established throughout time and advocates the rupture with essentialisms that until recently dominated our culture.

The vision of the constitution of the Black Atlantic from the perspective of the south reiterates the importance of the black diaspora in the formation of transcultural and hybrid Americanness and, at the same time, takes on the importance of a voice many times made subaltern, and concretizes a postcolonial focus through the agency of female opposition incarnated in the figure of the woman writer, Kehinde. Thus, *Um defeito de cor*, by giving the space of enunciation to Kehinde, de(re)constructs the history of black presence in Brazilian literature and establishes itself as a precursor of this insubmissive imaginary.

Notes

1. The concept of narratives of historical extraction adopted in this study was used by André Trouche to encompass a broader range of narratives that are

constructed and fed by historical material, converting them into a form of production of transgressive knowledge.

2. Note that this translation and all others are mine unless otherwise noted.

3. Note that the sources for the construction of this chart are Tejada (2004), Esteves (2010), Figueiredo (1994), Lobo (2008), and Weinhardt (2006).

4. The literary production of female authorship in Brazil can be divided into various phases. According to Constância Lima Duarte, the first phase begins at the beginning of the nineteenth century, when women vindicate their right to read and write. Nísia Floresta Brasileira Augusta (1810–1855), one of the first Brazilian feminist icons, was at the forefront of this process. In addition, Beatriz Francisca de Assis Brandão (1779–1860), Clarinda da Costa Siqueira (1818–1867), and Delfina Benigna da Cunha (1791–1857) stand out as important figures. Shortly thereafter, in 1870, women came to occupy a more significant space in the cultural sphere, whether through literary or journalistic production, inaugurating the second phase of feminine insertion in literature. For Muzart, owing to the process of exclusion and marginalization that women were subjected to, the literary production was feminist, since it was impossible to separate the literary labor from the current feminine condition. The third phase initiated at the beginning of the twentieth century is characterized by the fight for the conquest of feminine citizenship—the right to vote, to education, to a university formation, and to professional training. Women writers came to occupy a more significant space and inserted themselves into Brazilian artistic activity. It is in this way that Rosalina Coelho Lisboa (1900–1975), in 1921, won the first prize in the literary contest of the Brazilian Academy of Letters with the work *Rito pagão* [*Pagan Rite*].

Representative of this period are Patricia Galvão-Pagu, as she was known; Gilka Machado (1893–1980); and Rachel de Queiroz (1910–2004). We should also point out the presence of Clarice Lispector and Cecilia Meireles, who, upon publishing *Romanceiro da Incondidencia* [*Ballads of Incondidencia*] (1953), won the respect of Brazilian critics. The production by Cecilia and Clarice marks a rupture with the past through deconstructive and metalinguistic language, which, according to Gotlib (1998), inaugurated a new time in the literary production of feminine authorship in Brazil, in which the search for the constitution of an identity intensified.

The last phase can be located, temporally, starting in the 1970s. The development of the studies of gender and of feminist literary criticism in Brazil made possible the creation of discussion forums, conferences, fields of investigation, and investigative groups, which allowed for reflection on the presence of women in Brazilian literature throughout time, realizing, through archaeological work, the revision of the instituted canon. In that moment, the literature of feminine authorship provoked the development of the discussion of institutional patriarchal norms, opening the way for the debate on gender by means of the insertion of feminine voices in historicized spaces, and proliferating the narratives of historical extraction by women writers in Brazil.

5. Haroldo de Campos, in the essay *O sequestro do barroco na Formçãao da literatura brasileira: o caso Gregorio de Matos,* published in 1989, deals with this question, rejecting the exclusion made by Candido. Luis Costa Lima, in *Concepção de história literária na Formação* (199), clarifies the concept of Candido's literary system and shows his motives for not including Gregorio de Matos in his work.

6. Francisco de Assis Barbosa, in the introduction to the 29th edition of the work *EU* by Augusto dos Anjos (São José Press, 1963), narrates, anecdotally, the story of the death of the poet. According to the author, Olavo Bilac, the prince of the Brazilian Paranassian poets, upon learning of the death of the great poet Augusto dos Anjos, asked who he was because he had never heard about his production. This episode portrays the rejection that Augusto dos Anjos faced and that was remedied after his death.

7. This work received the Jabuti Prize and the Prize of the Brazilian Academy of Letters in the Novel category in 2003.

8. When referring to the work *Um defeito de cor,* I will use the abbreviation UDC.

9. Wisnik also cites *Quarup,* by Antonio Callado; *Incidente em Antares* [*Incident in Antares*], by Érico Veríssimo; *Catatau,* by Paulo Leminski; and *Romance da Pedra do Reino* [*Stone's Kingdom*], by Ariano Suassuna.

10. It is important to underscore that the ideas defended in the work use the experience of North America as a departure point for discussion. Thus, by using the term "Black Atlantic" to designate contemporary Brazilian literary production, an amplification of the concept is realized. By criticizing the "absent presence" of blacks in the formation of Western culture, Gilroy forgets that black transit did not only operate in the North. Thus, the rescue of the term and its application to the confrontation and analysis of southern literary production assumes an equally de-colonizing character.

11. This taxonomic division is proposed by Bernd in the dictionary of *Mobilidades Culturais* (2011) and has the following characteristics: Space: trips, displacements, flâneries, time: temporal jumps and holes in the narrative, discourse: change of narrative voices and multiple enunciators, language: the use of linguistic figures and aesthetic techniques that displace the denotative sense.

12. In this type of work, the slave was free to do whatever work was available in the streets, but had to pay his owner a certain quantity of money on a monthly basis.

13. For more information on rhizomatic identity, see Deleuze and Guattari (1997) and Glissant (2005), who deal with the African diaspora in the Americas.

14. This concept of black literature was presented by Ironides Rodrigues in an interview given to Luiza Lobo in 2007.

15. The studies on black literature in Brazil begin to develop after 1970, when the writers came to assume their ethnic identity.

16. Kehinde herself, conscious of this situation, takes advantage of the opportunity to buy her freedom in a controversial maneuver: she drugs her owner with herbs to make her sleep and then asks Sebastião, her lover, to go to bed with

her mistress and seduce her. While this is happening, she removes her mistress's clothing and calls the priest. By means of this artifice, she manages to buy her liberty and that of her son for a reduced price.

Works Cited

Assis Barbosa, Francisco. "Introdução." In *Eu by Augusto dos Anjos*. Rio de Janeiro: Editora São José, 1963.

Azevedo, Elciene. *Orfeu de carapinha: a trajetória de Luiz Gama na imperial cidade de São Paulo*. Campinas: Editora da UNICAMP, 1999. Print.

Bernd, Zilá, ed. *Escrituras híbridas, estudos em literatura comparada interamericana*. Porto Alegre: Editora da UFRGS, 1998. Print.

———. *Dicionário das mobilidades culturais: percursos americanos*. Porto Alegre: Universidade Federal do Rio Grande do Sul, 2011a. 9–16. http://www.msmidia.com/conexao/06.pdf. Web.

———. "Vestígios memoriais: fecundando as literaturas das Américas." In *Revista Conexões*. Porto Alegre: Universidade Federal do Rio Grande do Sul, 2011b. Print.

Campos, Haroldo de. *O sequestro do barroco na formação da literatura brasileira: o caso Gregório de Matos*. Salvador: Fundação Casa de Jorge Amado, 1989. Print.

Castro-Klaren, Sara. "La crítica feminista y la escritora en América Latina." In *La sartén por el mango*. Eds Patricia Elena González and Eliana Ortega. Puerto Rico: Ed. Huracán, 1985. 27–46. Print.

Deleuze, Gilles and Felix Guattari. *Mil Platôs*, vol. 5. São Paulo, 34th ed., 1997. Print.

Duarte, Constância Lima. Feminismo e literatura no Brasil. Esud. Av. 17.49 (2003): 151–172. http: dx.doi.org/10.1590/S0103-40142003000300010. Web.

Esteves, Antonio Roberto. "O novo romance histórico brasileiro." In *Estudos de literatura e linguística*. Ed. L. Z. Atunes. São Paulo: Arte & Ciência; Assis, SP: Curso de Pós-Graduação em Letras da FCL/UNESP, 1998, 122–158. Print.

———. *O romance histórico contemporâneo*. São Paulo: Ed. UNESP, 2012. Print.

Figueiredo, Vera Lúcia Forrain. "Da alegria e da angústia de diluir fronteiras: o romance histórico hoje na América Latina." *Cânones e contextos:* Anais do 5º Congresso ABRALIC. Rio de Janeiro, ABRALIC, 1998. v.1. http://filipe.tripod.com/Vera.html. Web.

Gaddis, John Lewis. *El paisaje de la historia: Como los historiadores representan el pasado*. Barcelona: Anagrama, 2002.

Gama, Luiz. "Carta a Lucio Mendonça." http://www.letras.ufmg.br/literafro/data1/autores/96/textosselecionados.pdf.

Gilroy, Paul. *O atlântico negro*. 34th ed., Rio de Janeiro. 2012. Print.

Glissant, Edouard. *Introdução a uma poética da diversidade*. Juiz de Fora: Editora UFJF, 2005. Print.

Gonçalves, Ana Maria. *Um defeito de cor*. Rio de Janeiro: Record, 2006. Print.

Gotlib, Nadia. "A literatura feita por mulheres no Brasil." In *Refazendo nós*. Eds Izabel Brandão and Zahildé Muzart. Florianópolis: Editora Mulheres, 2003. 19–72. Print.

Guerra, Lucía. *La mujer fragmentada: historias de un signo.* Chile: Editorial Cuarto propio, 1995. Print.

Hutcheon, Linda. *Poética do pós-modernismo.* Trans. Ricardo Cruz. Rio de Janeiro: Imago, 1991. Print.

Lima, Luiz Costa. *Sociedade e discurso ficcional.* Rio de Janeiro: Guanabara, 1986. Print.

Lobo, Luiza. "A literatura de autoria feminina na América latina." In *Revista Brasil de Literatura* (Rio de Janeiro), ano I, Julho-setembro 1997. http;//www. cesargiusti.bluehosting.com.br/Centralit/Textos/semi1.htm. Web.

Lukács, Georg. *A teoria do romance.* São Paulo: Duas Cidades, Editora 34, 2000. Print.

Medeiros–Lichem, María Teresa. *La voz femenina en la narrativa latinoamericana: una relectura crítica.* Santiago: Ed. Cuarto Propio, 2006. Print.

Miranda, Ana. *Boca do inferno.* São Paulo: Companhia das Letras, 1989. Print.

———. *A Última quimera.* São Paulo: Companhia das Letras, 1996. Print.

———. *Clarice.* São Paulo: companhia das Letras, 1999. Print.

———. *Dias e Dias.* São Paulo: Companhia das Letras, 2002. Print.

Muzart, Zahilé Lupinacci. "Feminismo e literatura ou quando a mulher começou a falar." In *História da Literatura, teorías, temas e autores.* Ed. Maria Eunice Moreira. Porto Alegre: Mercado Aberto, 2003. 35–44. Print.

Sáenz de Tejada, C. "Brasil." In *La narrativa histórica de escritoras latinoamericanas.* Ed. Glória Cunha. Buenos Aires: Corregidor, 2001. 69–98. Print.

Talpade-Mohanty, Chandra. *Third World Women anda the Politics Feminism.* Bloomington: Indiana University Press, 1991. Print.

Trouche, André. *América: história e ficção.* Niterói: Ed. UFF, 2006. Print.

Viu, Antonia. *Imaginar el pasado, decir el presente.* Santiago: Ril Editores, 2007. Print.

Weinhardt, Marilene. *Considerações sobre o romance histórico.* Revista de Letras. Curitiba/PR: Ed. UFPR, n⁰ 43, 1994, 49–59. Print.

Wisnik, Miguel. "O biscoito fino e a massa: um defeito de cor, de Ana Maria Gonçalves." http://www.idelberavelar.com/archives/05/lancamento_nacional_um_defeito_de_cor_de_ana_maria_goncalves.php. Web.

Woolf, Virginia. *A Room of One's Own.* http://ebooks.adelaide.edu.au/w/woolf/virginia/w91r/. Web.

White, Hayden. *Meta-História.* Trans. José Lourênio de Melo. São Paulo: EDUSP, 1992. Print.

10

El sueño del celta: Postcolonial Vargas Llosa

Helene Carol Weldt-Basson

In 2010, the Peruvian writer Mario Vargas Llosa achieved two major successes. First, he won the Nobel Prize for literature, and second, he published his most recent novel, *El sueño del celta* [*The Dream of the Celt*]. *El sueño del celta* is a historical novel based on the life of Roger Casement, an Irish patriot who also served as British consul and fought against human rights abuses in the Congo and Amazon during the late-nineteenth- and early-twentieth-century colonization of these areas. *El sueño del celta* follows a line of historical novels written by Vargas Llosa in which a tendency to metaphorize one historical event through another reveals itself through both a careful textual analysis and an intelligent contextualization of his work. We have already noted in Chapter 1 of this volume that, in 1981, Vargas Llosa published *La guerra del fin del mundo*, a novel based on the revolt against the Brazilian government in Canudos. The revolt was led by the fanatical Antonio Conselheiro, who opposed the collapse of the Brazilian Empire and the concomitant establishment of a national republic during the nineteenth century. Seymour Menton has astutely pointed out that Vargas Llosa uses the Brazilian fanatic as a departure point to reflect on other fanaticist actions, such as that of Castro's curtailment of freedom of artistic expression in Cuba (Menton, 40). Similarly, in 2000, Vargas Llosa published *La fiesta del chivo*, a novel ostensibly about the Trujillo dictatorship in the Dominican Republic, but that also draws many parallels with the Alberto Fujimori government in Peru during the late 1990s. *El sueño del celta* inserts itself within this group of works by Vargas Llosa, because the novel explicitly connects a series of colonized areas—the Congo, the

Putumayo region in the Amazon, and Ireland before Home Rule (or Irish Free State)—so that the first two become symbolic of the third, in order to present a criticism and commentary on colonization that lends itself to a postcolonial analysis of the novel.

However, the connection between *El sueño del celta* and postcolonial theory is, as we are about to see, not quite as simple as a mere denunciation of colonization through the figure of Roger Casement. Although Casement was known for his human rights work, both for his Congo Report and for the Blue Book written about abuses in the Putumayo region, he was put to death as a traitor to the British government in 1916, allegedly for enlisting Irish patriots to help the Germans during World War I and aiding the Irish rebellion against Great Britain in obtaining German arms. Moreover, Casement's private diaries revealing his homosexual encounters had been confiscated by Scotland Yard, and were used to besmirch his reputation and ultimately to obtain a death sentence for him despite international pleas for clemency.

Thus, Vargas Llosa has chosen a highly polemical and ambiguous figure as the subject of his latest novel. As I hope to show in the following pages, Casement, although romanticized to a certain degree within the novel, is portrayed as both saint and sinner, as both colonizer and colonized, and thus is the embodiment of postcolonial contradiction, as understood by such theorists as Homi Bhabha, as well as a *par excellence*, postmodern figure. Thus, Vargas Llosa's most recent work illustrates the theory put forth in this book, that the most current work in Latin American historical fiction has ultimately been influenced and shaped by the ideas and concerns developed by postcolonial theoretical discourse. According to Nicholas Harrison, postcolonial studies are characterized by "An attention to the history of colonialism and imperialism and its aftermath, and may be in many instances distinguished from traditional historical or political writing on the colonial or post-independence era by the particular attention that is paid to the role within that history of 'representation' or 'discourse' " (9).

This postcolonial shift in the focus of contemporary historical fiction is summed up well by Homi Bhabha's statement regarding the change in emphasis of the representation of national traditions:

> Where once, the transmission of national traditions was the major theme of world literature, perhaps we can now suggest that transnational histories of migrants, the colonized, or political refugees, these border and frontier conditions, may be the terrains of world literature.... For the critic must attempt to fully realize and take responsibility for the unspoken, unrepresented pasts that haunt the historical present
>
> (Bhabha, 17).

In other words, as we saw in Chapter 1, the historical novel's focus on national identity has shifted to the notion of a plurality of national identities that includes those of the previously "unspoken, unrepresented" groups—such as women, people of color, and the colonized.

To fully comprehend the postcolonial bent given to the manner in which Casement is portrayed in *El sueño del celta*, we must first contextualize the novel within the historical debate surrounding Casement. In *Roger Casement in Death*, W. J. McCormack indicates that after Casement's death in 1916, there was a

> widespread, low-intensive belief that five diaries associated with Casement preserved in the Public Record office at Kew are forged. In Ireland, it is an article of faith with some older patriots who hold that, at the time of Casement's trial for treason in 1916, the British authorities manufactured a record of frequent and promiscuous homosexual acts involving payment for money.
>
> (McCormack, 1)

Lucy McDiarmid notes that this controversy over the diaries was "initiated by William Maloney's book *The Forged Casement Diaries*, which argued that the British had interpolated into Casement's innocent, consular diaries those of one of the Peruvian criminals he had been investigating in 1910, so that all the homosexual acts mentioned were those of the rubber agent, Armando Normand" (McDiarmid, 179). This vision of Casement as martyr and saint was further cultivated by the poem written by William Butler Yeats, "The Ghost of Roger Casement". In the poem, Yeats suggests that Casement was unfairly executed: "I say the Roger Casement / Did what he had to do . . . . They turned a trick by forgery / And blackened his good name" (Yeats, 306).

Despite such claims, both the contemporary hand-writing analysis done by Dr. Audrey Giles and the paper analysis done by Peter Bower confirm that the so-called "Black Diaries" were indeed authentic and written by Roger Casement (Bower, 250; Giles, 233). Biographies written about Casement, such as William Bryant's *Roger Casement: A Biography*, affirm Casement's homosexual promiscuity at the same time that they acknowledge and praise his humanism and achievements.

In order to deconstruct both the presence of colonialist ideology and the theoretical underpinnings of postcolonialism that expose and criticize such discourse and ideology in *El sueño del celta*, the present study will focus on four principal aspects of the novel: (1) the novel's historical symbolism, conflating the Congo, Amazonian Putumayo region, and pre–Home Rule Ireland; (2) the novel's portrayal of racial minorities and the protagonist, Casement's, attitudes toward them (essentially Casement's role as both colonizer and colonized); (3) the portrait of Roger Casement in general as saint and sinner; (4) the novel's all-pervading sense of postmodern contradiction as evidenced not only by Casement (as discussed in points two and three), but also through a series of minor figures such as Henry Morton Stanley and Joseph Conrad. Many of these points overlap at different junctures of the novel's development.

In the opening paragraph, I alluded to the symbolic use of events in Vargas Llosa's novels. Nowhere is this symbolic conflation of different historical situations more evident than in *El sueño del celta*. On numerous occasions throughout the novel, the narrator explicitly signals the "identity" between any two of the three main scenarios: Congo, Putumayo, and Ireland. For example, after Casement writes his Congo report in the novel, he states: "este viaje a las profundidades del Congo me ha servido para descubrir a mi propio país. Para entender su situación, su destino, su realidad . . . ¿No era también Irlanda una colonia, como el Congo?" (109–110) ["but this journey into the depths of the Congo had been useful in helping me discover my own country and understand her situation her destiny, her reality . . . . Wasn't Ireland a colony too like the Congo?" (80)].[1]

Similarly, further along in the novel, Casement states: "los irlandeses somos como los huitotos, los boras, los andoques, y los muisanes del Putumayo. Colonizados, explotados, y condenados a serlo siempre, si seguimos confiando en las leyes . . . de Inglaterra para alcanzar la libertad" (239) ["We Irish are like the Hitotos, the Boras, the Andoques, and the Muinanes of Putumayo. Colonized, exploited, and condemned to be that way forever if we continue trusting in British laws, institutions, and governments to attain our freedom" (186)]. Indeed, although we cannot conflate the narrator with the author, comments of this nature are so frequent in the novel that at times the reader has the sense that the novel's most pressing point is not the denunciation of colonization in Africa and South America, but rather the criticism of Ireland's colonial status in the early twentieth century. The character Roger Casement, although a clear denouncer of colonialist abuse both in the Congo and in the Putumayo region, interprets these geographical regions from a Eurocentric perspective and seems at times more concerned with European politics and his own nationalist agenda, than with Third-World realities.[2]

Moreover, the conflating of different colonial scenarios, without taking into account their particular historical differences, is one of the chief criticisms leveled against colonial discourse. Nicholas Harrison cites the renowned African postcolonial writer Chinua Achebe's criticism of such historical vagueness with regard to Joseph Conrad's novel *Heart of Darkness* in his study of postcolonial criticism. According to Harrison, Achebe points out that

The setting for the story has appeared to be a vague and perhaps metaphorical "Africa" exploited by a vague and perhaps metaphorical "Company." . . . such vagueness and such metaphoricity in themselves amount to a form of racism and contribute to the ongoing and active history of Eurocentricity and racial discrimination. Achebe . . . contends specifically that the "age-long attitude" embodied in *Heart of Darkness*'s use of Africa as undifferentiated backdrop has fostered and continues to foster "the dehumanization of Africa and Africans." . . . on one level, Conrad (or the text) is guilty of a sort of racism of omission or abstraction, such that the colonial reality on which the action rests comes to seem unimportant, and on another level, Conrad's text will encourage readings and actions that similarly degrade Africa and Africans. (38–39)

Although Vargas Llosa does adhere to historical details and specifics of each region, I would argue that, to a certain degree, his constant symbolic emphasis on the identity of the colonization of the Congo and Putumayo regions with Ireland has much the same effect, detracting from the specificity so crucial to postcolonial criticism and thus falling, to a certain extent, into the colonizer's worldview (or at least portraying Casement of being guilty of the same). Indeed, some historical/postcolonial texts have raised the issue of whether Ireland should be included at all as a colonized nation in the history of world colonization because it lacks Third-World status. Thus, the symbolic conflation of distinct colonial realities in the novel appears at odds with the narrator's ironic repetition of colonialist discourse throughout the pages of the novel.

The intention to deconstruct such colonialist discourse in a postcolonial fashion can be seen in many passages of the novel, especially in the narrator's representation of Roger Casement's initial idealism and subsequent disillusionment with Stanley's African expedition, as well as with the company that initially sends him to Africa, allegedly on a civilizing mission. Casement's ingenuous belief in the company's rhetoric and failure to comprehend the company's mercantilist motivations contribute to the novel's romanticizing portrait of Casement as an idealistic saint:

Luego repetía convencido las ideas que impregnaban esos textos. Llevar al África los productos europeos e importar las materias primas que el suelo africano producía era, más que una operación mercantil, una empresa a favor del progreso de pueblos detenidos en la prehistoria, sumidos en el canibalismo y la trata de esclavos. (26)

[Then he would repeat with conviction the ideas that permeated those texts. Bringing European products to Africa and importing the raw materials that African soil produced was, more than a commercial operation, an enterprise in favor of the progress of peoples caught in prehistory, sunk in cannibalism and the slave trade. (13)]

This discourse is later followed by confirmation of Roger Casement's innocent beliefs when he blushes at the thought of his previous "blindness" (38). Thus, on the one hand, *El sueño del celta* exposes the economic motivation of colonialist "civilizing" discourse, while on the other, the novel falls into the colonialist trap of de-emphasizing national peculiarities in favor of a generalizing discourse that runs the risk of being racist and essentialist through eliding ethnic, racial, and social differences between nations and favoring the European "First-World" problematic versus the Third-World reality.

A second important aspect of *El sueño del celta* that exposes postcolonial contradiction is the portrayal of the racial minorities that constitute the Congo and Putumayo regions. Although Casement defended the rights of these populations and did much to help reform the treatment of the native populations of each region, both in the novel and in history, the novel's Roger Casement character is represented ambivalently in this regard. Although Casement is the defender of blacks and indigenous peoples in the novel, he treats the native populations as objects of his sexual desire, a role that converts him from defender of the colonized into the colonizer who views the colonized as sexual object. Casement's treatment of the native populations as sexual object directly ties into Homi Bhabha's theory of ambivalence toward the colonized subject through both processes of stereotyping and fetishism. According to Bhabha, the fetish or stereotype fixes identity based on a series of contradictory beliefs; it is simultaneously the recognition of difference and the disavowal of the same. In other words, the black man is both cannibal and the most obedient of servants; he is both as innocent as a child and the embodiment of rampant sexuality (Bhabha, 118). Bhabha explains how the sexual fetishization of the colonized subject is based on what he terms "voyeurism," "surveillance," and the "scopic drive" and manifests the master's fantasy and ambivalence toward the colonized "Other." Bhabha states:

> One has to see the surveillance of colonial power as functioning in relation to the regime of the scopic drive ... that represents the pleasure in "seeing"— Like voyeurism, surveillance must depend for its effectivity on the "active consent which is its real or mythical correlate" .... The ambivalence of this form of "consent" to objectification—real as mythical—is the ambivalence on which the stereotype turns (...)

> The stereotype can also be seen as that particular fixated form of the colonial subject which facilitates colonial relations and sets up a discursive form of racial and cultural opposition in terms of which colonial power is

exercised .... By acceding to the wildest fantasies of the colonizer, the stereo-typed Other reveals something of the "fantasy" (as desire, defense) of that position of mastery. (109–118)

Bhabha's ideas also mesh with those expressed by Edward Said in *Orientalism* regarding Western ideas about the sexuality of the colonized "Other." Hema Chani builds on Said's ideas from *Orientalism* and points out in her article "Colonial Fantasies" that places like the Orient and Africa were locations that one could "look for sexual experience unobtainable in Europe" and "procure a different type of sexuality" (278). Chani asserts, when studying colonized India vis-à-vis its colonizer Great Britain, that the colonized Indian is

> The object of European male desire fulfilling the powerful erotic fantasies of the colonizers in its project of subordination of men by men ... the gaze of the imperial voyeur is directed elsewhere, not necessarily or always on the female, but glancing askance on the colonized men .... Colonial power sustained its domination and status by appropriating a contradictory but systematic process of avowal and disavowal of sexual desire between men in the colonies. (279)

Much of what Chani states with regard to India, particularly the notion that male sexuality was part of a "voyeuristic spectacle impacting the dynamics of colonial appropriation" (280), is highly applicable to the relationship between Roger Casement and the native populations in *El sueño del celta*.

Vargas Llosa's novel affirms this role of Africa as the scene of alter-native sexuality in the following passage, placed prior to the description of Casement's initiation of homosexual activity: "El África ... era tam-bién tierra de libertad, donde los seres humanos podían ... manifestar sus pasiones, fantasías, deseos, instintos y sueños, sin las bridas y prejuicios que en Gran Bretaña ahogaban el placer" (280–281) ["Africa ... was also the land of freedom, where human beings could ... show their passions, fantasies, desires, instincts and dreams without the restraints and preju-dices that stifled pleasure in Great Britain" (220)]. It is interesting that Vargas Llosa places Casement's first sexual experience in Africa (although this does not appear to be historically true),[3] and above all, that in addition to the physical relationships described in his diaries, Casement is fre-quently represented as a photographer who photographs the natives who are the objects of his sexual desire. In this way, Casement enacts the role of voyeuristic colonizer who sees the natives of both Africa and the Putumayo as sexual objects through the scopic drive so aptly described by Bhabha:

> Uno de ellos, el más joven, era muy hermoso. Tenía un cuerpo alargado y atlético, músculos que asomaban en su espalda sus piernas y brazos con el

esfuerzo que hacía. Su piel oscura, algo azulada, brillaba de sudor. Con los movimientos que hacia al desplazarse con la carga al hombro desde la carreta al interior del depósito, el ligero pedazo de tela que llevaba envuelto en la cadera se abría y dejaba entrever su sexo, rojizo y colgante y más grande que lo normal. Roger sintió una oleada cálida y urgentes deseos de fotografiar al apuesto cargador. (113).

[One of the youngest was very beautiful. He had a long, athletic body, muscles that appeared on his back, legs, and arms with the effort he was making. His dark skin, gleaming with sweat, had a blue tinge. With the movements he made as he carried the load on his shoulder from the wagon to the interior of the storehouse, the light piece of cloth he wore around his hips opened and offered a glimpse of his sex, reddish and dangling and larger than normal. Roger felt a warm surge and an urgent desire to photograph the handsome porter. (83)]

This emphasis on Casement as a photographer is also present in Casement's real diaries and has been commented on by the historian McCormack as a phenomenon specifically provoked by Casement's experiences in the Congo and Putumayo: "Photography was not a feature of his [Casement's] hidden life in Dublin, London, or Paris, nor indeed of his non-hidden life. But it emerges in prolific and ambiguous form in the tropics" (McCormack, 128). Casement's use of photography is another highly ambivalent element of the novel, since in other sections photography is also used to document the abuses against the native populations.

Other passages of the novel emphasize the exoticism of Putumayo Indians from Casement's perspective, a description that fits perfectly with the postcolonial notion of the European colonialist's racist view of the colonized subject as exotic Other. Casement describes the mestizo Alcibíades Ruiz as a beautiful man and compares him to the Brazilian "caboclos," whom he describes as "hombres de rasgos ligeramente exóticos" (316) [men of slightly exotic features].[4]

The issue of Roger Casement's homosexuality leads us to the third principal aspect of *El sueño del celta*, the novel's portrayal of the historical figure Casement vis-à-vis his image in historical texts. In general, despite the already mentioned myth of Casement's forged Black Diaries, historical texts tend to represent Casement as a romantic idealist in terms of his anti-colonialist stance, but also as a promiscuous homosexual whose sexual behavior represented scandalous comportment for the time period in which he lived. For example, the biography *Roger Casement* written by William Bryant provides ample detail about Casement's sexual activities:

The Puritanism of Protestantism was severe in Ulster, as was that of the Catholic church. The austere sexual code led to frustration, and a desire to escape . . . . The conflicts of religion, social status and occupation were obviously profound. The "working class" boys were debased, as they were in Britain. Roger Casement had excellent pickings in the "lower" orders, where boys fairly openly committed sodomy in defiance of the rules of the church. Casement arrogantly defied the social conventions of his class . . . . Economics was the rule. As his cash ledger for 1911 clearly recorded, he generally paid his Irish tricks a little less than usual. (7)

Bryant also acknowledges Casement's eye for sexual descriptions in his diaries (19). However, it appears that the historical record is at odds with many of the fictional representations that tend to idealize Casement and deny his sexual promiscuity, converting him into a saint. In "The Afterlife of Roger Casement," Lucy McDiarmid mentions not only the aforementioned poem by Yeats that terms the Black Diaries forgeries, but also discusses another, more recent poem "Casement's Funeral" (1965) by Richard Murphy that portrays Casement as a saint (182) as well as a 1995 novel by Michael Carson, *The Knight of the Flaming Heart*, in which Casement returns from the dead to perform miracles in the town Kerry, Ireland. To a certain degree, Vargas Llosa's novel inserts itself within this romanticizing tradition. Although Vargas Llosa adheres to strict historical detail throughout the entire novel, frequently culling information from Casement's Congo and Putumayo diaries,[5] Vargas Llosa ultimately contradicts historical discourse and romanticizes the figure of Casement, with regard to Casement's homosexual activity. Although *El sueño del celta* does not depict Casement's Black Diaries as forgeries, the novel suggests that what is written in these diaries is largely Casement's fantasy, rather than authentic promiscuity. Several passages of the novel portray Casement writing about sexual encounters that never actually occurred (see, e.g., pages 299 and 303),[6] while the epilogue explicitly states the following faced with the unceasing controversy surrounding Casement and his Black Diaries:

> Mi propia impresión—la de un novelista, claro está—es que Roger Casement escribió los famosos diarios pero no los vivió, no por lo menos integralmente, que hay en ellos mucho de exageración y ficción, que escribió ciertas cosas porque hubiera querido pero no pudo vivirlas. (449).

> [My own impression—that of a novelist, obviously—is that Roger Casement wrote the famous diaries but did not live them, at least not integrally, that there is in them a good deal of exaggeration and fiction that he wrote certain things because he would have liked to live them but couldn't. (355)]

To a certain degree, Vargas Llosas's statement here contradicts what is generally considered historical "truth," since contemporary history acknowledges both the authenticity of the Black Diaries and the reality of Casement's sexual activity. If we understand this passage in a literal sense, it seems that Vargas Llosa cultivates a romanticized portrait of Casement as anti-colonialist and sexual dreamer rather than promiscuous homosexual.[7] Nonetheless, this romanticized sexuality may indeed be contradicted in the novel's first chapter, in which Scotland Yard first discovers and reveals Casement's Black Diaries to the public. Casement's attorney's assistant scolds him for writing down "such things" in his diary and this view of Casement's sexuality (although the reader does not yet know to what the assistant is referring) is supported by Casement's desire to take a bath. The juxtaposition of a dirty Casement desiring to bathe and be cleansed symbolically suggests a need to be purified and absolved from his sexual "sins."

There are other portions of the novel that further elaborate this romanticized portrait at the same time that they contradict historical discourse on Casement. In particular, Casement's relationship with Eivand Adler Christensen, a homosexual partner whom he met while wandering the streets of New York City, undergoes significant elaboration in this direction within the pages of the novel. For example, Casement's relationship with Eivand is described in terms of a romantic love that Casement had never before known: "Pero con el 'bello vikingo' ... había establecido, por fin, una relación afectiva que podía durar" (407) ["But with the 'beautiful Viking' ... he had at last established a loving relationship that could endure" (320)]. This insistence on Casement's desire for true love with Eivand Adler Christensen turns Casement into an even more sympathetic and pathetic figure when we learn that Eivand Adler is a traitor who attempts to sell information regarding Casement's revolutionary activities for Irish independence to the British government. Moreover, this representation of Casement's relationship with Adler is in sharp contrast to William Bryant's and Peter Singleton-Gates's portrayals in their biographies of Casement. According to Bryant, Casement was well aware that Adler was a petty criminal known to the police but ignored the risks (218), while Peter Singleton-Gates indicates that Adler's appearance in Casement's life was "the sign, if not the beginning, of an accelerated and non-resisted degradation in Roger Casement's character which was, thenceforth, only checked on rare occasions" (Singleton-Gates, 340).

These sections and relationships in *El sueño del celta* give us a somewhat false impression of a purely idealistic portrait of Roger Casement by Vargas Llosa. However, as we have already seen, and other passages from the novel show, Vargas Llosa ultimately portrays Casement as a contradictory, ambiguous, and postmodern figure. This postmodern portrayal is clearly in keeping with the most contemporary trend of the Latin American historical novel. Vargas Llosa points the reader in this direction at the very beginning of the novel, with its opening epigraph, a line from José Enrique Rodó's *Motivos de Proteo* that signals the changing and contrasting personalities of each one of us. Thus, *El sueño del celta* ultimately mixes the two visions of Roger Casement that we have observed thus far in this article: Casement as a promiscuous homosexual colonizer who views the colonized Congo Africans and Putumayo indigenous people as the objectified, exotic, Other versus Casement, the pathetic romantic who fantasizes about sex and love, and is ultimately betrayed by his one potential love in life. Moreover, Casement's personal life is contrasted with his public service as a heroic anti-colonialist advocate.

Many other aspects of Casement's life and its development in the novel suggest postmodern contradiction, notably Casement's religious beliefs. In the second chapter we are told that his mother, Anne Jephson, was a Catholic who converted to Protestantism because his father, the elder Roger Casement, followed that religion. However, Jephson secretly had Roger baptized and covertly continued her Catholic beliefs. Thus, before his hanging in 1916, Roger returns to Catholicism and is seen confessing to a Catholic priest while in prison. Casement's vacillation between religious sects is yet another postmodern contradiction within his life.

Similar postmodern contradiction equally characterizes the portrayals of several of the more minor characters in *El sueño del celta*. In particular, the novel's representations of both the historical explorer, Henry Morton Stanley, as well as the famous novelist, Joseph Conrad, illustrate the novel's postmodern conception of historical figures. The vision of Henry Morton Stanley as a heroic explorer who civilized Africa is counterpoised to a deconstruction of such a myth in favor of Stanley seen as an opportunistic adventurer who sought fame and economic gain. For example, Stanley is enlisted by King Leopold II of Belgium in his imperialistic efforts to take control of Africa, which are clearly criticized within the novel. We are told: "el explorador era capaz por igual de grandes hazañas y formidables villanías si el premio estaba a la altura de sus apetitos" (39) ["the explorer was equally capable of great deeds and formidable villainies if the prize was on a level with his appetites" (25)]. This vision of Stanley as both heroic and evil is developed throughout the early pages of the novel in which Casement is first recruited to accompany Stanley on his mission. In one scene, after Stanley forces native Africans to sign contracts written in a language they do not understand, and in which they agree to work and provide services for the Belgium Company sent to develop the region, Casement confronts Stanley regarding the ethics of such contracts. Stanley responds with the traditional racist and paternalistic colonialist discourse that the novel frequently attempts to expose and deconstruct. He states that "todo esto es por su bien" (43) ["all this is for their good" (28)] and that the Europeans will convert the pagans, teach them "civilized languages," provide the people with jobs, and generally modernize their country, which is why it is justifiable for them to make them sign such contracts (42–43).

However, in another passage, we are told that Roger has seen Stanley perform many humanitarian actions, which include offering his water canteen to indigenous people who are dying from contagious illnesses (46). Stanley is presented as an ultimate contradiction or indecipherable postmodern mystery: "Roger Casement aprendió también que el explorador era un misterio ambulante. Todas las cosas que se decían de él estaban siempre en contradicción entre ellas" (44) ["Roger also learned that the explorer was a walking mystery. The things said about him were always contradictory" (29)].

Similarly, the writer Joseph Conrad, whom Roger Casement met on one of his African expeditions, and whose novel *Heart of Darkness* (1899) is based on his own experiences in Africa, is also portrayed in a contradictory manner in *El sueño del celta*. It is important to note that Conrad's novel has been the frequent object of postcolonial studies, which have criticized the novel as presenting a racist view of Africa, both for its treatment of Africa as a nonspecific geographical region and for its notion of Africa as an uncivilized zone that ultimately turns barbarous the Europeans who colonize the region.[8] At the beginning of the novel, Conrad is portrayed as Casement's close friend, and the two develop an intimate friendship in Africa that continued for many years thereafter. The initial description of a sincere friendship between Casement and Conrad is later contradicted by Conrad's refusal to sign the petition for clemency when in 1916 Casement is tried for treason by the British government and hanged to death. When Roger asks his friend, the historian Alice Stopford Green, if Conrad signed the petition, she replies that for unknown reasons, he refused to sign, showing himself to be "spineless" with regard to contemporary politics (70–71). Conrad's reasons for not supporting the petition remain unclear and contribute to this ambiguous vision of the friendship between Casement and Conrad that is contradicted by the failure of the latter to attempt to save his friend from a death sentence.

Moreover, the character of Casement in Vargas Llosa's novel directly engages with the postcolonial criticism of Conrad's novel as racist discourse. We have already seen how Achebe criticized Conrad's novel for racist portrayals of Africa and Africans. In *El sueño del celta*, Casement discusses this interpretation of *Heart of Darkness* with the historian Alice Stopford Green who confirms it: "Esa novela es una parábola según la cual África vuelve bárbaros a los civilizados europeos que van allá. Tu Informe sobre el Congo mostró lo contrario más bien" (76) ["That novel is a parable according to which Africa turns the civilized Europeans who go there into barbarians. Your Congo report shows the opposite" (54)].

The complexity and ambiguity of *Heart of Darkness* in contemporary literary criticism is brought to light by studies such as those by Terry Collits (*Postcolonial Conrad*) and Nicholas Harrison (*Postcolonial Criticism*). The interesting point here is not so much whether Conrad's novel is indeed racist, but how Vargas Llosa's novel ultimately replicates this ambiguity toward the colonized through the figure of Roger Casement and the conflation of colonial territories. Just as *Heart of Darkness* simultaneously denounces European imperialism and mimics racist discourse, so does Casement denounce imperialism and mistreatment of both the Congo and Putumayo natives and at the same time lusts after the native men and objectifies them through his photography.[9] The sexual encounters described both in Vargas Llosa's novel and in the Black Diaries result in an image of Casement that contradicts the romanticized, humanitarian portrait. This undermining of Casement's postcolonial heroic image is well summarized by Angus Mitchell in "The Riddle of the Two Casements":

> The Black Diary narrative trivializes Casement to the level of low-life, bad health and bitterness: the type of petty-minded consular status that Casement despised and spent his life deliberately rising above. It constructs the type of man the British felt justified in executing in 1916. While the contested diaries give Casement a voracious sexual identity, they also alter his meaning and significance on several other levels. They destroy his mystical role as both imperial knight and the moral standard-bearer of advanced nationalism. He is turned from being the investigator of the system into the exploiter, the sexual colonizer, the crude fantasist. It is impossible to champion Casement's worth as a human rights campaigner and in the same hand uphold the diaries as the master narrative in the telling of the key moments of his human rights campaign. (112).

It is thus particularly interesting that Vargas Llosa, as we have already seen, attempts to somewhat erase Casement's inherent postcolonial contradiction, through an interpretation of his Black Diaries as an innocent fantasy. If Casement's sexual activities were mere fantasies, this would significantly diminish his aspect of colonialist abuser although it would not entirely abolish Casement's ambivalence as colonizer, nor his dualistic role as colonized and colonizer in the novel.

In summary, *El sueño del celta* is an excellent example of how the contemporary Latin American historical novel is influenced by and in turn engages itself with issues of postcolonial theory. Vargas Llosa's earlier historical novels, *La guerra del fin del mundo* and *La fiesta del chivo,* have been interpreted as more realist in nature, although arguably with some postmodern overtones.[10] In contrast, *El sueño del celta* focuses on a much debated and therefore postmodern historical figure, Roger Casement, and history is treated in a highly postmodern fashion throughout the novel.[11] Moreover, the manner in which the novel portrays and interprets Roger Casement can be concretely understood in terms of key concepts explicated by Homi Bhabha in his landmark book, *The Location of Culture*. Bhabha's notion of stereotyping through fixity is important for comprehending how the history of Roger Casement is represented in *El sueño del celta*. Although Vargas Llosa's novel appears to deconstruct colonialist discourse through its ironic replication in the mouths of historical figures such as Henry Morton Stanley and King Leopold II, his focus on the anti-colonialist hero Roger Casement inevitably illustrates Bhabha's notion of colonialist stereotyping. According to Bhabha,

> Colonial discourse depends on the concept of fixity, the ideological construction of otherness. Stereotype, a major discursive strategy, also vacillates between what is always in place and already known, and something that must be anxiously repeated. It is this process of ambivalence, central to the stereotype, that this chapter explores as it constructs a theory of colonial discourse.... The function of ambivalence as one of the most significant discursive and psychical strategies of discriminatory power, whether racist or sexist, peripheral or metropolitan remains to be charted... the stereotype is a complex, ambivalent, contradictory mode of representation.
>
> (Bhabha, 100)

In other words, colonialist discourse describes the colonized subject as both same and other, a process that we have observed in the character Roger Casement's treatment of the inhabitants of the Congo and Putumayo throughout *El sueño del celta*. At the same time that the fictional Casement seeks to aid Africans and Putumayo Indians, recognizing the capitalist ideology behind the colonizer's "civilizing" discourse of the natives, Casement regards these colonized subjects as exotic, racial, and sexual "Others" to be sexually dominated by the European colonizer. This results in a literary paradox: the Casement that Vargas Llosa represents as anti-colonialist hero and romanticized character is at the same time guilty of viewing native populations through the processes of fixity and stereotyping discussed by Bhabha. Consequently, *El sueño del celta* enacts a postcolonial and postmodern contradiction, simultaneously constructing and deconstructing colonialist discourse and illustrating the inherent ambivalence of the colonizer. The important point here is that whether consciously or unconsciously, Vargas Llosa has constructed a novel that can only truly be understood within the postcolonial framework that has both shaped its discourse and can be used to deconstruct it. This is the essential mark of the contemporary historical novel in Latin American, whose focus on women and people of color has clearly changed and defined new directions for the genre.

Notes

1. This translation of *El sueño del celta* has been taken from the recent translation by Edith Grossman, *The Dream of the Celt*.
2. Some historians point out that Casement's experiences in the Congo and Amazon helped to shape his subsequent Irish nationalist stance, a fact that might also explain to a certain degree the conflation of the different regions as portrayed in the novel.
3. William Bryant suggests that Casement was already visiting male brothels in Ireland in 1877, at least six years prior to his first African voyage in 1883 (see Bryant, 27–28).
4. Note that in Grossman's translation, this sentence, which I have translated literally, is changed to "in whom indigenous gentleness and sweetness mixed with the coarse virility of the descendants of the Spanish" (247). This changes the original sense of the Spanish and erases the Orientalizing view of the colonizer present in the quotation's original language.
5. A careful comparison of *El sueño del celta* and the Congo and Amazonian journals clearly reveals that Vargas Llosa consulted these sources in the construction of his novel. For example, one of the minor characters, Víctor Israel, is taken directly from the Putumayo diary. Vargas Llosa replicates the fact that Israel is the only English-speaking interlocutor that Casement finds while traveling on the ship to the Putumayo region. However, there are many other historical facts in the novel that correspond to information from the diaries. See the *Amazonian Journal*, 79–83, and *El sueño del celta*, 199–209. Moreover, the descriptions and tones of the erotic diary passages in the novel appear to mimic those of the actual *Black Diaries* (see Singleton-Gates, *The Black Diaries*).
6. On page 303 of the novel, the narrator explains that imagining exaggerated sexual encounters in which he has three lovers in one night lifts his spirits and counteracts his feelings of powerlessness.
7. Note that this portrayal of Casement as a dreamer rather than a promiscuous individual may, in fact, be a wink from the novelist indicating the ultimate fictionality of his portrayal since he claims to be offering this interpretation from his position as a novelist.
8. The character Kurtz's relentless pursuit of ivory as well as his abuse of the natives as seen through a series of shrunken African heads discovered when Marlow arrives at his residence suggests a criticism of colonialist greed and capitalism (see Conrad, 60). On the other hand, many of Marlow's descriptions of the natives portray them as inferior to Europeans and are racist in nature (see Conrad, 44).

9. McCormack cites early texts (1908) in which Casement is guilty of making racist remarks: "hideous cross breeds . . . a very large admixture of native blood . . . the resultant human compost is the nastiest form of black-pudding you have ever sat down to" (112).

10. See the studies by Robin Lefere: "Lectura crítica de *La fiesta del chivo*" and "*La fiesta del chivo,* mentira verdadera?" for the realist interpretation of *La fiesta del chivo,* and Helene Carol Weldt-Basson, "Mario Vargas Llosa's *La fiesta del chivo*: Fiction, History, or Social psychology?" for a more postmodern vision.

11. This postmodern view of history can be observed in numerous quotations from the novel. For example, at one point, the narrator states: "Eso era la historia, una rama de fabulación que pretendía ser ciencia" (274) ["That was history, a branch of fable-writing attempting to be science" (215)]. In another passage, when the historian Alice Stopford Green and Casement discuss events, Alice states that there is no such thing as "black" and "white"—everything is gray—to which Roger responds that life is complex and full of contradictory and uncertain circumstances (354).

Works Cited

Bhabha, Homi. *The Location of Culture.* London: Routledge Classics, 2004. Print.

Bower, Peter. "Paper History & Analysis as Research Procedure." In *Appendix: Roger Casement in Irish & World History.* Ed. Mary E. Daly. Dublin: Royal Irish Academy, 2005. 243–251. Print.

Bryant, William. *Roger Casement: A Biography.* New York: I Universe Incorporated, 2007. Print.

Collits, Terry. *Postcolonial Conrad.* London: Routledge, 2005. Print.

Conrad, Joseph. *Heart of Darkness.* Madison: Cricketuse Books, 2010. Print.

Chani, Hema. "Colonial Fantasies and Postcolonial Identities: Elaboration of Postcolonial Masculinity and Homoerotic Desire." In *Post-Colonial, Queer: Theoretical Intersections.* Ed. John C. Hawley. Albany: State University of New York Press, 2001. 277–304. Print.

Gilles, Dr. Audrey. "Report of Audrey Giles." In *Roger Casement in Irish & World History.* Ed. Mary E. Daly. Dublin: Royal Irish Academy, 2005. 203–237. Print.

Harrison, Nicholas. *Postcolonial Criticism.* Cambridge: Polity Press, 2003. Print.

Lefere, Robin. "La fiesta del chivo, mentira verdadera?" *Actas del XIV Congreso de la Asociación Internacional de Hispanistas.* Ed. Isais Lerner, Robert Nival and Alejandro Alonoso. Newark [Delaware]: Juan de la Cuesta, 2001. 331–338. Print.

———. "Lectura crítica de *La fiesta del chivo.*" In *Literatura y música popular en Hispanoamérica.* Ed. Angel Esteban, Gracia Morales and Alvaro Salvador. Granada: Universidad de Granada, 2002. 541–546. Print.

Menton, Seymor. *Latin America's New Historical Novel: 1949, 1979, 1992.* Austin: University of Texas Press, 1993. Print.

McCormack, W. J. *Roger Casement in Death: Haunting the Irish Free State.* Dublin: University College Dublin Press, 2002. Print.

McDiarmid, Lucy. "The Afterlife of Roger Casement." In *Roger Casement in Irish & World History*. Ed. Mary E. Daly. Dublin: Royal Irish Academy, 2005. 178–188. Print.

Mitchell, Angus, Ed. *The Amazon Journal of Roer Casement*. London: Anaconda, 1997. Print.

Mitchell, Angus. "The Riddle of the Two Casements?" In *Roger Casement in Irish & World History*. Ed. Mary E. Daly. Dublin: Royal Irish Academy, 2005. 99–120. Print.

Said, Edward W. *Orientalism*. New York: Vintage, 1979. Print.

Singleton-Gates, Peter, Ed. *The Black Diaries*. Paris: The Olympia Press, 1959. Print.

Siocháin, Séamas O. and Michael O'Sullivan, Eds. *The Eyes of Another Race: Roger Casement's Congo Report and 1903 Diary*. Dublin: University College Dublin Press, 2003. Print.

Vargas Llosa, Mario. *La guerra del fin del mundo*. Barcelona: Seix Barral, 1981. Print.

———. *La fiesta del chivo*. Madrid: Punto de lectura, 2000. Print.

———. *El sueño del celta*. Doral [Florida]: Santillana USA Publishing Company/Alfaguara, 2010. Print.

———. *The Dream of the Celt*. Trans. Edith Grossman. New York: Farrar, Straus and Girox, 2012. Print.

Weldt-Basson, Helene Carol. "Mario Vargas Llosa's la fiesta del chivo: Fiction, History, or Social Psychology"? *Hispanófila* 156 (2009): 113–130. Print.

Yeats, William Butler. "The Ghost of Roger Casement." In *The Collected Poems of W.B. Yeats*. Ed. Richard J. Finneran. New York: Scribner, 1996. 306. Print.

Contributors

Fernando Burgos is a Professor of Spanish and Latin American Studies at the University of Memphis. He completed his BA at the Universidad de Chile and received his PhD in Romance Languages from the University of Florida, where he was awarded a *Recognition for Outstanding Contribution*. His area of research includes nineteenth- and twentieth-century Latin American narrative. In addition to delivering more than 80 papers at international and national conferences, he has been invited as a keynote speaker to the Universidad Nacional Mayor de San Marcos, Lima, Perú, and the University of Cincinnati. He has published 12 books, including *La novela moderna hispanoamericana: un ensayo sobre el concepto literario de modernidad* (Madrid), *Vertientes de la modernidad hispanoamericana* (Caracas), *Cuentos de Hispanoamérica en el siglo XX* (Madrid), and *Los escritores y la creación en Hispanoamérica* (Madrid). He has also published 70 articles in European, North American, and Latin American professional journals. Professor Burgos has received many awards, including the Alumni Association Distinguished Teaching Award, the Fellowship for Visiting Scholars Program to conduct research at the University of Illinois at Urbana-Champaign, the SPUR (Superior Performance in University Research) award, the Alumni Association Award for Distinguished Research and Creative Achievement in the Humanities, and the Dunavant Professorship.

Marcelo Coddou is a Professor Emeritus at Drew University. In addition to publishing numerous critical essays on Latin American literature in professional journals in the United States, Europe, and Latin America, he has edited books on Gabriela Mistral (1979), Juan Rulfo (1981), Julio Cortázar (1980), and Isabel Allende (1985). He has published several books on the Chilean poet Gonzalo Rojas, winner of the Cervantes Prize in 2003. These include a critical edition of Rojas's *La miseria del hombre* (1995) and Biblioteca Ayacucho and Fondo de Cultura Económica's editions of Rojas's *Selected Works* (1998). He is also the author of *Poética de la poesía activa* (1985), *Nuevos estudios sobre la poesía de Gonzalo Rojas* (1986), *Para leer a Isabel Allende* (1988), *Veinte estudios sobre la literatura chilena del siglo*

XX(1989),*"Hija de la fortuna" de Isabel Allende: rediagramación fronter-iza del saber histórico* (2001), and *Gonzalo Rojas: los poetas son niños en crecimiento tenaz* (2007). He has recently finished writing a book titled *Escritura en el borde de la realidad—Tomás Eloy Martínez: Variaciones críticas sobre su prosa narrativa.*

María Josele Bucco Coelho received a master's degree in literatura from the Universidad Estadual de Sâo Paulo and is currently a doctoral candidate in Comparative Literature at the Universidad Federal de Rio Grande de Sur. She is an Assistant Professor at the Universidad Federal do Paraná and coordinates the research group on "The Feminine in Contemporary Historical Narratives." She is also a member of the Nucleus on Gender Studies of the UFPR and of the research team on "Questions of Hybridization in the Literatures of the Americas."

Víctor Figueroa is an Associate Professor of Latin American and Caribbean literatures in the Department of Classical and Modern Languages at Wayne State University in Detroit, Michigan. He obtained his BA in Compara-tive Literature at the University of Puerto Rico, Rio Piedras, in 1992. He completed his PhD, also in Comparative Literature, at Harvard Univer-sity, in the year 2000. His articles on writers such as José Martí, Alejo Carpentier, C. L. R. James, Derek Walcott, and Aimé Césaire, among others, have appeared in *Latin American Literary Review, Afro-Hispanic Review, Twentieth Century Literature,* and *The French Review.* His book *Not at Home in One's Home: Caribbean Self-Fashioning in the Poetry of Luis Palés Matos, Aimé Césaire, and Derek Wacott* was published in 2009 by Fairleigh Dickinson University Press. His poetry collection, *El regicida y su sombra,* was published by Terranova Editores in 2011.

Ester Gimbernat González is a Professor of Spanish and Latin American literature at the University of Northern Colorado. She obtained her MA and PhD from Johns Hopkins University. She has published numerous books, including *Paradiso: entre los confines de la transgresión* (Universidad Veracruzana, 1982); *Aventuras del desacuerdo: escritoras argentinas de los 80* (Buenos Aires, Danilo Vergara, 1992); *Utopías, Ojos azules, bocas suici-das: la narrativa de Alina Diaconu* (Fraterna, 1993, co-edited with Cynthia Tompkins); *Boca de dama: la narrativa de Angelica Gorodischer* (Feminaria, 1995, co-edited with Miriam Balboa Echeverría); and *La poesía de mujeres dominicanas a fines del siglo XX* (Mellen Press, 2002). She has also com-piled the book *Luisa Futoransky y su palabra itinerante* (Editorial Hermes Criollo, 2005). Her numerous articles on Latin American contemporary women authors have been published in academic journals in the United States, Latin American, Europe, and Korea. She has participated in more than 200 national and international professional meetings. Since 1993 she is the editor of *Confluencia: Revista de Cultura y Literatura Hispánicas.*

Fátima R. Nogueira is an Associate Professor of Spanish and Portuguese at the University of Memphis. She specializes in twentieth-century Latin American literature and received her PhD from Vanderbilt University. Her publications include articles in academic journals such as *Revista Chilena de Literatura, Alpha, Confluencia, Inti, Luso-Brazilian Review, Arizona Journal of Hispanic Cultural Studies, Amaltea,* and *Afro-Hispanic Review.* She has presented 30 papers at national and international professional meetings and written various book chapters. Professor Nogueira is the co-author of the book *Productividades posmodernistas en la obra de Enrique Jaramillo Levi.* She is currently working on a book titled *Poéticas del devenir en la obra de Clarice Lispector y Luisa Valenzuela.*

Elda Stanco holds a PhD in Hispanic Studies from Brown University, where she specialized in city literature and Venezuelan authors. During her doctoral studies, she was an Exchange Scholar at Harvard University and an Exchange Fellow at the Universidad de Salamanca. Her research also focuses on transatlantic subjects, bilingual writings, and the new genera-tions of authors from Venezuela. She currently teaches at Roanoke College in Virginia.

Patricia Varas is a Professor of Spanish and Latin American Studies at Willamette University. She is the author of *Las máscaras de Delmira Agustini* (2003) and *Narrativa y cultura nacional* (1993) as well as the co-editor of *Identidades americanas más allá de las fronteras nacionales: ensayos en homenaje a Keith Ellis* (2012). She has published extensively on Latin American modernity, film, culture, and women's writing.

Helene Carol Weldt-Basson is a Professor of Spanish and Latin American literature at Michigan State University. She is a noted specialist on the Paraguayan writer Augusto Roa Bastos, about whom she has published two books: *Augusto Roa Bastos's I the Supreme: A Dialogic Perspective* (University of Missouri Press, 1993) and the edited collection titled *Postmodernism's Role in Latin American Literature: The Life and Work of Augusto Roa Bastos* (Palgrave/Macmillan, 2010); she has also published numerous articles in such journals as *Texto Crítico, Chasqui, Hispanic Jour-nal, Inti,* and *Hispanófila.* She recently received an honorary doctorate for her work on Roa Bastos from La Universidad del Norte, in Asunción, Paraguay. She has also published a book on Latin American women writers and feminism: *Subversive Silences: Nonverbal Expression and Implicit Nar-rative Strategies in the Works of Latin American Women Writers* (Farleigh Dickinson UP, 2009).

Index

9 781137 277565